Ann Sheridan

Ann Sheridan

The Life and Career
of Hollywood's Oomph Girl

MICHAEL D. RINELLA

McFarland & Company, Inc., Publishers
Jefferson, North Carolina

ISBN (print) 978-1-4766-9418-4
ISBN (ebook) 978-1-4766-5204-7

Library of Congress and British Library
cataloguing data are available

Library of Congress Control Number 2024013781

Front cover image: publicity photograph of Ann Sheridan
from the 1939 "Oomph Girl" campaign (author collection)

Printed in the United States of America

*McFarland & Company, Inc., Publishers
Box 611, Jefferson, North Carolina 28640
www.mcfarlandpub.com*

This book is dedicated to my
"Favorite Mother-in-Law,"
Midge Stanton.
I treasure our conversations about the old movies
and your memories of them as a child.

Table of Contents

Acknowledgments

First, I would like to thank my wife, Julie; my son, Paul Rinella, and his wife, Gretchen Mattern; my daughter, Martha Liberti, and her husband, Mike Liberti; and my daughter, Faith Rinella, for their continued support and encouragement through this whole process. I continue to be grateful to Tracy Whitney and the staff at Marion Public Library for their invaluable assistance. I am deeply appreciative to Cheryl Blue for cheerfully fulfilling my never-ending requests for books through the interlibrary loan system; without Cheryl's assistance, this book would not be as complete as I had envisioned. I am grateful to Kathryn Riedener, the Collection and Resource Coordinator at the OWWL Headquarters. I am deeply indebted to Christopher Frank and James Hallahan, formerly of the Association for the Blind and Visually Impaired (ABVI) of Rochester, for their assistance with adaptive technology. I would also like to thank Jim Costanza for his invaluable assistance with editing the final manuscript. I owe a debt of gratitude to James Robert Parish for his words of encouragement and guidance every step of the way. I am also appreciative of Lynn Kear, another author who has encouraged my writing endeavors. I am grateful for the assistance provided by Manvitha Doma of the University of North Texas library. I thank the staff of the following New York public libraries: Rochester; Fairport; Greene; and Pittsford, as well as the following universities: SUNY Brockport; SUNY Cortland; SUNY Geneseo; Cornell University; Syracuse University, and the University of Rochester.

I am grateful for the assistance of my family in obtaining photographs for this book, with Martha playing a critical role in this area.

Finally, I am grateful to God, in whom all things are made possible.

Introduction

More Than Just Oomph

When my career is over, I'll be able to wave it Godspeed with a grin.[1]

Ann Sheridan had reason to smile. Hers was a story of determination and grit with a healthy dose of humility, a sense of fun and a strong desire to work. During a 1965 interview conducted by Ray Hagen, she was asked her opinion on her overall position in motion picture history. Her response was modest and sadly prophetic: "There's no position, really. It'll be just one of those things that's written off, for heaven's sake. It won't mean anything."[2]

While her movie fame has been eclipsed by the mega-watt glare of Bette Davis, Katharine Hepburn and Joan Crawford, Sheridan is no less revered by film historians and classic movie buffs of Hollywood's Golden Age. She is perhaps the most versatile and talented of all the great movie actresses from that era. This was evident throughout her 32-year career in the entertainment industry. That she achieved stardom at all, despite overwhelming odds, is a testament to her indomitable Texan spirit and appealing screen personality.

Like three other stars, Betty Grable, Rita Hayworth and Lucille Ball, Sheridan began her long career in small parts. After a few years, she graduated to playing leads in mediocre "B" films and small supporting roles in the occasional "A" productions. She then achieved stardom in a spectacular fashion, with critics and moviegoers sitting up and taking notice. For Grable, it was the warm, tuneful Technicolor musicals beginning with *Down Argentine Way* (1940) that made the audience feel good. For Hayworth, it was the complicated interplay between luscious beauty and smoldering femme fatale sex appeal that flowered in full bloom in *Blood and Sand* (1941) and *Gilda* (1946). For Ball, always an accomplished performer, film stardom proved elusive—but then came the beloved *I Love Lucy* television series. After that, everybody loved Lucy.

Unlike these ladies, Sheridan cannot be reduced to a single role or genre as she excelled in so many of them. In the hard-hitting dramas *They Drive by Night* (1940) and *Kings Row* (1942), she was the no-nonsense, street-smart heroine who knew her way around in difficult situations; while we were on the lookout for a strong man to rescue her, we always knew that she would be just fine on her own. With her gift of tossing sarcastic, biting lines at a hapless recipient, she proved equally at home in comedy. Her comic performance in *Torrid Zone* (1940), which pitted her against two masters of fast-talking wisecracks (James Cagney and Pat O'Brien), is a gem.

1

Likewise, her tart portrayal as Cary Grant's wife in *I Was a Male War Bride* (1949) is sheer delight from the beginning to the final credits.

Not to be overlooked are her complex, conflicted characters in the unjustly neglected film noir classics *The Unfaithful* (1947) and *Woman on the Run* (1950). If that wasn't enough, it turned out the lady could sing in a voice pleasantly reminiscent of Alice Faye's warm contralto. When she sang, she elevated the silliest plot contrivance in films like *Navy Blues* (1941) into a moment of unadulterated joy.

Ann Sheridan had a tremendous appeal that went beyond a striking beauty and shapely figure. Exotic gals Maria Montez and Veronica Lake capitalized on their unique screen allure and achieved great (but brief) popularity. Not so with Sheridan. Just as she wouldn't fit into a screen type, she would not be hampered by efforts to mold her into a sex symbol via the "Oomph Girl" label. As pal Humphrey Bogart noted in 1943, the label "has not affected her a bit; by hard work and determination to be a good actress she has managed to rise above it."[3]

"Without ever achieving the mythic status of a super-star, [Ann Sheridan] was always a pleasure to watch, and, as with all true stars, was never quite like anyone else."—*London Times* obituary, 1967.

Yet it was the "Oomph Girl" designation that highlighted Sheridan's zest for living life to the fullest. When Joseph Breen's Production Code took effect in mid–1934, the sexy, playful and naughty qualities of actresses like Norma Shearer and Kay Francis were sanitized and a veneer of respectable glamour was heavily applied. Sexual playfulness was reserved only for the "bad women," who would pay a heavy price for their carnal desires and indiscretions.

With her breakthrough turn in *It All Came True* (1940), Sheridan flipped glamour off its high heels. In one fell swoop, the "Oomph Girl" brought sex back at full force and paved the way for others like Hayworth and Grable to showcase their own special brand of fun and intoxicating screen qualities. These ladies showed that "good girls" could have fun too.

In 1944, at the peak of Sheridan's fame, gossip columnist Hedda Hopper examined her appeal. She noted that she is "tremendously popular with all the men at Warner's. From cameramen to press agents, they're solidly behind her. They like her. She's down to earth; completely natural, and can joke along with the best of them—and does." Then Hopper touched upon Sheridan's Achilles heel: "I think Annie gets along better with men than with women. Her own sex often gets Annie peeved. She knows their little tricks and duplicities and doesn't like them. She comes clean and expects others to do the same."[4]

Her lifelong friend Ida Lupino observed that Sheridan was different because she was "honest, feminine, and yet had masculine directness."[5] Pal Ann Sothern echoed that sentiment: "She's such a straight-shooter, such a good guy. There's no nonsense about her.... Sometimes, she's so regular, she reminds me of a man."[6] Director Howard Hawks marveled at how, despite the odds, she attained Hollywood success. "[S]he outlived some of the worst pictures you've ever known.... People liked her. They made her a star in spite of the bad pictures."[7]

In the book *Margaret Sullavan: The Life and Career of a Reluctant Star*, I described the actress' intangible quality as clarity of vision, "that rare ability to clearly communicate to the audience the purpose of his or her very existence. It is the inherent ability of knowing who they are and remaining steadfastly true in that conviction no matter what life may throw in their paths."[8] Sheridan had this trait in spades. This quality is evident in many of her performances. If this is lacking in some early works, we can blame Sheridan's inexperience. In a handful of later performances, we point the finger of blame at the director's misunderstanding of her appeal.

It is this "clarity of vision" appeal I first encountered as a teenager when I caught *City for Conquest* (1940) on the Late Show. With the simple yet raw emotions of her tenement dweller who desires fame and fortune, I was transfixed by the impact she had on me. More than that, I was hooked. In the years since that introduction to the delectable Ann Sheridan, I have sought out and watched all but two of her film appearances (*Home on the Range*, 1934, and *Just Across the Street*, 1952, both of which have been difficult to find). The impression remains the same. As an ardent fan of classic films, I have many favorite performers, but I continue to be amazed by the depth and scope of her talent.

As for Sheridan's assertion that her film career would mean nothing to future generations: Perish the thought. Once you have seen Ann Sheridan in her prime, there's no turning back. Fortunately, most of her films are available for viewing through Turner Classic Movies, streaming websites and the DVD market. There's no excuse for her to remain a shadowy, faded image from cinema's past. She's too special to be relegated like that.

Noted film historian David Shipman once wrote, "She really was too warm, too lush, and too genuinely glamorous to compete with the other tinny girls.... At all events, she never quite received her due."[9] Here's hoping to change all of that.

ONE

Denton's Own
"Personality Girl"

Never thought of pictures at all, that was too far out.[1]

Ann Sheridan was born Clara Lou Sheridan on February 21, 1915, in Denton, Texas (not in Dallas, Texas, as commonly reported in various biographical sources). Denton, the county seat of Denton County, is 47 miles south of the Oklahoma-Texas border and 49 miles northwest of Dallas. Sheridan was named after a neighbor, Clara Evans, and her mother Lula. Sheridan's family background was a mix of Irish, Scottish and Cherokee heritage. The Sheridan name is believed to be derived from O'Sheridan ("descendant of Siridean").[2]

Her father, George Washington Sheridan, was born on February 19, 1875, in Springfield, Missouri. Hollywood publicists claimed he was the grandnephew of famed Civil War Union general Philip Sheridan (Ann confirmed this in a 1952 interview with Louella Parsons). Known as "Little Phil" or "Fightin' Phil," General Sheridan was notable for his rapid rise to the rank of major general and his close association with General-in-Chief Ulysses S. Grant during the Civil War.

George Sheridan was the son of William Thomas Sheridan (1853–1929) and Nancy Rachel Stanley (1855–1925). George was the eldest of seven children. He moved to Texas at age 17 and settled in Cedar Hill, where he met Lula.

Lula Stuart (some sources spell it Stewart) Warren was born in Addington, Virginia, in 1877. Her father, Spencer White Warren (1855–1938), was related to the Warrens of Virginia clan. Sheridan once joked that her mother "was of the Warren family of Virginia, so you see on one side I was good old Confederacy stock, and on the other we fought the Civil War."[3] Lula's mother was Margaret A. Roberts (1855–1919). Lula was the second oldest of eight children. In 1895, her family moved to Dallas.

Married on August 5, 1900, George and Lula moved to Denton in 1901. The couple had six children: R.L. Sheridan (who died in infancy in 1902), Ida Mae "Kitty" Sheridan Kent (1902–79), Mabel Lane Sheridan Rowton (1905–97), George B. Sheridan (1908–56), Georgia Pauline "Polly" Sheridan Day (1911–88) and Clara Lou.

In Denton, George opened a machine shop on East Oak Street. He was widely regarded as a pioneer in the automobile garage business for opening his first garage in 1904. This was located on 144 West Sycamore Street. He worked as a mechanic and a supervisor.

The Sheridan family belonged to the First Baptist Church. Well respected in their community, they were often featured in the local newspaper's society pages.

Ann later said she was grateful to her parents "for the fearless outlook on life they gave me."[4] In other interviews, she revealed that her parents were strict, God-fearing Baptists. "Since I was a kid, religion ... has always scared me to death—all that hellfire and damnation."[5]

Throughout Sheridan's show biz career, Hollywood publicity painted a rather rosy picture of a loving and devoted family. As late as 1953, Sheridan stated that although her mother "found out ... our attitude to boys as well as our smoking ... she must have figured she was hitting a pretty good average in bringing us up properly. Our father, who wasn't half as aware as Mother about our minor sins, was proud of us." She said, "I needed my father's pride in me to give me confidence and I needed my mother's more accurate appraisal to forestall my having any illusions about myself."[6]

Even as a teenager, Clara Lou was quite the beauty and in possession of all the traits that later made her a beloved star.

The truth of the matter was more complicated. Sheridan's parents frowned upon the entertainment business and the manner in which their youngest child conducted her life. Their disapproval contributed to a strained relationship between Sheridan and her family. When George died unexpectedly on May 20, 1938, Sheridan took a few days off from film work to fly home, but left before the funeral. In early January 1946, Sheridan flew to Texas to visit her ailing mother at a Fort Worth hospital. After the hour-long visit, Sheridan attended a family dinner at her sister Kitty's house before heading back to Hollywood. When Lula passed away on January 27, Sheridan did not fly back for the funeral; she claimed she was unable to get away from her current movie set. Even after the deaths of both parents, remnants of family friction persisted. At the time of Sheridan's own death, Kitty told reporters that her famous sister made infrequent visits to her siblings even though she constantly traveled to other parts of the world.

According to many biographical sources, Clara Lou's family lived on a cattle ranch. One of the earliest textual bits of evidence dates to a 1939 *Movie Mirror* magazine article, "Texas Bombshell." This claim, however, has been refuted by several local sources. According to records, the family resided at 59 Bernard Street as of the 1920 census. They relocated to 402 Elm Street in 1930. Neither one of these homes stand today. An article dated December 12, 1933, "From Main Street to Hollywood in Few Months Is Remarkable Record Made by Local Personality Girl," confirms the second address.[7] The stories of life on a ranch frequently surfaced throughout Sheridan's career. Perhaps she even got in on the gag. There is no doubt she experienced life on a local ranch; it isn't likely that she lived on a ranch growing up.

As a child, Clara Lou was described as a tomboy and was nicknamed "Lulu" and "Ludie." She was an active child who enjoyed physical activities. Years later, she recalled for *Movieland* magazine that she had fond memories of "[m]y whole childhood, which was just a normal 'everybody's kid's' existence."[8] She called the hunting trips she took with her dad "the brightest spot in my bright childhood."[9] Due to her upbringing, Sheridan later proudly proclaimed, "I can whistle through my fingers, bulldog a steer, light a fire with two sticks, shoot a pistol with fair accuracy, set type, and teach school."[10]

Of her siblings, Clara Lou's playmates were her brother George and sister Polly. Kitty and Mabel were considerably older and they married early on during Clara Lou's childhood years. Sheridan recalled having a special fondness for Mabel, a "gentle girl [who] used to take my part against the others when they would tease me."[11]

Sheridan attended Robert E. Lee Grade School, located at 800 Mack Street. It was the smallest of three grade schools (Stonewall Jackson and Sam Houston being the other two) and the lowest-rated school in Denton. In 2017, it was announced that the school would be renamed the Alice Moore Alexander Elementary School in honor of a beloved teacher.

In a 1957 interview, the family's onetime neighbor Elizabeth Chilwood described Sheridan as an

> earnest, straightforward youngster who was always friendly, always eager to do her part.... If she came in while youwere sweeping, she'd say "Give me the broom and you go do something else".... She was brought up at home to work. She was so full of life that she was kind of noisy, but she was well liked.... [Her] red hair was really too curly, but her ivory complexion was beautiful and did not need makeup.... In the neighborhood, we all used to say "Ludie's a pretty kid."[12]

Sheridan attended Denton Junior High School, located at 1007 Fulton Street. At this school, she enrolled in acting classes. An active member of her class, she participated as an understudy in school plays. In her senior year, she was voted class president.

Lula once stated that Clara Lou's desire to act in motion pictures surfaced early. "From the time of her first attendance of a movie, when she was just a few years old, Clara Lou has always stated her intentions of being a movie actress."[13] Such hypocrisy on Lula's "pride" infuriated her daughter to no end. Known for her straightforwardness and honesty, Sheridan had little patience for deceit.

Growing into young womanhood in a small, conservative town proved a challenge for the restless child. As she recalled to Robert Higgins in 1966, "I finally got over things like 'vanity is bad' and 'marriage is the only way for a woman.' That's when I started to fight my own battles. But I guess I started fighting as a kid. Otherwise, I'd never have gotten out of Denton."[14]

On Sheridan's yearbook page is this quote: "Dancing grey eyes and a smile that's worth while"—an apt description.[15]

After graduating from Denton Junior High School, Sheridan enrolled at North Texas State Teachers College. "My parents merely had to send me to some school and this one was handy," she recalled.[16] The college was formerly called Texas Normal

Sheridan and her sister Polly, circa 1938.

College and Teacher Training Institute when it first opened in 1890; today, it is known as the University of North Texas. Following in one sister's footsteps, Sheridan "planned" to pursue a teaching career, as sanctioned by her parents. She intended to major in art, but soon found it unsatisfying. She decided to switch to dramatics because she thought it would be more interesting. She loved her dramatic teacher, Myrtle Hardy, who cast her in a few college plays, including *Playgoers* (April 1933). Sheridan was also on the women's basketball, swimming and tennis teams.

Secretly, Sheridan aspired to be a band singer, "[b]ut that meant I thought I was pretty, and vanity was bad." At age 17, "I was very young and pudgy fat with kinky hair and a space between my teeth."[17] There seemed to be no point in seriously contemplating a career outside of teaching, as her parents would have opposed any other aspirations.

One day, Sheridan was visiting her friend Gwendolyn Woodford at a Denton dance studio. As she waited for Gwendolyn, she hummed a few bars of "Mood Indigo," a 1930 Duke Ellington jazz song. She was interrupted by a stranger who demanded, "Sing that through for me!" After Sheridan sang the song in its entirety, the stranger unexpectedly announced, "You get the job!"[18] The stranger was Bill Ardis, a local dance instructor, and he is credited for discovering Clara Lou Sheridan.

Ardis introduced her to Floyd Graham, conductor of the college band. After an audition, Graham hired her to sing with the band at college functions and other music venues in nearby cities. Sheridan became popularly known as the "Personality Girl." Her local appearances were frequently covered in the college newspaper, *Campus Chat*, and in the *Denton Record-Chronicle*. In one variety show reviewed by *Campus Chat*, Sheridan's singing voice was characterized as "original Harlem manner."[19]

With this experience, Sheridan began to seriously consider career options other than teaching—but knew she had to keep her parents in the dark. She even harbored the dream of being a glamorous member of a Broadway chorus line in faraway New York City. As Sheridan admitted a few years later, "I'm afraid teaching school was only a rare possibility. The teachers college was a good school to attend. We had a lot of fun and I doubt that any of us ever gave serious thought to the fact that someday the responsibility of teaching would be staring us in the face."[20]

During this time, a nationwide contest was underway that would spell the end of any further attempts at an actual teaching career.

Two

The Beauty Contest Winner

The fault of beauty contests is that the winners believe that they have won a chance at an acting career. They soon learn that this is far from true.[1]

In 1932, Paramount sponsored a nationwide search for an unknown girl to play "The Panther Woman" in their upcoming motion picture *Island of Lost Souls*. Kathleen Burke, a dental assistant in Chicago, was declared the winner. With the box office success of the film and the tremendous amount of publicity generated by the contest, Paramount dreamed up a new publicity stunt: an international search for 30 young men and women, at the peak of their physical beauty, to play small roles in a production called *Search for Beauty*. Contestants would be chosen from England, Scotland, Ireland, South Africa, Australia, New Zealand, Canada and the U.S. A typical ad such as this one popped up in national newspapers:

"I'd give anything to go to Hollywood!"

How many thousands of young men and women have expressed this wish, the desire to see the City of the Stars, to rub elbows with the greats, to enter the magic studio gates!

Perhaps this is your chance—now. To go not merely as a guest, but to enter Hollywood as one of its members with a contract in your pocket to appear in one picture—and maybe more!

The Majestic theater "International Search for Beauty" Contest may be your opportunity.[2]

Such a siren's call was irresistible to star-struck youngsters yearning for a way out of their bleak existences. Unbeknownst to Sheridan, her sister Kitty submitted her (Clara Lou's) picture to the *Dallas Morning News* office in the fall of 1932; later publicity claimed that this was done as a joke. The *Dallas Morning News* was one of hundreds of English-language newspapers worldwide that participated in Paramount's contest.

Sheridan heard of the contest but didn't think much of it. Then she saw her picture in the newspaper and found that she was listed as one of several contestants in that region of the state. She confronted John Rosenfield, drama editor of the newspaper. He informed her that Kitty had submitted her photograph. Sheridan did not believe she had much of a chance: "I did not think ... I was pretty enough."[3] She soon forgot about the whole thing.

After winning the local contest, Sheridan went on to win the statewide contest. After Sheridan's death, Dallas Palace Theater manager James O. Cherry vividly recalled: "Her application came in just at the deadline. I think the reason the judges picked her was because of her distinctive voice." Cherry recalled an "attractive girl who was very surprised to win a big thing like a statewide contest. She said she had no idea of becoming an actress. She was an ordinary girl then—except for that voice of hers."[4]

After winning the contest, Sheridan's application and photograph were sent to Paramount in Hollywood. Several judges culled through hundreds of entries in order to select 30 of the best-looking finalists. LeRoy Prinz, a choreographer, served as one of the judges and had to choose between three contestants for a finalist position. He simply threw the photographs in the air and, when Sheridan's picture landed face up, she was declared the lucky finalist!

In mid–July of 1933, Sheridan received the shock of her life. She recalled in 1944 that she was "studying to be a teacher at North Texas State Teachers College in Texas, when I got word to pack up and leave for Hollywood." Sheridan's parents "didn't like it worth a cent. They thought that I was too young to leave home. They'd Heard Things about Hollywood."[5]

Also chosen to represent Dallas was Alfred Delcambre, aged 32. Delcambre was the star center for the Southern Methodist University Mustangs football team from 1929 to 1931 and an all-star conference player in 1931. He graduated from college in 1932 with a degree in commerce. Based on the amount of newspaper coverage about Delcambre, the handsome young man was the favored candidate for screen stardom.

Bursting with pride, the *Denton Record-Chronicle* reported,

> Miss Clara Lou Sheridan, daughter of Mr. and Mrs. G.W. Sheridan, 402 South Elm Street, has been named joint winner with Alfred J. Delcambre of Dallas in the "Search for Beauty" contest sponsored during the last month by the Palace Theater of Dallas and a Dallas newspaper in conjunction with Paramount Pictures designed to find material for the screen and especially for the film, *Search for Beauty....* Screen tests were made of Miss Sheridan and Delcambre Monday afternoon and were sent to Hollywood where they will be judged along those of the other winners. Each contest winner has a chance to win a role in the screen production.... Miss Sheridan is well known in Denton, having appeared in several local productions, both in Denton High School and in Teachers College.[6]

Regarding her screen test, Sheridan admitted she was ill-prepared and only spoke her name for the camera. During the walking scene, she claimed that she stumbled and almost fell. By all indications, the disastrous test should have disqualified her from the competition. Sheridan was shocked when notified in early September that she was one of 15 women chosen from the worldwide contest; Delcambre was one of the male winners. The 30 contest winners were given five-week contracts at $50 per week, lodging at the Roosevelt Hotel and guaranteed small roles in *Search for Beauty.*

Once again, Delcambre dominated the local news coverage: "Alfred Delcambre, former all-conference man, leaves today for Hollywood to appear in the Paramount picture, *Search for Beauty.* This panther man will be accompanied by Clara Lou Sheridan, who with body-beautiful Del won the contest from this territory."[7]

Clara Lou's mother told the hometown reporters, "Clara Lou was thrilled to death, of course, but I really don't believe that she was half as pleased as I was. I'm so proud of her and so glad she is to have this chance."[8]

The winners arrived in Hollywood in mid–October and underwent strenuous preparation for their motion picture debut. As Sheridan recalled in 1939,

> I guess I thought this place would bring me a tremendous good time, with a few hours sacrificed here and there for work. I soon learned how wrong I was. Within a few days after arriving they put me into a school.... They kept me there for eight or nine hours a day for months. I had to study diction, and all the hundreds of ways of conveying thought and ideas through gestures and facial expressions. It sounds easy, but it was a nightmare. I soon felt that everything about me was wrong, and that my wonderful opportunity was crumbling because of it.

The worst part of all this preparation "was relearning the English language. I was born and reared in Texas, where speech is picturesque and filled with colloquialisms. The accent is broad, and, well, it's just Texas."[9] The whole experience of moviemaking was overwhelming to the novice; Sheridan later admitted, "I thought I'd never live through it."[10] She recalled the most terrifying moment occurred when she was supposed to speak her big line ("It's time to get up") in front of the camera. "Well, I rehearsed my lines—pardon me, my *line*—all right, but when they tried to make it a 'take,' I couldn't utter a sound. The director was disgusted, but I guess he was used to being patient and finally I got through it."[11]

While Sheridan was grateful to be in Hollywood, she had mixed feelings about how she got there. As she reflected in 1937,

> A few like Joan Blondell, Mary Astor, Corinne Griffith and Clara Bow have won great success on the screen, but for these few are scores lost in the shuffle of Hollywood.... Too often a beauty contest winner has nothing exceptional save her face and figure. Of course the opportunity offered is marvelous, one that hundreds of girls would like to have, for it opens the studio gates and places the girl before a camera.[12]

By 1966, she had a less charitable view on the studio-inspired beauty contests: "They're horrible on kids, because they break so many hearts."[13]

Search for Beauty, based on the obscure play *Love Your Body* by Schuyler E. Grey and Paul R. Milton, was earmarked as a showcase for two promising young actors, Larry "Buster" Crabbe and an English actress making her American film debut, Ida Lupino. Lupino, billed as the "English Jean Harlow" with a bleach dye job, later called the film "a darling little thing" and noted, "The greatest thing about it was that I met my best girlfriend, Ann Sheridan.... We were both so homesick. We didn't want to be stars, we just wanted to meet some nice guy and settle down."[14] Sheridan likewise had fond memories of her association with Lupino. "Ida is a dear, close friend," she told interviewer Ray Hagen. "I adore her. And she's a damn fine actress, too."[15]

Upon completion of the film, only five other contest winners (aside from Sheridan) were given new Paramount contracts with the standard six months' options: Delcambre; Julian Madison of Minnesota; Colin Tapley of New Zealand; Gwenllian Gill of Scotland, and Eldred Tilbury of South Africa. Tilbury and Gill were each awarded a $1000 bonus for being the standout male and female performers in the picture. The rest of the contestants were given tickets to return home. The problem was that many of them refused to leave and instead ran up big bills at the studio's expense. Paramount never ran such a large-scale contest again.

Sheridan's first screen appearance was in a Paramount short, *Hollywood on Parade No. B–5,* released in December 1933. The 15 "Search for Beauty" females are prominently featured throughout the nine-minute running time. Sheridan is

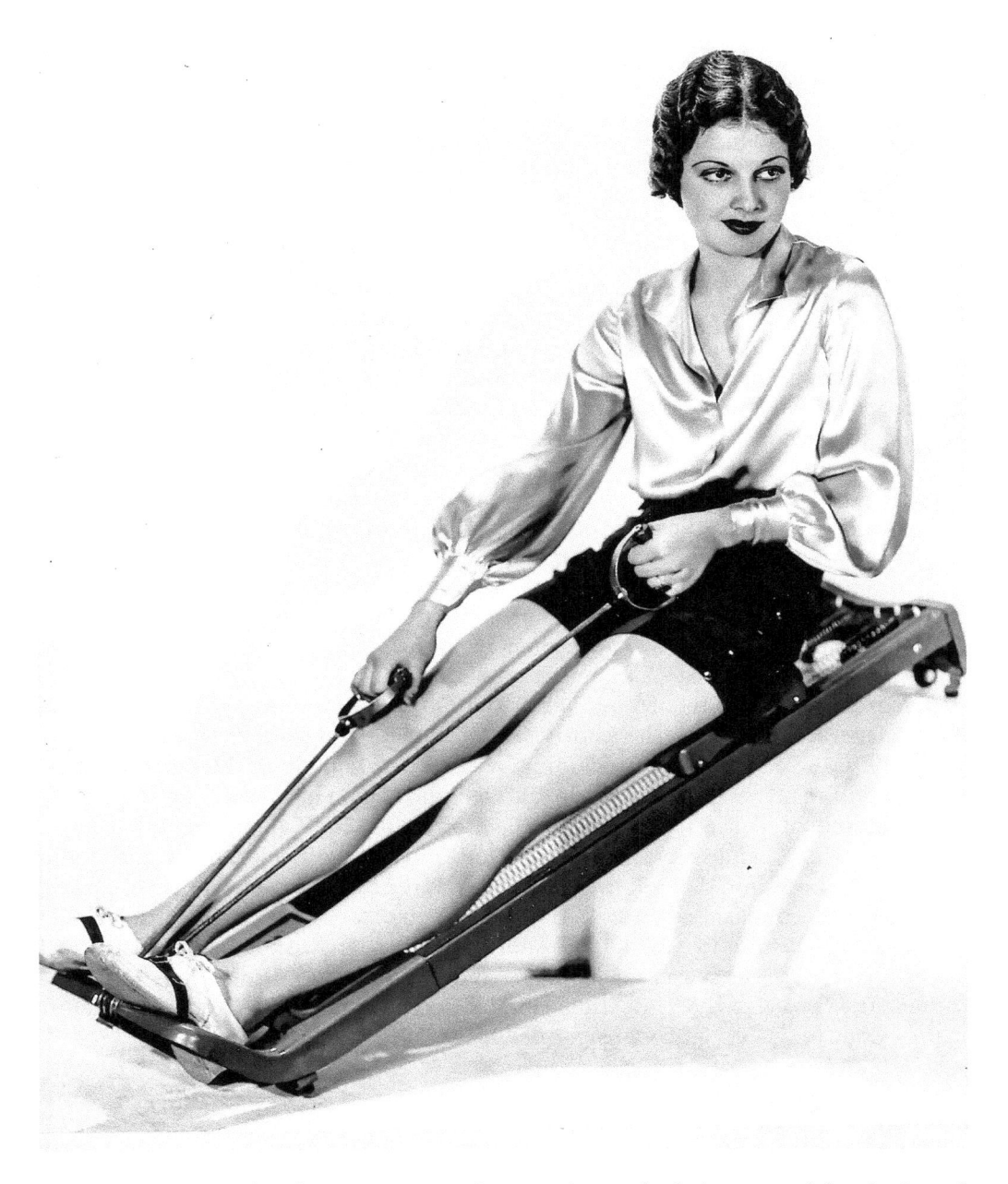

Sheridan was one of 30 beauty contest winners who made their screen debut in *Search for Beauty* (1934). Only Sheridan achieved film stardom.

generally hard to spot, but she is visible looking over silent comedian Lloyd Hamilton's left shoulder during the middle segment.

While many of the girls have lines, Sheridan remains quiet; perhaps the Texan accent was still too strong?

In January 1934, columnist Dan Thomas informed his readers of a potential new star:

Did you ever hear of Clara Lou Sheridan? Probably not. But look up somebody from Dallas ... and he'll tell you that Miss Sheridan is now a big movie star in Hollywood. As a matter of fact, Clara Lou has appeared in only one picture, *Search for Beauty*, and her part in it was a very small one. However, that makes no difference to the folks in Dallas, whence Clara Lou hails. To them, she already is a film celebrity, and when the film is shown there her name will probably go up in electric lights above those of Robert Armstrong and James Gleason, who have the leading roles. That's the way things work out in the movies. Players who make scarcely a ripple in Hollywood cause a big splash in their home towns, even though they only play small bits.[16]

Texas pride ran deep and, when *Search for Beauty* was previewed in Denton on January 27, 1934, locals were excited to see their hometown girl on the screen. However, there was a mix-up, and the reel containing her scenes did not arrive in time for the preview. Toward the end of its Denton run, in late February, the missing reel finally arrived and "the present version gives Miss Sheridan a number of speaking parts."[17] This is not the case in the current available print.

Search for Beauty involves a trio of con artists (Armstrong, Gertrude Michael, Gleason) who cash in on the health fitness craze by publishing raunchy magazines that promote sex under the guise of "Health and Clean Living." They enlist the aid of two unsuspecting Olympic gold medalists, Don Jackson (Crabbe) and Barbara Hilton (Lupino). The screenplay incorporates actual "Search for Beauty" contest winners when Don sets up a similar contest to promote the magazine. However, the golden pair quickly catches on to the trio's scheme and thwart their efforts. It all works out in the end thanks to Barbara's intervention.

Search for Beauty turned out better than it should have and the reviews were mostly favorable. However, the feature ran into censorship trouble. Due to the prevalence of pre–Code elements (including brief rear male nudity), this form of "family entertainment" was condemned by the Catholic Legion of Decency for its morally offensive content. With enforcement of the Production Code starting on July 1, 1934, *Search for Beauty*, and several other pre–Code movies, were relegated to the studio vaults. If, in the period that followed, a studio wanted to reissue any of these features, the offensive scenes had to be cut. In the case of *Search for Beauty*, such editing would have reduced the film to a 20-minute short. This film languished in obscurity until 2009 when it was released as part of the six-movie DVD set *Pre-Code Hollywood Collection.* The release of this collection, coupled with film historians' renewed interest in pre–Code films, brought *Search for Beauty* back into the spotlight.

Three

Clara Lou, Extra Girl

Being a contest winner gets you to Hollywood ... but it doesn't keep you there.[1]

After her inauspicious debut in *Search for Beauty*, Sheridan began what she termed a "series of fast exits" or bit parts.[2] In her next film, *Bolero*, she was most likely present in the dance hall or night club sequences, but it's hard to tell. The musical-drama, starring George Raft, Carole Lombard and an up-and-coming British actor, Ray Milland, was based on the life of Maurice Mouvet, one of the most successful male dancers of dance teams prior to the World War I period in the United States and Europe. Of particular interest is the presence of legendary burlesque star Sally Rand, who performs her trademark ostrich fan dance that conceals her suggested nude form for titillated moviegoers.

Of all the stars on the Paramount lot, Sheridan had the fondest memories of Carole Lombard: "I was only a stock girl at Paramount where she was a big star. But she would always stop and speak to me on the lot—as though I were important, too."[3] It was that same kind of warmth and generosity that Sheridan demonstrated in her days as a star.

Released in late February, *Bolero* was well received by critics and filmgoers. With its box office success, the feature spawned a follow-up film, *Rumba*, the following year.

While learning film acting techniques, Sheridan honed her skills by performing in the studio's stock plays. Paramount executives could attend these plays and watch potential screen stars like Ida Lupino and "Buster" Crabbe give live performances. These plays were presented on the lot for a day or two, and players who excelled often found themselves assigned roles in upcoming films. "Most of us were pretty horrible, because we'd had no training whatsoever," Sheridan told Hagen.[4] Compounding the issue: "[T]he teachers would come to watch us on the set and would usually end up arguing with the directors about how a certain scene should be played, so we ended up more confused than ever."[5]

Crabbe had a different view of this experience. "It was more like an actor's workshop, where we could practice reading lines or ask questions. We could study different techniques, play different characters in little skits and learn how to play our best sides to the camera—anything that would ease us out of our amateurism into passable professionals."[6]

In one studio play, *Double Door*, Lupino and Crabbe got the leading roles and Sheridan appeared as a maid. But Sheridan's performance was noticed and she was awarded a featured role in the rowdy military comedy *Come On Marines!* Apart from the opportunity to work with one of her favorite directors, Henry Hathaway, it wasn't much of a break. Sheridan was incorrectly identified as playing Shirley in both *Variety* and *The New York Times* even though the film's final credits list her (thirteenth) as playing Loretta.

The original screenplay had collected dust at Paramount since early August 1931. In January 1934, production began with a revised script but no male lead; executives were pondering whether to cast the established Richard Arlen or the up-and-coming Crabbe. Arlen won the part opposite a newly dark-haired Ida Lupino (in her second movie for Paramount). *Come On Marines!* did not mean much to the players or to audiences. The critics did not find much to cheer about either.

Sheridan's next film, *Murder at the Vanities*, has become something of a cult film due to its salacious pre–Code elements. It was based on a successful, but critically panned, Earl Carroll–Rufus King 1933 Broadway play which had featured Bela Lugosi in a supporting role. It was not the play's murder mystery–musical hybrid plot that drew customers; rather, it was the scantily clad (in some cases, downright nude!) show girls prominently on display. When Paramount bought the screen rights, the censors were apprehensive that too much would be seen of girls wearing too little. Several scripts were submitted to Joseph Breen at the Association of Motion Picture Producers (AMPP) for approval. The resulting film gleefully illustrates that the producers ignored many of Breen's suggestions and it is this impertinent attitude that makes this film so entertaining today.

Released in late May, the picture was a hit and most critics saw its box office potential. Like other pre–Code films, *Murder at the Vanities* disappeared from view for many years until resurfacing in the previously mentioned DVD set.

With all of the action in the film, the viewer has to resort to freeze-framing to spot Sheridan in a fleeting shot during the last production number. One gets a better glimpse when she is seen standing behind stars Carl Brisson and Kitty Carlisle during the denouement.

Sheridan received her first fan magazine coverage in a ten-starlet pictorial spread in *The New Movie Magazine*. It has been reported that both Lucille Ball and Lynn Bari appeared as chorus girls; Alan Ladd supposedly appeared as a chorus boy, but this has not been substantiated.

Many Happy Returns, Sheridan's next feature, was a musical farce starring Gracie Allen, George Burns, Ray Milland and Guy Lombardo and His Royal Canadians (Lombardo is top-billed, but the film really belongs to Allen). The zany plot was based on Lady Mary Cameron's 1933 novel *My Dayton, Darling* (some publications cite Cameron's story "Once a Bridegroom" as the source). *Many Happy Returns* was met with mixed reviews, but proved highly popular among moviegoers. Sheridan is not easily spotted amidst the chaos.

Shoot the Works, starring Jack Oakie, Ben Bernie and Dorothy Dell under Wesley Ruggles' brisk direction, offered Sheridan some dialogue and a piquant close-up. The film is based on a sordid Ben Hecht–Gene Fowler play, *The Great Magoo*, that closed after 11 performances on Broadway in 1932. The film's title, however, came from a 1931 musical revue. The screenplay was considerably revised in order to meet the newly enforced Production Code.

What sparks the film is the performance of Dell, who made a great impression here and in two other early films, *Wharf Angel* and *Little Miss Marker*. Dell showed promise of becoming a major star for Paramount. The studio had recently cast her in an important role opposite Gary Cooper and Shirley Temple in *Now and Forever.* But fate dealt a cruel blow: The 19-year-old actress was killed in an automobile accident before *Shoot the Works* reached theaters.

The song "With My Eyes Wide Open, I'm Dreaming," introduced by Oakie and Dell, became a big hit and was later recorded by artists Patti Page, Dean Martin and Natalie Cole. In 1939, *Shoot the Works* was remade as *Some Like It Hot* (no connection to the Billy Wilder comedy classic), with Bob Hope and Shirley Ross.

In Sheridan's next film, *Kiss and Make Up*, she has a fleeting moment near the beginning. Alongside Sheridan in small parts were the WAMPAS Baby Stars of 1934, who were given prominent billing in the credits. The WAMPAS Baby Stars was a promotional campaign that selected a group of actresses who the Western Association of Motion Picture Advertisers felt were on the brink of stardom. Previous WAMPAS stars included Jean Arthur (1929), Loretta Young (1929), Joan Blondell (1931) and Ginger Rogers (1932). The winners featured here were the last group as the WAMPAS disbanded the following year. Some of the future "stars" included Judith Arlen, Lu Ann Meredith and Jacqueline Wells (who fared better later as Julie Bishop).

This romantic farce, based on the play *Kozmetika* by István Békeffy, stars Cary Grant, Helen Mack, Genevieve Tobin and Edward Everett Horton. There is very little to this bubbly froth to entice today's viewer except for the fact that Grant, singing for one of the few times in his career, croons "Love Divided by Two."

As an extra, even Sheridan's *hands* were seen in insert shots in several Paramount films. "I used to go to Grauman's Chinese or Pantages," she told interviewer John Kobal, "and sit there waiting to see my faceless body on the screen."[7]

Sheridan recalled that there were concerns that she was not serious about her career. "They always wanted you to be seen as to be serious at Paramount," she told Kobal. "When they caught you laughing, the front office would say you weren't serious."[8] Her drama coach, Nina Mouise, even advised her to return to Texas as she doubted Sheridan could succeed. Her advice spurred Sheridan to action. "[T]he minute she said go back," Sheridan told Hagen, "that gave me the incentive to prove to her that I was serious about my career."[9]

Despite the occasional discouragement, Sheridan called working at Paramount "sheer fun. It was hard work, but this was the glitter, the glamour, the stars in your eyes. I didn't care if I worked all night and started on another picture the next day. I was dead tired, but there was always the energy."[10] Throughout, Sheridan remained grateful to be employed. "All those bits and extra work I was shoved into taught me something. And of course this was the middle of the Depression and, though I didn't know it at the time, I was damn lucky to be making $50 a week."[11]

When Sheridan got word that Paramount was about to drop her option, she acted quickly. She spoke with Max Shauer, the executive in charge of new players, and convinced him to keep her on the payroll. Her contract was renewed for another six months, still at $50 per week.

The studio executives began to feel that she was a starlet worth cultivating. In the June 20 *Hollywood Reporter*, a four-page Paramount ad pronounced, "[T]he old cry for new faces is ever in the air. New faces for old box-offices, new attractions to stimulate business ... new personalities to capture public fancy."[12] Clara Lou Sheridan was touted as one of the 16 new screen personalities for 1935; among the few to achieve later success were Fred MacMurray, Lloyd Nolan and Claude Rains. The rest of the "promising players" quickly faded into obscurity. Fellow "Search for Beauty" winner Gwenllian Gill eventually returned to England in search of better film roles.

The publicity department began to work overtime to get Sheridan's face and name out to the public with innocuous photo captions such as this one: "Clara Lou Sheridan, lovely Paramount player ... is the embodiment of all that is fresh and youthful."[13] In a news item entitled "Clara Lou Sheridan Possesses Perfect Camera Face," she was judged by Lee Tover, one of Hollywood's best cameraman, to have the perfect "camera face." Tover said that her face was "one of the very few unusual cases where perfection is appreciated. Her eyes are the perfect color for photography, hazel, and are ideally spaced. Her mouth is so well proportioned that it needs no change with makeups."[14]

In this photograph, Sheridan looks very much like "the It Girl" Clara Bow, to whom she was often compared. Then Ann's own title, "the Oomph Girl," came along.

Despite Paramount's bold proclamations of stardom, Sheridan continued to appear in the "fast exits" roles. Near the conclusion of *The Notorious Sophie Lang* (released in mid–July), she appears as one of the many mannequins in a fashion show. Gertrude Michael was fabulous in the title role; at the time, Paramount was beginning to build her up as an important star. The critics were generally impressed and the film was popular enough to spawn two follow-ups. But none of these films turned Michael into a star, which is a pity since she had proven to be a talented and versatile performer.

Sheridan received tenth billing in *Ladies Should Listen*, which starred Cary Grant, Frances Drake, and Edward Everett Horton. In a brief scene, she plays Adele, a telephone operator, and speaks her lines with clear diction and tonal control. The vocal coach had obviously helped her overcome her Texas drawl.

There is some confusion as to the original source for this romantic farce. On-screen credits state that the film is based on a play by Alfred Savoir and Guy Bolton. However, studio records indicate that the play's original title was *Le demoiselle de Passy* (written by Savoir), which was later adapted by Bolton and performed at a summer stock theater.

Of sole interest is the appearance of former silent star Charles Ray in a small role as Henri. Some of the reviews were favorable, but the film was not financially successful.

Next in line was an effective little gem displaying the darker side of small-time vaudeville, *You Belong to Me*. One of the memorable actors in the cast was Helen Morgan, the ill-fated blues singer of *Show Boat* fame. As an added treat, Morgan sings a blues song, "When He Comes Home to Me." Despite Morgan's lovely appearance, the viewer senses tragedy behind her large, sad eyes, which only adds to her poignant appeal.

Most impressive, however, is the outstanding performance by young David Holt, whose character is the film's emotional centerpiece. Upon the movie's release in early September, Holt was widely proclaimed as serious competition for Shirley Temple. Instead, he was relegated to small supporting roles and bits for the remainder of his motion picture career. As for Sheridan, you have to look quickly during the wedding party scene. Her face is not always visible but her thick, unruly hair is a dead giveaway.

It is much more difficult to spot Sheridan in her next film. *Wagon Wheels*, based on Zane Grey's 1929 novel *Fighting Caravans*, was Sheridan's first Western. The film, starring Randolph Scott and Gail Patrick, was a remake of Paramount's *Fighting Caravans* (1931) with Gary Cooper and Lily Damita. Westerns were then popular with the action crowd and, running 56 minutes, *Wagon Wheels* was a satisfactory second feature on most theater bills.

In *The Lemon Drop Kid*, Sheridan handles a few lines of dialogue with snappy sarcasm while she engages in a conversation with Alfred Delcambre (now occasionally playing bit parts) in the early racetrack scene. Her face is fuller than usual, but there's no mistaking that voice. In this instance, we get an early glimpse of the future master of zingy retorts. The film, written by Damon Runyan, was not successful. There was a revamped remake with Bob Hope and Marilyn Maxwell in 1951.

Sheridan makes a fleeting appearance as a theater patron in *Mrs. Wiggs of the Cabbage Patch*. The film was based on a 1904 play by Anne Crawford Flexner, who had combined two novels by Alice Hegan Rice, *Mrs. Wiggs of the Cabbage Patch* (1901) and its sequel, *Lovey Mary* (1903). The popular play spawned four film versions; the 1914 and 1919 films primarily focused on "Lovey Mary" (which, in turn, inspired the 1926 film of the same name). By the time of the sound versions in 1934 and 1942, "Lovey Mary" had disappeared from the storyline and Mrs. Wiggs (Pauline Lord in 1934 and Fay Bainter in 1942) stepped into the spotlight. Much of the plot is sentimental claptrap. Fortunately, W.C. Fields makes a most welcome appearance in the last 15 minutes. Due to Fields' popularity, the feature was one of Paramount's highest grossing films of the year.

In every respect, Sheridan's next feature, *Limehouse Blues*, was the entertainment and box office antithesis of *Mrs. Wiggs*. Sheridan appears in the final minutes, uttering one line in an English accent (no doubt coached by her friend Ida Lupino) as she enters the night club with two gentlemen. The dismal box office results of this George Raft film surprised no one.

College Rhythm, a musical comedy starring Jack Oakie, Mary Brian, Joe Penner

Like most young Hollywood starlets, Sheridan posed for many cheesecake stills. It was all part of the game.

and Lyda Roberti, has often been cited as the breakthrough film that got Sheridan out of the extra ranks. As Connie, the gloves salesgirl, she was filling in for an ailing Roberti. That scene was rewritten to fit Sheridan's character. According to a press release, "Her performance surprised the company. She did her bit so well that Director [Norman] Taurog ordered her part to be enlarged."[15] Taurog told the executives that Sheridan should receive a bigger build-up. His recommendation convinced

Paramount to renew her contract in late September for another six months (again with no pay raise). This was fortunate, as another news item reported, "[A]fter a year ... she was in danger of joining her other beauty contest winners in oblivion."[16] Other holdovers from the "Search for Beauty" contest who received contract renewals were Gwenllian Gill, Alfred Delcambre, Julian Madison and Colin Tapley. Sheridan always professed her gratitude to Taurog for his interest in helping her fledgling career along.

College Rhythm, a typical, raucous Oakie musical comedy, proved to be a popular feature.

Sheridan's next movie, *Ready for Love*, came from a most unlikely source. This lighthearted froth, with a strain of screwball comedy, was inspired by the dramatic play *The Whipping* by Eulalie Spence; the play in turn was based on the 1930 novel of the same name by Roy Flanagan. The novel was a "fierce and biting" story of a small Southern town in which a promiscuous white girl retaliates when the Ku Klux Klan tries to run her out.[17] Spence, a black writer from the British West Indies, was unable to get her play performed due to its controversial theme, so she sold the property to Paramount. The play was heavily reworked to conform to the Production Code. Released as *Ready for Love*, the film stars Ida Lupino and Richard Arlen in a slight story that details the madcap romantic adventures of a young woman who is mistaken for an older man's mistress in a conservative small town—quite a departure from Spence's original work.

Sheridan can be spotted in a brief scene at the beginning of the Basket Social. Her character, Priscilla, looks very fetching in her Pilgrim outfit. The other notable aspect of this movie is that it features the first screen appearance of Terry, the terrier who achieved fame as Toto in *The Wizard of Oz* (1939).

Sheridan's final bit for 1934 was in MGM's three-strip Technicolor short *Star Night at the Cocoanut Grove*. Stars like Gary Cooper, Bing Crosby and Jack Oakie are trotted out for audience amusement; Mary Pickford makes a showing to the delight of her legion of fans, who did not know that this would be "America's Sweetheart's" final screen appearance. Sheridan, appearing fourth in line as one of the Sands of the Desert models, looks stunning in a skimpy Egyptian gown, plumed headdress and a red cape. Also present is Edward Norris, who would soon play a major role in Sheridan's romantic life.

Four

The Big Paramount Build-Up

I was paid $50 a week by that studio and all I did for two and a half years was to show my knees in swim suits and play bits in B pictures.[1]

After Paramount took up the second six-months option in November, executives decided that "Clara Lou" would not work for the marquee. Sheridan was asked to choose a different first name (her suggestion of "Lou" sounded too masculine). The name "Ann" was suggested, and the executives liked the sound of "Ann Sheridan." A press release notified the world of the name change. In the *Denton Record-Chronicle*, the headline read, "Clara Lou Sheridan shortens name, lengthens contract with movies simultaneously."[2]

Her first film as Ann Sheridan was *Behold My Wife!*, an "A" film that starred Sylvia Sidney and Gene Raymond. Sheridan recalled to Hagen, "Mitchell Leisen, the director, was a very good friend of mine and he went to the front office and got this part for me."[3] Leisen, one of Sheridan's favorite directors at Paramount, was among the studio's leading directors and held considerable clout.

Behold My Wife! was based on a successful 1893 novel, *The Translation of a Savage* by Sir Gilbert Parker, a Canadian novelist and British politician. The novel spawned two early motion pictures. The first, which retained the novel's title, was produced by the Edison Company in 1913 and starred Mary Fuller. This short followed the basic plot of the novel, in which the hero, jilted by his English fiancée, vows vengeance on his snobbish family. He travels to the Hudson Bay in Canada and marries a Native American princess. He exacts his revenge when he sends her to his family in London. Initially horrified, the family soon embraces and transforms the "savage" into a respectable woman who can now live among them.

The second version, entitled *Behold My Wife*, was produced in 1920 by the Famous Players–Lasky Company, which later became Paramount Pictures. The film starred Mabel Julienne Scott, Milton Sills and Elliott Dexter. Both films are considered lost.

The story's incarnation was briefly and offensively titled *Red Woman* during production. Recently ousted studio head B.P. Schulberg produced the film as a showcase for his mistress, Sylvia Sidney. The plot was considerably reworked and the locale was moved from London to New York City and from the Canadian wilderness to the American Midwest. The most significant change was the transformation of the English fiancée to the working-class girl played by Sheridan.

Sheridan is ninth-billed as Mary White, the stenographer who loves Michael Carter (Raymond), the perpetually drunk scion of a wealthy New York family. She makes her appearance early and it is a compelling one. It is her wedding day and she is frantically trying to locate Michael. Michael's sister (Juliette Compton) sympathetically tells her that she is not the first girl Michael has abandoned like this. "I don't believe it. He loves me! I know he does!" Mary hysterically protests. When she is told that Michael sailed for France, Mary collapses on the bed, sobbing. Diana tries to console her with a large check and a ticket to California. After Diana leaves, Mary stares plaintively at the curtained window, which seems to beckon...

After Mary's suicide, the film quickly deteriorates into improbable melodramatic foam and viewers should not bother watching this feature to its painful end.

Behold My Wife! was not well received by the critics. Released in early December 1934, it did not make its way to New York City until mid–February due to poor reviews and box office results—a sure sign that Paramount had a real turkey on its hands.

Sheridan made a strong impression in her brief scenes. According to Kobal, Sidney believed the best thing about the film was "a kid named Ann Sheridan."[4] Sidney's biographer, Scott O'Brien, agreed: "Sheridan was the only one who came out ahead in this opus" due to her "standout turn."[5] As Sheridan reflected to Kobal, "Committing suicide was the great thing, you know. Makes everybody look at you and think you're serious about your career."

Due to her big moment, Sheridan received attention from some of the major critics. *Variety* prophetically noted, "There's a girl in an earlier sequence bit, Ann Sheridan, who should be an important screen personality someday if her work here is any criterion."

With the favorable comments, Sheridan thought she was finally on her way out of the extra ranks. However, "[n]othing happened after that.... Nothing."[6] It was back to "fast exits" and a minor supporting role.

A definite step up, Sheridan's next film was *One Hour Late*, an unpretentious, consistently enjoyable romantic comedy. In the leading role was Joe Morrison, a radio star who became a sensation with the song "The Last Round-Up." After a featured role in *The Old Fashioned Way*, Morrison seemed earmarked for stardom and given a big build-up in *One Hour Late*. But he did not fare well with the public despite his good looks, personable acting style and beautiful tenor voice. There was room at Paramount for one singer and that was reserved for popular crooner Bing Crosby. After a few more minor pictures, Morrison gave up his movie career and returned to radio. Sheridan can be seen in the office background in several scenes.

Next up was a minor supporting role in a Zane Grey Western, *Home on the Range*, in which Sheridan was seventh-billed as Elsie Brownly. The top-liners in the cast were Jackie Coogan (the child star of the 1920s in a comeback bid), Evelyn Brent (a former Paramount star on a career downslide) and rising star Randolph Scott. Previewed in October as *Code of the West*, the film was held back for retakes after Paramount acquired the rights to the song "Home on the Range." A new sequence with Joe Morrison singing this song was inserted prior to the film's release in late December. The low-budgeted feature was a Western with a racetrack background and most critics and moviegoers were not impressed. It has been called the worst of Paramount's Zane Grey–Randolph Scott features. Today, *Home on the Range* is either lost or extremely hard to find.

In *Enter Madame*, Sheridan's first release in 1935, she had another inconsequential bit. The romantic comedy with opera sequences was based on a successful 1920 play of the same name. Gilda Varesi, who co-wrote and starred in the play, based the leading character on her mother, opera singer Elena Boccabadati Varesi. *Enter Madame* was heralded as one of the best plays of the 1920–21 season. The first film version was produced in 1922 with Clara Kimball Young, Elliott Dexter and Louise Dresser. Prints of this film exist in a few European archives.

The 1935 version was Paramount's attempt to cash in on Grace Moore's phenomenal success with Columbia's *One Night of Love* (1934), but the end results fell considerably short of the mark. Its one plus is the engaging presence of Cary Grant.

The next feature, *Rumba*, was a poor rehash of *Bolero* that had the same leading actors but none of its entertaining pre–Code touches. The movie never quite catches fire and did nothing for those associated with it.

Sheridan finally got a big break as Randolph Scott's leading lady in another Zane Grey Western, *Rocky Mountain Mystery*. She recalled that she got the part because she lied to the casting director about her ability to ride a horse. Although she quickly learned, her fib caught up with her when she back-flipped off a horse that was galloping wildly through a field. In 1949, Sheridan joked, "It was wonderful training. Actors working in Westerns have the stiffest competition there is—the hero's horse."[7]

Sheridan was fortunate to be cast in a film based on Grey's work as he was a highly popular American author of adventure novels and stories commonly

Sheridan's break came when she played her first important role opposite Randolph Scott in a Zane Grey Western, *Rocky Mountain Mystery* (1934).

associated with the Western genre during the early 1900s. His books and short stories have been adapted into over 110 features dating back as early as 1911.

Rocky Mountain Mystery was based on Grey's unpublished story "Golden Dreams." The plot of the 1922 movie *Golden Dreams* was suggested by an unidentified Zane Grey story, but its plot is vastly different from two other versions. The first, *Golden Dreams*, an independent production distributed by Goldwyn Distributing Corporation, starred Rose Dione and Norris McKay. The second, Paramount's *The Vanishing Pioneer* (1928), based on the same story, featured Jack Holt, William Powell and, in his film debut, Tim Holt, age 9. This film's plot is also markedly different from the 1935 version. Both of the silent versions are considered lost.

The *Rocky Mountain Mystery* screenplay was a collaborative effort between Edward E. Paramore, Jr., and Ethel Doherty. Grey's story was reworked and updated with modern-day elements. It was shot on location at the Doble Mine and the stamping mill on Gold Mountain in Big Bear Valley, California. The shooting title was *The Vanishing Pioneer* and, when it was previewed by *Motion Picture Herald* in early November 1934, it bore this title. The reviewer noted that Ann Sheridan was previously known as Clara Lou Sheridan. When the film was released in early February under the new title, it was expected that the Zane Grey-Randolph Scott combination would prove as popular as other previous outings.

The convoluted plot involves mining engineer Larry Sutton (Scott), who teams with Deputy Sheriff Murdock (Charles "Chic" Sale) to investigate the murder of Adolph Borg, a ranch caretaker. Living at the ranch are an assortment of suspicious characters: the invalid Jim Ballard (George F. Marion), his nieces Rita (Sheridan) and Flora (Kathleen Burke) and nephew Fritz (Howard Wilson); Flora and Fritz are anxious for the old man to die so they can collect their inheritance. Other characters include Ling Yat (Willie Fung), the widowed housekeeper Mrs. Borg (Mrs. Leslie Carter) and her son John (James Eagles). Sutton is suspicious of the whole lot—except for Rita, of course. After two gruesome murders, the true killer is finally revealed and the pretty Rita is rescued in an exciting climax.

Rocky Mountain Mystery emerged as a routine mystery–Western "B" film that has some interesting touches, but the incoherent direction and overacting by supporting cast members reduce the feature to a head-scratcher. This must have been quite a letdown for the esteemed stage actress Mrs. Leslie Carter (known in her heyday as "the American Sarah Bernhardt"), who gives an overwrought, hammy performance.[8] Fourth-billed Sheridan has little to work with and fails to make much of an impression. She reflected to Hagen, "Nothing to do, no acting, it was just playing a lead, that's all."[9] At least she had something to put on her résumé.

The 68-minute feature, found on the bottom half of most theater bills, garnered scant attention from the trade papers. Many reviewers did not even acknowledge Sheridan's performance. *Rocky Mountain Mystery* was reissued in the late 1940s as *The Fighting Westerner*. This is the version that is available today on various DVDs. In his book on Randolph Scott, Robert Nott astutely noted, "Heroine Ann Sheridan is plump and pale, displaying little acting talent and none of the sensuous 'oomph' that she would be associated with a few years later."[10]

Sheridan's career took another step forward opposite Fred MacMurray in an entertaining but minor "B" action film, *Car 99*. This was MacMurray's first solo film after making a splash as Claudette Colbert's leading man in *The Gilded Lily* (1935).

Car 99 was based on a short story, "Hue and Cry," by Karl W. Detzer, an investigative journalist who often rode with the Michigan State Police on calls. Several of Detzer's stories based on these experiences were published in *The Saturday Evening Post* and eventually garnered national attention. Paramount hired Detzer to write a screenplay with C. Gardner Sullivan; Detzer also served as the technical advisor.

The shoot proved a challenge for Sheridan and director Charles Barton was of little help. MacMurray said,

> I remember we were working outside with the reflectors and the lights and the poor girl, where we were standing, had to look up a little bit and she just couldn't do it. The tears ran down her eyes; they put up screens to try to get the lights down, but she just couldn't face them. We all thought that the poor girl wouldn't make it. That girl was Clara Lou Sheridan.[11]

Veteran actor Sir Guy Standing was sympathetic to the youngster and helped build her confidence by reading the script with her and coaching her on her line readings. A few years later, Sheridan gratefully recalled to Gladys Hall that Standing was "simply wonderful to me. He was the first to give me a warm and helping hand."[12]

The plot concerns Ross Martin (MacMurray), a new recruit for the Michigan State Police, assigned to a small rural town where his girlfriend Mary Adams (third-billed Sheridan) is the telephone operator. Professor Anthony (Standing), a newcomer to town, is actually the mastermind behind a gang that just committed a big bank robbery. Ross accidentally stumbles upon the truth, but the professor and his "daughter" (Marina Schubert) escape. After Sergeant Barrel (William Frawley) forces Ross to turn in his badge, Ross loses heart and becomes an auto mechanic. Anthony and his gang rob the local bank and kidnap Mary. Ross manages to capture the crooks and is reinstated on the police force.

As one of "Paramount's Protégées" in 1935, Sheridan (top right) was destined for better things—before being fired. Clockwise after Ann: Katherine DeMille, Wendy Barrie, Gertrude Michael, Gail Patrick and Grace Bradley.

Car 99 is a low-budgeted film that has a generous amount of folksy humor mixed in with plausible dramatic action. Despite its designation on the lower half of movie bills, it was well-received by critics upon its release in early March. In some cases, Sheridan was referred to as one in a group of "promising youngsters" in the cast. Further down the cast list was the once highly touted Alfred Delcambre, who was about a year away from ending his less-than-stellar screen career.

A few years later, Sheridan revealed her flair for dramatics and self-deprecating humor (two traits that endeared her to those who worked with her) when she judged her performance in *Car 99* as "terrible. Simply awful. When the word went around for the second time that I was on the way out, I didn't even try to fix things up."[13]

According to publicity, the positive notices for the last two pictures convinced Paramount that Sheridan had the makings of a star. In March, she was named one of the six "Paramount Protégées" of 1935 who showed the most promise; the others were Gail Patrick, Gertrude Michael, Katherine DeMille, Grace Bradley and Wendy Barrie. The six were selected by nearly 300 studio executives, directors, writers and actors who believed these actresses were "the most likely starring material among the studio's eighteen young actresses." And there was more: "Executives have announced that particular pains will be taken to advance them as rapidly as possible during the coming year."[14] Sheridan recalled a few years later that "[b]eing one of the six chosen to remain gave me another little shot in the arm of hope."[15] The *Denton Record-Chronicle* trumpeted this headline: "Ann Sheridan, Denton Girl, One of 'The Paramount Protégées' of 1935; Gets Important Film Roles."[16]

Unfortunately for Sheridan, the "important film roles" failed to materialize. Her next film, *Mississippi* with Bing Crosby and W.C. Fields, released later in March, found her back in a bit as one of leading lady Joan Bennett's finishing school friends. She appears in three brief scenes and has only a few lines—hardly a showcase for a "protégée."

The pre–Civil War musical comedy was based on Booth Tarkington's play *Magnolia*, which had a short Broadway run in 1923. The first motion picture version of that play was produced by Paramount as *The Fighting Coward* (1924), with a teenage Mary Astor as the feminine lead. The second version was the early talkie *River of Romance* (1929) with Charles "Buddy" Rogers and Mary Brian. It's believed to be a lost film.

The 1935 version was considerably revamped to conform to Crosby's genial screen image and afford him a few songs to croon. Fields is the biggest provider of laughs as the showboat captain who capitalizes on Crosby's popularity as the fictional "Notorious Colonel Steele, the Singing Killer." Although the movie was an odd blend of the standard Crosby musical and Fields comedy, it was a successful box office attraction.

Sheridan was next loaned out for a leading lady role in *Red Blood of Courage*. This feature was produced by the Maurice Conn production unit for Ambassador, a company that began operations in 1934. Although Sheridan received second billing, the impact was mitigated by the fact that Ambassador was a Poverty Row studio, primarily known for its low-budget features. *Red Blood of Courage* was hardly noticed by critics in the metropolitan areas.

The stalwart hero of the photoplay was Kermit Maynard, the younger brother of popular cowboy star Ken Maynard. Kermit was a stuntman who had doubled for

George O'Brien and Warner Baxter during the 1920s. During the shoot, Maynard was nearly burned alive during the log cabin fire sequence when the set caught fire prematurely during filming. Sheridan was thrown from a horse and required a few days of bed rest before returning to work.

Red Blood of Courage was Maynard's fourth in a series of 17 films based on James Oliver Curwood stories. Curwood was a renowned American action-adventure author and conservationist. His books ranked among the top-ten best sellers in the U.S. in the early 1920s. At the time of his death in 1927, he was considered the highest-paid (per word) author in the world. There is some confusion as to the original source. Some websites refer to it as a novel but in the opening credits, it is listed as an original story. The 1914 short film *Caryl of the Mountains* has been cited as the first version of this work. However, while *Red Blood of Courage* has some similarities to that short, there are many differences.

Jim Sullivan (Maynard) of the Northwest Mounted Police goes undercover to search for a missing Mountie. He arouses the suspicions of the unscrupulous Bart, a member of a gang headed by Pete Drago. Drago is masquerading as Mark Henry (the real Henry is being held prisoner) in order to gain control of some oil-rich property. Henry's niece Elizabeth (Sheridan) has not seen her uncle in many years. When she overhears Drago and Bart discuss their nefarious scheme, she runs away but is followed by Bart. She is rescued by Jim, who assures her that he is one of the good guys. The melodramatic plot comes to a boil with a cabin fire, a runaway wagon and a last-minute rescue by the Northwest Mounted Police.

Only a handful of critics bothered to review *Red Blood of Courage* when it was released in mid–April. The movie did little to advance the careers of anyone involved. Despite the lack of significant progress in Sheridan's career, columnists announced that the actress "was being built up by Paramount."[17]

Then came the surprise. When it was time to renew Sheridan's option for another six months, Paramount dropped her. In the dismissal memo, it was asserted that Sheridan was being let go because she was lazy, fat and prone to raucous laughter. All of this was proof that she did not take her career seriously. Sheridan believed that the real reason boiled down to finances. Since she was making between $75 and $100 per week, she would have gotten a $25 raise with the renewal. As Sheridan reasoned, "They had other people at fifty dollars they could use for the same things, so why bother with me?"[18]

The Glass Key, released at the end of May, was the first movie version of Dashiell Hammett's 1931 novel. Paramount bought the screen rights to use it as a Gary Cooper feature in 1931, but constant negotiations between the movie company and the Hays Office (due to the story's depiction of state officials) held the production up until it was finally cleared for production in early 1935. George Raft was better cast than usual and the movie emerged as one of his biggest hits of the '30s. Sheridan appears briefly as a nurse who tends to Raft's injuries.

Released in late August, the ten-minute short *Hollywood Extra Girl* depicts Suzanne Emery, Extra Girl #1472, reporting to Central Casting one day for Cecil B. DeMille's production of *The Crusades*. Although Emery is given her "big chance" in this short, her actual appearance in *The Crusades* is nothing more than a bit. Sheridan appears fleetingly as an extra who impatiently awaits her big break. When the short was reissued in the 1940s, Sheridan was given second billing below DeMille.

Cecil B. DeMille's epic *The Crusades*, released nationally in late October, was Sheridan's final Paramount feature. Of all the productions in which Sheridan appeared, this was the biggest and most expensive. Movie audiences loved the spectacle and it was one of Paramount's highest grossing films that year.

Sheridan reminisced to Kobal about her experience: "I had to wear this awful brown wig—which I thought was going to make me look glamorous, wonderful, like Dietrich. Well, I looked horrible."[19] As a Christian girl on the auction block, Sheridan speaks her lines ("The cross, the cross! Let me kiss the cross!") just before a close-up of her tear-drenched face. Later, there was much publicity on how this little moment caused a minor delay in the shoot

Sheridan wears the infamous wig in a studio portrait from *The Crusades* (1935).

(and Sheridan loved telling this anecdote in interviews). This account is from 1963: "I cried out in my best Texas accent, 'The cwuss! The cwuss! Let me kiss the cwuss!'" DeMille called a halt to things and asked, "Young lady, what's your name?"

"Clara Lou Sheridan."

"Where are you from?"

"Denton, Texas."

"Well, then, I want you to rehearse for a while with the voice coach."

"DeMille thought it was very funny and told it at a luncheon I attended 17 years later.... He loved me after that."[20]

Sheridan recalled to *Modern Screen* in 1940, "I was still so hopeful that when I finished at Paramount, I thought it was merely a matter of testing at another studio to be signed up again." Her resentment toward Paramount is evident: "Paramount thought I was so good, they let me work out my contract in bit parts."[21] Paramount did not have a good track record of building up their starlets during the 1930s: Ida Lupino, Gail Patrick, Marsha Hunt and Frances Farmer, to name a few. Only Dorothy Lamour fared well with her build-up during the 1930s.

Despite her tendency to make light of the situation, Sheridan remained bitter about her treatment at Paramount and never worked for that studio again.

FIVE

In Professional Limbo

I wasn't going to go home and admit I was licked.[1]

After a couple of months idle, Sheridan was offered a small but pivotal role in Universal's *Off Sides*. For three weeks of work, she was paid $125.

The feature was based on an original idea by Stan Meyer, which was adapted into a screenplay by Henry Johnson, Florabel Muir and Hamilton MacFadden, the director of the film. The plot blends two opposing themes in popular entertainment: the rah-rah college football film (nearing the end of its profitable cycle) and radical activities on college campuses. *Fighting Youth* (as the movie was retitled) was the second of three films released in the 1930s that dealt with the impact of Communism on college youths (the others were *Red Salute*, 1935, and *Soak the Rich*, 1936). This element added a little punch to an overworked plot derived from a few previous Universal films, *The Spirit of Notre Dame* (1930), *The All-American* (1931) and *Saturday's Millions* (1933). Andy Devine, who appeared in all of these features, is on hand here to reprise his character of the oafish, bumbling comic relief. Several All-American football players from various universities were also featured. A low-budget affair, the film was shot in four weeks and previewed in Hollywood in early September.

Sheridan received fourth billing as Carol Arlington, the spoiled daughter of a wealthy business tycoon. She has been recruited to State College to assist the campus' radical group, the Student League of Freedom (based on the real-life American League Against War and Fascism). She sets her sights on the football hero, Larry Davis (Charles Farrell), and tries to get him to join the movement. Despite concerns by his longtime girlfriend Betty (June Martel), Larry falls into Carol's trap and leaves Betty and the team. It all works out with Carol being exposed by a Department of Justice agent (masquerading as a student) and Larry reunited with Betty after scoring the winning touchdown at the big game.

Fighting Youth was released at the end of September to mixed reviews. While Sheridan garnered some positive notices, the feature did little to advance her prospects. "[I]t's strange how all the dozens of screen tests I took in every studio didn't impress executives. It looked for a long time as though I just wasn't movie material."[2]

In late 1935, director Howard Hawks tested Sheridan for the role of a French girl in *The Road to Glory* (1936). "[S]he was fresh out of Texas, with a real Texas accent," he recalled. The test was far from a success and the role was given to June Lang. Still, Hawks noticed something special. "I went over to talk with Jack Warner," Hawks reminisced, "and I said, 'Jack, I made a test of a girl today who can be *really* good. She's no good for what I want, but you should sign her.'"[3] Warner, the top executive at Warner Brothers, agreed to test her. But Sheridan failed to impress. Warner felt she too closely resembled contract player June Travis, who was being groomed for stardom as James Cagney's leading lady in *Ceiling Zero* (1936).

It was a year before Sheridan was offered another movie role. She often referred to this period as a dark time in her life. "Fortunately, my pride died slowly," she told Wood Soanes in 1937, "so long as I was able to eat with fair regularity and I decided I wouldn't go back home until the last money I had paid out for groceries was exhausted. Don't say I suffered, because I didn't. But I was scared—and a little ashamed."[4] Her refusal to give up and return home was deeply rooted in "Texan pride." "You'd be a pretty shallow person if every break

Sheridan had a rare unsympathetic role as a communist college campus vixen in *Fighting Youth* (1935); it was another year before she got another acting role.

came your way," she later mused. "If you didn't have to keep your chin up now and then, you'd never develop tolerance and understanding."[5]

Her agent Bill Meiklejohn offered to find extra work for her, but a friend advised her against it. It was reasoned that, once she took extra work, she would never break out of the extra ranks. So Sheridan dropped Meiklejohn and signed with Dick Pollimer, whose clients included Anita Louise, Tom Brown and Ida Lupino.

Sheridan's personal life took an upswing in early 1936, when she spotted actor Edward Norris in the lobby of the Canterbury Apartments. She was instantly attracted to his dark good looks and wanted to meet him. "I thought him the handsomest man I'd ever seen," she reminisced, "and I liked him too, though I didn't know him at all."[6]

The next day, they were introduced by a mutual friend. Her appearance was less than memorable as she wore slacks, an old checked coat, flat heels and no makeup. She praised his performance in *Show Them No Mercy!* (1935). In her mind, the introduction meant little beyond polite conversation. To her surprise, however, Norris telephoned the next day and asked her to the President's Ball at the Biltmore Hotel. Sheridan later learned that Norris was involved with Alice Faye at the time and had a date with her on the same evening. After a fight with Faye, Norris broke off that date, and kept his date with Sheridan. In an interview with Dan Van Neste for *Classic Images*, Norris said, "I'll never forget how astounded I was when I saw how beautiful she looked when she came down the stairs in a black outfit and that red hair!"[7] The evening went well and their mutual attraction led to a romantic relationship. It was just the diversion she needed to take her mind off her stalled career.

Norris was born Septimus Edward Norris on March 10, 1911, in Philadelphia. His father, Richard C. Norris, was a renowned gynecologist and obstetrician; his mother, Grace Vogt, was the daughter of the president of Southern Railway. Norris was expected to follow in his father's footsteps but, at 16, he dropped out of the Culver Military Academy to marry Virginia Bell Hiller, the daughter of a socially prominent physician. This marriage produced his only son. The marriage ended after a few years.

Edward Norris, Sheridan's first husband, was an MGM contract player who never got his lucky break once Robert Taylor arrived on the lot.

In 1927, a chance encounter with director William A. Wellman led to Norris performing as a double for actor Charles "Buddy" Rogers in the World War I classic *Wings*. Wellman advised the youngster to get some acting experience on the stage, so Norris went back to Pennsylvania in 1928 and joined two stock companies. For four years, he acted in a variety of plays and traveling shows. Later studio publicity falsely asserted that, after acting jobs became scarce in the early 1930s, Norris worked as a deck hand on a round-the-world freight ship. The less exciting truth was that Norris found himself back in Hollywood with another stage gig. After he was introduced to director Rouben Mamoulian, Norris was given his first film role in Greta Garbo's *Queen Christina* (1933). Edward's performance landed him a long-term MGM contract. Norris mainly appeared in bit parts in MGM productions. In 1935, he married actress Lona Andre. The marriage was annulled after five months.

Norris attracted attention with his performance in the unpretentious yet remarkable 20th Century production *Show Them No Mercy!* As a result of the positive notices, Norris was recognized as a possible "threat" to Hollywood's "King,"

Clark Gable (other "threats" included Errol Flynn, Ross Alexander and former tennis player Frank Shields). This kind of attention should have bolstered Norris' stock at Metro. Instead, the studio began grooming Robert Taylor, while Norris remained in bit roles and an occasional loan-out to other studios. Norris became bitter about this turn of events; he remarked to Van Neste, "*Show Them No Mercy!* really did me a lot of good, but MGM responded by giving me bit roles. Every time I would get a good role on loan, they would give me a walk-on to reprimand me. To not appreciate what you had accomplished on another lot! It was a big comedown."[8]

Sheridan got her lucky break when her agent introduced her to Max Arnow, the casting director at Warner Brothers. Arnow arranged another screen test for a small part in *Always Leave Them Laughing*. Her test was deemed good enough and she was given her first part in over a year. During the early days of the shoot, Sheridan's performance so impressed director Ray Enright that he persuaded the studio to put her under contract. Sheridan always claimed Enright was her favorite director at Warners since he gave her her first real chance. She was offered a contract with the standard six-months option at $75 a week. She joined the ranks of other female players (Beverly Roberts, June Travis, Anne Nagel) who were being developed into stars. Columnist Elizabeth Yeaman noted, "A change of studio will sometime work miracles in the career of an actor.... Now Warners are crowing over the acquisition of Ann Sheridan, who was signed up by Paramount about two years ago in a beauty contest. She never did anything worth mentioning at Paramount."[9]

Perhaps it was their professional circumstances that drew Norris and Sheridan together. Their relationship was based on a mutual desire to help each other achieve stardom. She recalled to Gladys Hall in 1938, "I can't say that it was love at first sight. I think that it was ... that we had such fun."[10] To Norris, it was more serious than that: "She was really great! She had such a wonderful sense of humor.... She was light-hearted and down to earth, a real breath of sunshine."[11] It wasn't long before Norris contemplated marriage. As he told *Movies* magazine in 1939, "I wanted marriage. I liked the idea of a home, a place to put down roots as it were. I met Ann Sheridan and fell madly in love with her." After seven months of dating, Norris "decided that here at last was a girl with whom I could always be happy. To me, Ann Sheridan was the loveliest thing in the world."[12]

On August 18, 1936, the couple eloped to Ensenada, Mexico. Norris' actor friends Ivan Lebedeff and Bruce Pierce served as witnesses as a Mexican judge performed a quick ceremony. Sheridan wore a white slack suit adorned with a paisley scarf, while Norris and the attendants wore sports clothes. After the brief ceremony, the wedding party headed back to Hollywood to resume their acting assignments.

The couple moved into a small house high on a hill in the San Fernando Valley overlooking Hollywood. There, Sheridan got "a sense of the unimportance of everything, except happiness."[13] The newlyweds were reportedly content to spend their evenings at home and were rarely mentioned in the gossip columns. The newlyweds settled into domestic bliss and looked ahead to a brighter future.

Six

Training Ground
at Warner Brothers

I had no parts worth remembering.... I did almost every B picture they made at Warner Brothers.[1]

During the 1930s, three studios dominated: MGM, Paramount and Warner Brothers. In terms of star power and box office revenue, no other Hollywood studios came close. Each had its specialty. MGM produced lavish prestige films; Paramount offered sophisticated dramas and comedies, and Warners specialized in backstage musicals, raucous comedies and gritty melodramas "ripped from the headlines." As child actor Sybil Jason reflected in her autobiography, "In the 1930s, Warner Brothers was like a well-cogged wheel that continually churned out a product that America and the rest of the world clamored for. While watching those movies today, we discover that a good percentage of them have a quality and an appeal that holds up in this era."[2] This is the main reason why many of Sheridan's Warner Brothers features still deserve to be seen today.

The driving force behind Warner Brothers was Jack L. Warner, a complex man who inspired a mixture of fear, derision and even respect from those working there. "He was the father," recalled one of the studio's most popular stars, Bette Davis. "The power. The glory. And he was in business to make money."[3] According to producer Hal B. Wallis, "Jack was a dynamo. Nervous, restless, he couldn't sit still a minute ... endlessly interested in everything that was going on." Like other studio heads, Jack was keenly aware of what movie fans wanted. "Jack was a showman who played his hunches," marveled Wallis. "I never saw him read a script, let alone a book. Just from glancing at a title or rifling through a few pages, he could sense whether a property would interest millions of people all over the world. He was usually right."[4]

Under Jack's management, Warner Brothers was primarily an actor's studio where James Cagney, Edward G. Robinson and Errol Flynn prospered. The actresses, on the other hand, had much tougher hurdles. In the mid–30s, Kay Francis reigned as the queen of the Burbank lot before being maliciously tossed into mediocre "B" films as "punishment" for daring to insist on better scripts. Other ranking actresses, like Joan Blondell and Ruby Keeler, would soon be on their way out. Oscar winner Bette Davis was embroiled in a legal case in England to terminate her contract. Olivia de Havilland appeared to be thriving, but she would wage a far-reaching court battle with the studio in 1943.

Sheridan's relationship with Jack Warner was complicated. "Professionally—if I was on suspension, I wasn't to be spoken to, either inside or outside the studio," she reminisced to Hagen. "I adore Jack socially. He's a lot of fun."[5]

Jane Wyman recalled in a 1995 Turner Classic Movies interview that working for Warner Brothers during this period was a valuable experience: "It was great training, with all its heartbreaks and everything." Wyman found that working at Warners was like working as a family. "We all helped each other ... and the big stars would help when we were working with them."[6]

James Cagney told *TV Guide* in 1966, "When Ann came to Warners, she was just a nice kid—chumming around with the working staff.... There was nothing aggressive about her." It wasn't long before established stars like Cagney, Flynn and Pat O'Brien "took Ann under our wings—sort of helped out."[7]

"The good thing about working at Warner Brothers was the spirit at the studio," Sheridan told Kobal. "It was a very good group. An absolute family. It was just incredible."[8] In this environment, Sheridan flourished and honed her craft as a movie actress of box office value.

Sing Me a Love Song (the release title for *Always Leave Them Laughing*) was the studio's second attempt to turn tenor James Melton into a singing superstar in the Nelson Eddy mold. Melton plays an heir to a department store fortune. When he learns that the store is failing, he flies to New York City to take over its management. He goes "Undercover Boss" and learns the business from the ground up. The slight plot had all the elements of a musical comedy with an attractive ingénue (Patricia Ellis) and solid comedy support from ZaSu Pitts, Allen Jenkins and Hugh Herbert (who played four parts) mixed in with musical interludes handled by Melton.

The box office results did nothing to make Warners think Melton had screen potential and soon his movie career was effectively over. He fared much better in other venues like radio, opera and night clubs.

Sheridan, seventh-billed, is Lola Parker, an aggressive woman who, with her matchmaking mother, pursues Melton. *Sing Me a Love Song* premiered in New York City and other cities on Christmas Day 1936. In ads, Sheridan's face was prominently displayed and she was called "One of the most delicious morsels of fascinating femininity on the screen!"[9] Despite her relatively short time on-screen, some critics praised Sheridan's performance. By mid–January, her name was no longer featured in the cast listing in some metropolitan areas. It appeared that, in some cases, her scenes were deleted when the studio cut three and a half minutes from the film. The edited film would fit into a double bill when the Melton name alone was not enough to generate healthy box office returns. The original version with the Sheridan footage does not appear to exist today; all that remains in the current print is one line, "That Parker dame is outside in the car and won't leave until you talk to her."

Sheridan was announced for several productions, including *Gold Diggers of 1937* (Joan Blondell appeared instead, acting opposite her real-life husband Dick Powell). She was also assigned the female lead in a low-grade "B" film, *The Shrinking Violet*, opposite Dick Purcell. She was taken out of that production when she was cast as Pat O'Brien's love interest in *The Making of O'Malley*.

Based on a Gerald Beaumont short story of the same name (serialized in *Red Book* magazine in 1924), *The Making of O'Malley* was previously produced in 1925 with Milton Sills and Dorothy Mackaill. Scenarists Milton Krims and Tom Reed updated the plot by incorporating criminal behavior and the need for justice system reform (a favorite theme at Warners). Under William Dieterle's direction, production began in late July with O'Brien, Humphrey Bogart, Frieda Inescort and Sybil Jason cast in the main roles. Sheridan appeared in a sizable role; she later admitted, "I was scared to death."[10] Fortunately for the actress, many on the set lent a helping hand and put her at ease. O'Brien was especially helpful, coaching her on the fundamentals of screen acting. Later, Sheridan gratefully acknowledged that he was "darned sweet."[11]

Many years later, Jason told author Laura Wagner that Sheridan was "one of my very favorite people.... Everybody loved her, from the wardrobe people on up the list. She was generous, had a great sense of humor, was quick to laugh and, as far as I could see, was warm to everyone that came within her sight."[12]

The most lasting friendship to come from this movie was with Bogart, whom Sheridan adored. "Bogie is very easy to work with," she said in 1943, "because he takes everything in stride."[13] Despite his cynical screen image, Sheridan found him to be "less temperamental than almost any star in Hollywood, but will fight hard for the rights of someone else." She said that another example of his consideration "is his kindness to young actors. He often gives them coaching quietly on the sidelines."[14] Bogart remained an important influence on her career while at Warner Brothers.

Bogart was likewise fond of Sheridan because of her raunchy sense of humor and ability to out-drink him. Of course, he could not disclose these aspects of her personality publicly. In a 1943 article titled "Sister Annie," Bogart said that when he met her for the first time on the set, she was a "scared kid ... self-conscious and unsure of herself."[15] He took the time to coach her on her lines and helped ease her nervousness. This act of kindness endeared him to her and they became fast friends. "[Sheridan is] one of the nicest girls in Hollywood," Bogart asserted, "because she is real, honest, unassuming, friendly, and ... natural."[16]

In the mid–1940s, Bogart listed Sheridan, Barbara Stanwyck, Mary Astor and Ingrid Bergman as his favorite actresses to work with. The reason he gave was delivered with a touch of that Sam Spade cynicism he was known for: "They aren't dames. Those dames who wet their lips and wiggle give me a pain."[17]

The only person who proved immune to Sheridan's charms was the *O'Malley* director, who was less than thrilled with the studio for assigning this picture after having directed several prestigious productions. As Jason recalled, "Dieterle seemed to take a particular dislike to her because she had a loud and boisterous laugh that always reached its peak during shooting breaks and lunchtime."[18]

Viewing the rushes, studio executives were so pleased with Sheridan's work that she was given a small role in an important film, *Black Legion*. Following the completion of her scenes in *The Great O'Malley* (as it was renamed), production on the new picture began in late August.

Black Legion is a fictionalized account inspired by a notorious incident involving the Black Legion, a white vigilante group based in Detroit. In May 1935, Charles Poole, a Works Progress Administration organizer, was found murdered. The testimony of Dayton Dean, the Legion's executioner, was the state's evidence at the trial and led to the conviction and life sentences of 11 men. After authorities prosecuted another 37 men for related crimes dating over three years, the Black Legion was disbanded.

Executive producer Hal B. Wallis wanted Edward G. Robinson for the lead role, a character loosely based on Dean. Producer Robert Lord felt that Robinson was too foreign-looking and preferred Bogart, who in his estimation was more American-looking. Warners executives had been impressed by Bogart's *Great O'Malley* performance, so he was given the role as a reward. Bogart, who had been with Warners since *The Petrified Forest* (1936), was tired of being typecast as the hoodlum and looked forward to playing a different type of role.

The movie tells the harrowing tale of a family man who finds himself embroiled in illegal activities perpetuated by a secret vigilante group. Frank Taylor (Bogart), a Midwestern factory mechanic, is bitter when he is passed over for a promotion in favor of a foreign-born co-worker. He joins the anti-immigrant Black Legion and they begin a reign of terror, targeting foreign-born citizens. Things take an ugly turn when Taylor kills his best friend Ed Jackson (Dick Foran); Bogart's performance of anguish illustrates his acting skills at its finest. Taylor is arrested and placed on trial. Despite threats by the Legion, Taylor remains guilt-ridden over Jackson's death and the emotional toll on his family. His confession on the witness stand results in the arrest and conviction of all the Legion members.

Although *Black Legion* was completed after *The Great O'Malley*, it reached the screen first with its premiere in New York City in mid–January 1937. The film's trailer proudly proclaimed "*The Black Legion* tells the whole dramatic truth behind the headlines that shocked the nation!" Bogart was praised by the *New York Times* for having "handled a difficult assignment flawlessly"; the critic also noted the "soundly executed portrayals by Dick Foran, Helen Flint, Ann Sheridan, Clifford Soubier, John Litel and many others." Upon *Black Legion*'s national release at the end of January, it continued to garner praise. Sheridan received positive notices.

The National Board of Review named *Black Legion* one of the ten best films of 1937, and Bogart was recognized for giving one of the ten best performances. *Photoplay* cited the film as one of the "Best Pictures of the Month" with Bogart giving one of the best performances. Robert Lord's original story received an Academy Award nomination. Despite the awards and critical raves, *Black Legion*, while profitable, was not the smash hit the studio expected. Perhaps its incidents hit too close to home for movie audiences. Despite his fine performance, Bogart was soon relegated to playing supporting roles (usually as the hoodlum) for a few more years before he finally became a bona fide star with *High Sierra* (1941).

Black Legion was not the first film to depict the Detroit case. Columbia had released *Legion of Terror*, starring Bruce Cabot, Marguerite Churchill and Ward Bond in November 1936. Another film, *Nation Aflame*, released later in 1937, was reportedly inspired by the same incident. Neither of these had the trenchant power of the Warner Brothers feature.

Fourth-billed as Betty Grogan, Jackson's fiancée, Sheridan plays with a direct manner and an appealing, natural quality that is a marked improvement over previous performances. According to Norris, it was more than just an insightful director who helped Sheridan loosen up on the screen. Norris told Van Neste, "Annie was scared of the camera, she used to walk around the set with a bottle of Coke which was really rum in a Coke bottle. She was very nervous and upset." During her Warner Brothers years, Sheridan was well-known for her excessive drinking on the set. "She used to be able to drink me under the table," Norris marveled. "It was unbelievable what she could consume, and you would never know it."[19]

The Great O'Malley was released in mid–February. Given the overall excellence of *Black Legion*, this feature was quite the letdown for all concerned. The sentimental plot deals with Policeman O'Malley (O'Brien), whose adherence to the smallest infractions of obscure laws causes him to be thoroughly disliked by his fellow officers and the community on his beat. The latest victim of O'Malley's misguided principles, John Phillips (Bogart), robs a pawn shop out of desperation and is sent to prison.

Due to the negative publicity generated by Phillips' trial, O'Malley is demoted to school crossing duty. He befriends a crippled girl, Barbara (Jason), unaware that she is Phillips' daughter. When he learns her identity, he is guilt-stricken and secretly arranges for an operation to fix Barbara's leg. O'Malley also secures Phillips' early release from prison. By the illogical ending, O'Malley has learned a valuable lesson and wins the affections of the community and schoolteacher Judy Nolan (Sheridan).

When the film was previewed in early December 1936, the original cast lineup listed O'Brien first, then Bogart, Sheridan, Frieda Inescort and Jason. After early screenings, the reception to Jason's performance was so great that she was elevated to second billing, thereby pushing Bogart, Sheridan and Inescort down one notch. The studio also added more scenes featuring Jason and O'Brien, while Bogart's scenes were trimmed to "bookend" status (appearing mainly in the beginning and ending scenes). It was Jason who showed the most promise as Warners' answer to Shirley Temple. Despite some favorable notices for Jason's performance, the less-than-stellar box office returns convinced Warners that perhaps Jason would never really be considered a threat to Temple's popularity and let her contract lapse the following year.

Sheridan's career took another step forward when she was taken out of the supporting cast of a comedy, *Her Husband's Secretary* (she was replaced by Beverly Roberts), and given third billing as Pat O'Brien's love interest in *San Quentin.* She replaced an actress who had proved to be unsuitable. Reporting on the casting change, Louella Parsons enthusiastically noted, "What a nice break this is for the little Sheridan girl, who is certainly making rapid strides."[20]

San Quentin was based on the original story "Captain

Sheridan's early roles at Warner Brothers were highly reminiscent of the kind her fellow actresses Beverly Roberts and June Travis played; it took a few years for Sheridan to come into her own.

of the Yard" by Robert Tasker, who specialized in hard-hitting prison melodramas, and John Bright. Even though only two screenwriters received screen credits, the screenplay was actually written by no less than six writers. Actual footage of San Quentin State Prison was utilized in long shots, while the main scenes were shot on the studio lot. With Lloyd Bacon handling directorial chores, the shoot lasted five weeks. When producer Hal B. Wallis expressed dissatisfaction with the ending, director Michael Curtiz was brought in to shoot a new ending in January. The new footage was deemed unsuitable and Bacon was brought back to reshoot the ending. An additional five minutes was added to the 65-minute running time.

San Quentin marked Warner Brothers' return to the cycle of prison films that had peaked in the early 1930s with films like *I Am a Fugitive from a Chain Gang* (1932) and *20,000 Years in Sing Sing* (1933). The film's socially conscious theme explores the need for prison reform, in which rehabilitation is emphasized to give criminals a second chance.

San Quentin is notable for showcasing Sheridan in the quintessential Sheridan role: the sassy, street-wise girl who keeps men at bay with her sharp retorts, while having a soft spot for the underdog. She is a woman who is awakened by the love of a worthy man. It's a beguiling and captivating combination. As a bonus, she is afforded the opportunity to sing a catchy Harry Warren–Al Dubin song, "How Could You?" She reveals a pleasant contralto similar in quality to Alice Faye's voice. Although her singing served her well in other media, such as radio and television, she always downplayed this talent. She later admitted to having worked with a few of the studio's vocal coaches, but "nobody can teach me to sing. I haven't got that kind of voice."[21] Although she was always modest about her singing talent, Sheridan's singing is always a treat.

Sheridan is May, a night club singer whose younger brother "Red" (Bogart, 15 years her senior) is sent to San Quentin, where Jameson (O'Brien) was brought in to institute reform after a series of riots under the leadership of sadistic chief guard Druggin (Barton MacLane).

Over time, Jameson earns the respect of May and the inmates. Although Red responds to Jameson's influence, he is shocked when he learns about Jameson's romantic relationship with his sister. Red escapes while working on a road gang. Red finds Jameson in May's apartment and shoots him, injuring him slightly. Red learns the truth about May's love for Jameson, and about Druggin's attempts to oust Jameson. He flees and is shot by the police. He makes it back to San Quentin just in time to prevent Jameson from being fired by the parole board.

Although *San Quentin* was previewed in late March, it was not released until early August. With its short 70-minute running time, it suited its purpose as an entertaining entry in double bills. After playing brother and sister in this film, Sheridan jokingly referred to Bogart as "Brother Bogie," while he called her "Sister Annie."

Despite some favorable notices in her previous movies, Sheridan was next assigned to the unit headed by Bryan Foy, Warners' "Keeper of the Bs."[22] Foy was adept at churning out low-budget features in a short period of time and making a profitable showing. While this seemed to be a comedown for Sheridan, the experience and exposure she gained in several Foy movies proved beneficial in learning the tricks of the trade in her craft.

Despite its humble pedigree, her next film, *The Footloose Heiress*, emerged as a pleasant, well-conceived screwball comedy boasting many of the studio's contract players. According to the *Motion Picture Herald*, "A group of Warner's younger players, going through that intensive training period out of which come the stars of tomorrow, are featured in this production."[23] William Hopper (son of columnist Hedda Hopper), Anne Nagel and Hugh O'Connell were the most prominent cast members, in support of the leads, Craig Reynolds and Sheridan (replacing Patricia Ellis). The studio was particularly interested in showcasing Reynolds, who had been with Warners since 1935. Reynolds was usually typecast as a heel or villain; his role in *Footloose Heiress* promised to give his career a boost. A caption in *Picture Play* magazine called him an "up-and-coming" leading man.[24]

The original screenplay (entitled *The Madcap Heiress*) by Robertson White was a screwball comedy variation of William Shakespeare's *The Taming of the Shrew* with additional elements borrowed from *It Happened One Night* and *My Man Godfrey*. Sheridan plays Kay Allyn (described in the trailer as the "Heiress with too much temper!"), errant daughter of advertising magnate John C. Allyn (O'Connell). She impulsively elopes with Jack Pierson (Hopper) to win a $5000 bet, but her efforts are thwarted through the intervention of a hobo, Butch Baeder (Reynolds).

Kay's father takes a liking to the young man after Butch develops a radio ad for an important client as well as being a strong match for Kay's temperament. Kay, despite her initial annoyance, finds herself attracted to Butch. More amusing slapstick situations ensue before the obligatory happy ending in which Butch and Kay profess their love.

With a 59-minute running time, the comedy graced the bottom half of most double bills, which meant that it got scant attention from the major critics. The lack of exposure also doomed Reynolds to remain in the "B" film groove.

In her first comedy, Sheridan is a revelation. She looks fetching in several Howard Shoup gowns, has a beguiling and appealing presence, and demonstrates a solid control of the comic situations. Her performance should have propelled her out of the "B" film category.

Sheridan's next movie, *Wine, Women and Horses*, was one of the worst films she did at Warner Brothers and a major step backward. It was loosely based on the 1933 novel *Dark Hazard* by W.R. Burnett, the prolific author of the crime novels *Little Caesar* and *Beast of the City*.

Dark Hazard was first produced as a movie bearing the same title in 1934, with Edward G. Robinson as "The Lovable Rogue of Every Woman's Dream." Robinson hardly ever qualified as "every woman's dream" and was ill-served by the attempt to pass him off as such. *Dark Hazard*, released in the months before the enforcement of the Production Code, was condemned by the Catholic Legion of Decency due to the glorification of gambling and the loose morals exhibited by the main characters.

Production of *Wine, Women and Horses* began under the title *Lady Luck*. Although not considered an official remake of the earlier film, there are many similarities. Warner Brothers was expert in passing off remakes as "originals" as evident in a few of Sheridan's later films. As Sheridan was still busy on the *Footloose Heiress* production, she was given a secondary role that had limited screen time, but offered name value for the box office.

Barton MacLane has a rare opportunity to play a leading role as compulsive gambler Jim Turner, who has the habit of losing all his money at the racetracks. He bids his old friend Valerie (Sheridan) farewell as he travels to Barrowville, a small Midwestern town. There he falls in love with Marjorie (the dour Peggy Bates), who opposes gambling. Jim promises to mend his ways through honest labor, and the couple marry.

Soon Jim is back into gambling and carousing with his old friends, including Valerie. Fed up, Marjorie leaves him. Jim's newest run of bad luck ruins him financially and he heads back to Barrowville to patch things up with his wife. Their reconciliation does not last long and Marjorie confesses her love for a former beau who can offer her a stable life. Jim marries Valerie and finds himself back on his feet with a racehorse, Lady Luck.

Wine, Woman and Horses was released in mid–September to mostly scathing reviews. Filmgoers were unimpressed by the low-budget feature.

Sheridan appeared in yet another inconsequential role as John Litel's love interest in the prison melodrama *Alcatraz Island.* Though Litel had the most important role, Sheridan received top billing in the ads as an indication of her rising star status. This was the first movie set in the prison on Alcatraz Island, which opened in 1934. The shoot took place at a studio-built, faithful partial reproduction of the prison located on a hill in San Fernando Valley. The feature, based on an original screenplay by actor-writer Crane Wilbur (a cousin of Tyrone Power), was produced by the Bryan Foy unit.

Litel is "Gat" Brady, a "respectable" racketeer who intends to use his ill-gotten wealth to start a new life in Europe with his daughter (Mary Maguire). After Gat is arrested by the FBI for tax evasion and sentenced to five years at Leavenworth Federal Prison, he asks his girlfriend Flo (Sheridan) to take care of his daughter.

After Annabel and Flo return from Europe, Annabel is kidnapped by "Red" Carroll (Ben Welden), a mug who bears a grudge against Gat. Red is captured by the police and sent to the same prison as Gat.

One day, Red is found stabbed and he implicates Gat on his deathbed. Annabel's new boyfriend, George Drake (Gordon Oliver), the young lawyer who once prosecuted Gat, decides to defend him. Drake uncovers the real killer and Gat is acquitted.

Alcatraz Island reached movie theaters in early November to mostly indifferent notices. Sheridan earned some positive notices but the general consensus among the critics was that she'd had better parts.

After the release of *Alcatraz Island*, playwright-screenwriter Milton Herbert Gropper filed a lawsuit against Warner Brothers, claiming that the film's plot was lifted directly from his unproduced 1934 play *Ex-Racketeer.* The studio maintained that the plot was derived from an original screenplay. In January 1941, the Southern District of New York judge ruled in favor of Warner Brothers:

> The main theme underlying both stories is old and any habitué of the theatre or moving pictures is familiar with [it]. It has been portrayed many times on the stage and screen.... I am convinced that while both authors consciously or unconsciously made use of a common fundamental plot, the stories told are not the same. There is a material difference in the characters and the episodes necessarily required in describing the gangster operations so familiar to the public. The fundamental plot, however, is the same, and of course is not copyrightable under the law.[25]

How Warner Brothers avoided another copyright infringement suit with Sheridan's next movie, *She Loved a Fireman* (originally titled *Two Platoons*), can be attributed to the fact that the screenwriters of the original source were current studio employees.

In 1934, the studio produced the popular *Here Comes the Navy* with James Cagney, Pat O'Brien and Gloria Stuart. *She Loved a Fireman* was supposedly based on an original story by Charleston Sand, but comparisons between the two films reveal several nearly identical plot elements, including the comic sidekick's desire to buy his mother a set of dentures! Apparently, switching the locale from San Francisco to New York and the occupation from sailors to firemen was enough to qualify the story as "original."

She Loved a Fireman, another low-budget product of Foy's unit, was intended as a step in building Dick Foran's career as a leading man. Foran, who usually starred in the studio's "B" Westerns, plays "Red," an obnoxious blowhard who decides to join the fire department to spite the fire captain, Smokey Shannon (Robert Armstrong). Red's overbearing manner alienates him from the other firefighters, with the exception of Skillet Michaels (Eddie Acuff).

Matters become complicated when Red dates the captain's sister Margie (Sheridan). Red continues to neglect his work duties until Skillet's leg is broken in a firetruck mishap. Red is demoted to working with a fire tug squadron. During a three-alarm fire at a waterfront warehouse, Red saves the captain's life and becomes a hero. Margie realizes that Red has reformed and marries him as her brother beams proudly.

She Loved a Fireman was released in mid–December and was barely noticed. Some reviewers noted that Sheridan was deserving of better material. Unfortunately, the studio failed to understand her screen potential and it would be years before she came into her own.

SEVEN

Building "Name Value"

I tested for every big picture on the lot, but I usually wound up, if I wound up at all, in a quickie.[1]

In early August 1937, Sheridan pointedly addressed the age-old issue of marriage interfering with one's film career. "It is all rubbish to think that a screen career is endangered in any way by marriage. My marriage to Edward has been the best thing that could have happened. It gave me incentive, it has renewed my confidence in myself."[2]

However, by the beginning of 1938, the Sheridan-Norris marriage was unraveling. As Sheridan's career continued its upward climb, Norris was frustrated by his inability to catch that elusive lucky break. When the couple moved into a ranch-style home in Burbank in early 1937, this newspaper headline said it all: "Burbank Home Purchased by Movie Couple: Ann Sheridan, Spouse Will Occupy Eugene Walsh Former House."[3] The slight must have galled Norris. His situation was certainly not lost on Hollywood insiders. Columnist Robbin Coons noted, "The strange case of Edward Norris can be blamed, in a way, on that fellow [Robert] Taylor. Or you may, if you prefer, ascribe it lightly to the vagaries of movie fortune."[4]

Although Norris received good notices for his performance as the schoolteacher killed by a vengeful mob in Warner Brothers' hard-hitting *They Won't Forget* (1937), it did not lead to better roles. Viewing his performance illustrates the main problem: While he delivers a solid acting job, he lacks the charisma that made Robert Taylor a star. None of this sat well with Norris and, many years later, he admitted to author Richard Lamparski, "I don't know how [Sheridan] stood me that long. I was trying to drown my disappointments with alcohol."[5]

Sheridan's first feature released in 1938 was *The Patient in Room 18*, based on a popular 1929 novel of the same name by Mignon G. Eberhart. The characters of Nurse Sarah Keate and her boyfriend, Detective Lance O'Leary, spawned additional novels, such as *While the Patient Slept* and *The Mystery of Hunting's End*. From 1935 to 1938, Warner Brothers produced 12 mystery films under the "Clue Club" franchise; six were based on books and original stories by Eberhart, but only three featured Keate and O'Leary: *While the Patient Slept* (1935), *Mystery House* (1938) and *The Patient in Room 18*. The most remarkable aspect of *The Patient in Room 18* is the glamorous transformation of the character after frumpy Aline MacMahon played Nurse Keate in the first feature and the equally frumpy Jane Darwell in *The Great Hospital Mystery* for 20th Century–Fox in 1937. Likewise, dapper Patric Knowles replaced buffoonish, middle-aged Guy Kibbee as O'Leary in *While the Patient Slept.*

The movie starts out amusingly enough with O'Leary (Knowles) found sleepwalking in the streets (an uncredited Carole Landis appears as the woman he bumps into on the stairs). Suffering from a nervous condition caused by his last case, he is sent to recuperate at Thatcher Hospital. O'Leary's girlfriend Sara (spelled without the "h") Keate works at this private hospital.

Norris and Sheridan pictured on a rare night out at a glitzy Hollywood event. By mid–1937, the marriage was already unraveling.

The patient in room 18 is wealthy Frank Warren, who is being treated with $100,000 worth of radium by his physician Dr. Lethany. On a stormy night, Warren is discovered dead from an overdose of morphine; the radium *and* Dr. Lethany are missing. The list of suspects includes Warren's nephew Jim; the doctor's unfaithful wife Carol; and Dr. Hajek, the intern. O'Leary and Keate work together to catch the killer. Non-discriminating trade paper critics found this humor-laden entry to their liking.

Warners next planned to develop a new romantic team with Sheridan and Humphrey Bogart (an intriguing combination which was never developed) in *Torchy Blane in Panama*, the fifth entry in Glenda Farrell and Barton MacLane's popular *Torchy Blane* series. Lola Lane and Paul Kelly, who appeared instead, were greeted with such negative public response that Farrell and MacLane were brought back into the series.

The last entry of the "Clue Club" series, *Mystery House*, was released in mid–May after a delay of four months. This was a clear sign that Warners had doubts about this film. Based on the 1930 novel *The Mystery of Hunting's End*, it had a short production shoot of only a few weeks under the novel's title. Dick Purcell had a rare leading role when he took over as O'Leary; Sheridan was a last-minute substitute for June Travis.

When a wealthy banker is found shot dead in his bedroom, it is ruled a suicide. His daughter Gwen (Anne Nagel) is certain that he was murdered. O'Leary is hired to investigate at a hunting lodge. Gwen is asked to invite all the people who were present when her father was found dead.

Sarah Keate, who is taking care of Gwen's crotchety aunt, is glad to have O'Leary around for protection and assists with his sleuthing. There are two more murders and nerves become frayed. O'Leary identifies the killer as the one who had embezzled money from the bank.

With a running time of just under 57 minutes, *Mystery House* settled into the lower half of double bills, where it received scant attention.

As a sign of the good fortunes in her personal life, Sheridan once again elaborated on the benefits of her marriage to Norris:

> Marriage is the best confidence builder I have ever found. I think I had lost my courage. I found that I was hesitating over decisions I should have been able to make at a moment's notice. There was no one to kick me in the shins and tell me to go to work. Then I found that I was in love. There is nothing to do in that situation except marry the man I did. I married in spite of the advice of my friends who believed that a young actress should avoid romantic entanglements until their careers are at least in intermediate if not in high gear. I am sure I'll go further in my screen work, such as it is, as a married woman than I would have gone as a single girl.[6]

She fooled no one as insiders predicted it was just a matter of time before the marriage crashed.

Sheridan's next film, *Little Miss Thoroughbred*, found her playing second fiddle to a precocious little moppet, Janet Chapman (in her screen debut). The feature began production as *Little Lady Luck*. Based on an original story, it was highly reminiscent of *Little Miss Marker*, the 1934 film that propelled six-year-old Shirley Temple to stardom. Having failed with Sybil Jason, Warner Brothers now believed that Chapman would be a stronger rival to Temple in a copycat vehicle.

In the Damon Runyonesque plot, little orphan Janet (Chapman) believes that her father is out there somewhere and leaves the orphanage to find him. After she faints on a busy city street, she is taken to the hospital by ambulance. Caught speeding behind the ambulance, Todd Harrington (Frank McHugh) tells the policeman that Nails Morgan (John Litel) is the girl's father. To avoid trouble, Nails plays along and takes Janet home. His girlfriend Madge (Sheridan) becomes enamored of Janet and prevents him from sending the child back.

Before long, Nails and Madge are forced to marry in order to keep Janet, who brings them luck when they win a racehorse. The police and gangsters are on their trail, resulting in Nails, Madge and Todd being arrested. Janet's emotional appeal convinces the judge that Nails would make a good father for her—as long as he promises to get a legitimate job.

Little Miss Thoroughbred was heavily promoted as a star-making vehicle for the four-year-old moppet, dubbed the "bundle of sunshine" in the theatrical trailer. The movie got positive reviews but Warners' advertising campaign failed to impress moviegoers. The critics noted that it was tough on the adult actors as they were shoved into the background. The feature proved a major disappointment at the box office despite the talented cast and an up-and-coming director, John Farrow.

While she was busy on the *Little Miss Thoroughbred* shoot, Sheridan was cast in a small part in *Cowboy from Brooklyn*. This was one of Warners' "lower A" productions, which meant more exposure for Sheridan despite her limited screen time. The musical comedy represented a change of pace for the studio's singing star Dick Powell. Having gained fame as Ruby Keeler's sweetheart in a few Busby Berkeley features and other musicals, Powell had begun to tire of the familiarity of both the material and roles. His *Cowboy from Brooklyn* character offered him a welcome change of pace as a comedian.

The musical comedy was based on the 1937 play *Howdy Stranger* by Robert Sloane and Louis Pelletier, Jr. In the *Variety* review of the stage production, it was noted that the play "won't linger long" on Broadway "[but] its chances, however, as a screen property are good." As it turned out, *Cowboy from Brooklyn* was a waste of time for all involved and another setback for Sheridan.

The foolish plot concerns Elly Jordan (Powell), a singer from Brooklyn, who arrives at Hardy's Dude Ranch in Two Bits, Wyoming. Despite his strong aversion to animals, the Hardy family hires him and his friends to perform for the ranch hands. When fast-talking theatrical agent Ray Chadwick (Pat O'Brien) hears Elly sing, he immediately signs him to a contract. Chadwick believes that Elly is a real cowboy, so Jane (Priscilla Lane) tries to teach him how to act like one. Elly is renamed "Wyoming Steve Gibson" and makes a successful screen test. After Chadwick learns the truth, he persists with the deception. They travel to New York for a radio appearance on *Captain Rose's Radio Hour*, where Elly makes a successful appearance. After a few more mishaps (none of which are very funny), Elly finally lands a Hollywood contract and Jane's love.

Most critics deemed the film to be pleasant, but decidedly lightweight, entertainment. Sheridan's role was so small, most critics failed to mention her at all.

The *Cowboy from Brooklyn* plot was later reworked for *Two Guys from Texas* (1948), starring Dennis Morgan and Jack Carson in roles that incorporated different aspects of Powell's character. The musical comedy, inspired by Bing Crosby and Bob Hope's *Road* series, features beautiful Technicolor photography, some humorous situations and even a cameo appearance by Bugs Bunny but little else of entertainment value.

Sheridan's career was heading for a major rut. Although she had received positive notices for her performances in several films, it appeared that Warners executives had no real plans for her. She was even slated for a loan-out to Columbia for a lead opposite Jack Holt in the low-budget *Crime Takes a Holiday*. Sheridan became ill and Marcia Ralston replaced her. She recovered in time to accept another loan-out assignment, a lucky break that changed the trajectory of her career.

John M. Stahl was a highly regarded director behind popular "women weepies" such as *Imitation of Life* (1934) and *Magnificent Obsession* (1935). Even with the disappointing results of *Parnell* (1937), Stahl's reputation was still solid. He contacted Warner Brothers to request an interview with Sheridan for a potential role in Universal's *Letter of Introduction*. The interview went well and Sheridan was given a small role as the temperamental, well-gowned fiancée of Adolphe Menjou.

Letter of Introduction, based on an original story, was designed as a Margaret Sullavan production to reunite her with Stahl, who had directed her smash debut *Only Yesterday* (1933). But the unpredictable Sullavan, who owed one film to Universal, had just signed a six-picture deal with MGM. Andrea Leeds, who gave a sterling performance as the suicidal actress in RKO's *Stage Door*, was given the role instead.

Kay Martin (Leeds), an ambitious young actress, arrives in New York City. She brings a "letter of introduction" with her when she meets stage and screen idol John Mannering (Menjou). The letter was written by her late mother, whose brief marriage to Mannering produced a child he never knew—Kay. Both keep their relationship a secret to protect his "Great Lover" image.

This deception arouses jealousy in Mannering's fiancée Lydia (Sheridan) and she breaks off their engagement. Mannering's decision to go public about his daughter goes awry when he drinks heavily before opening night of their joint play. Distraught that he has lost his daughter's respect, Mannering steps out in front of a taxi and dies before he has the chance to introduce Kay as his daughter. Kay finally reveals her secret to her boyfriend Barry (George Murphy).

Letter of Introduction was released in early August and received respectable reviews. The feature was one of *Photoplay*'s "Pictures of the Month" with Menjou, Leeds, Edgar Bergen and Charlie McCarthy(!) cited for giving the best performances. It was the presence of Bergen and McCarthy that propelled the silly film into a box office success.

Sheridan enjoyed working with Menjou. She recalled her overall impression of the debonair actor for *Liberty* magazine in 1940: "He's so meticulous, so fastidious, so sophisticated ... he taught me the importance of clothes and the right way to do your hair."[7] Apparently, Menjou, nine times cited as the Best Dressed Man in Hollywood, knew what he was talking about, because Sheridan was awarded the Best Dressed Woman in Motion Pictures in 1945 and one of the Ten Best Dressed Women in America three times between 1946 to 1951.

Despite her limited footage in *Letter of Introduction*, seventh-billed Sheridan received good notices. According to a *Photoplay* writer, she "stole the show" by successfully blending a glamorous appearance with a no-nonsense personality.[8] While this part is a variation of roles she played at Warners, *Letter of Introduction* was considered her first "A" film with a notable director and was the catalyst her career needed. "I was thrilled to death at the opportunity to work with a big director like John Stahl," Sheridan stated a year later. "He gave me the confidence I so badly needed."[9] Stahl saw potential in the young actress. He edited her scenes together and sent the print to Jack Warner. "I've got a find for you," Stahl told Warner, "and she's in your own studio."[10] Sheridan credited Stahl with her getting an important role in *Angels with Dirty Faces*.

"There will be bigger and better things for Ann Sheridan at

In 1938, Warner Brothers began capitalizing more on Sheridan's physical appearance and less on her acting talents. With the increasing amount of such coverage, critics viewed her as a "publicity actress" badly in need of good parts.

Warner Brothers from now on," announced *Hollywood Citizen-News*.[11] Instead of appearing opposite Boris Karloff in *Devil's Island* (1939, with Nedda Harrigan replacing Sheridan), the studio announced that she would be given the feminine lead opposite Jon Hall in the Technicolor adventure film *Hearts of the North* (eventually made with Dick Foran and Gloria Dickson). Sheridan was also slated to assume the leading role previously designated for Kay Francis in *Gay Nineties*, with an all-star cast including Dick Powell, Olivia de Havilland and Janet Chapman.

As Sheridan's career continued to gain momentum, her marriage to Norris finally collapsed. In late August, it was reported, "Another movie marriage broke up today with [Sheridan and Norris] heading for the divorce courts. Miss Sheridan will probably file the divorce suit, based on grounds of incompatibility and temperamental differences."[12] Columnist Jimmie Fidler observed, "The separation of Ann Sheridan and Edward Norris is just one more example to prove the old Hollywood adage that marriages can't last when the wife out-shines the husband professionally."[13] The column mentioned other acting couples who found themselves in a similar situation, including Ruth Chatterton and George Brent (who would become Sheridan's second husband). In court, Sheridan told the judge that Norris "told me ... that our marriage was a mistake."[14] According to another report, she stated that Norris' conduct "made me nervous and I lost weight and couldn't eat."[15] In some articles, this was, in all seriousness, referred to as Sheridan's weight loss plan!

The divorce was granted in early October with Sheridan moving into an apartment after Norris was awarded the house. Some months later, she told *Photoplay*, "If two people can't agree, the best thing to do is get out of it." She shared her philosophy of life after divorce: "Once your original plan is disrupted, you have to work it all out again—and differently. It seems life can change, things can be different—although once you thought they never could be. A new set of ideas has to be worked out. Before it was two people planning a future—now it is one."[16]

Norris continued to play supporting roles for various studios. The gossip columnists noted that Sheridan and Norris were still friendly; in fact, the exes remained friends until her death in 1967. "It broke my heart when I heard of her passing," Norris told Dan Van Neste. "She was such a great gal, the love of my life!"[17]

During the divorce proceedings, Sheridan's next film, *Broadway Musketeers*, was released. It was a remake of *Three on a Match* (1932), which had featured Bette Davis and Humphrey Bogart. The remake was produced by the Foy unit with John Farrow directing. It began production under the title *Three Girls on Broadway*; the shooting lasted a month. Upon its completion, Sheridan's contract was renewed for three more years.

Sheridan is Fay Reynolds, a radio singer whose strip tease act lands her in jail. She is bailed out by Isabel Dowling (Margaret Lindsay) and Connie Todd (Marie Wilson), childhood friends from her orphanage days. Isabel, married to wealthy Stanley Dowling (John Litel), is the mother of little Judy (Janet Chapman), but she is dissatisfied with her predictable life.

After Isabel leaves her family, Fay begins a romantic relationship with Dowling and becomes his second wife and Judy's stepmother. Meanwhile, Isabel's life deteriorates as her new husband Philip gambles their savings away. Philip fails to pay gambling debts, and the situation leads to a gangster (Dick Purcell) kidnapping Judy for ransom money from Dowling. As the police search for Isabel and Judy, the baddies plan to kill them. To save her daughter, Isabel jumps out the window, clutching a newspaper article about the kidnapping. The police engage in a shootout and rescue Judy.

Broadway Musketeers made its way around the bottom half of double bills, garnering some favorable opinions. Sheridan, as the brassy, street-smart singer, performs two songs ("Has It Ever Occurred to You?" and "Who Said That This Isn't Love?") well and does a semblance of a strip tease that reeks of the fabled "oomph" quality.

Sheridan's next film, *Angels with Dirty Faces*, provided her with the big chance she needed to step into the next level on the lot. Cast as the love interest of the studio's #1 star, James Cagney, Sheridan stood to gain from the exposure in a highly anticipated "A" film. She gratefully acknowledged, "My first picture on this lot was *The Great O'Malley....* But my first good picture was *Angels with Dirty Faces*—that was the real start of my movie career."[18]

Angels was scripted by Rowland Brown, known mostly for his screenplays for the pre–Code crime films *The Doorway to Hell* (1930) and *Quick Millions* (1931). He peddled the script to Grand National as a vehicle for Cagney, who was working at that studio after a major dispute with Warners. Brown was originally assigned to direct but, after two less-than-successful features for Grand National, Cagney returned to Warners to score a better deal than was previously offered. Cagney pitched the script to studio heads. Director Mervyn LeRoy believed it would suit the Dead End Kids, who made a hit in the stage and screen versions of *Dead End*. Michael Curtiz, one of Warners' most versatile directors, was chosen to direct. Pat O'Brien, who worked with Cagney in several highly popular films, was given the role of Father Connolly. Humphrey Bogart and George Bancroft handled other major supporting roles.

Sheridan was initially nervous about being in such elite company but found the cast and crew made her feel at home. She recalled, "I was a brat running around who [Cagney and O'Brien] could pick on. I was certainly fond of them and they seemed pretty fond of me."[19] Cagney proved especially helpful in coaching the young actress. "He was grand to me.... I was so

Sheridan was cast opposite the studio's number-one star, James Cagney, in *Angels with Dirty Faces* (1938). Cagney became a lifelong friend and a strong advocate for her career.

nervous about everything," Sheridan told *Modern Screen* in 1940.[20] In another interview, Sheridan revealed her admiration for Cagney's professional conduct to other cast members: "He's the sort of star who will sit down with you and explain in detail why you should do a thing a certain way. He'll give you the benefit of everything he's learned."[21] Sheridan later became known for exhibiting the same kindness and courtesy to other actors.

During the filming, Sheridan recalled having a particularly difficult time when she had to slap Cagney hard. There were dozens of takes before director Curtiz was satisfied. Although he had a headache by then, Cagney reassured Sheridan, "I don't mind your hitting me so much as long as we get the scene right."[22]

Years later, Cagney wrote in his autobiography that Sheridan was "a lovely, talented girl" with "so much to offer"—but he was distressed by her three-packs-a-day smoking habit: "Years later when the lung cancer hit, she didn't have much of a chance, and what a powerful shame that was."[23]

Angels with Dirty Faces begins in 1920s New York City when two youths, Rocky Sullivan and Jerry Connolly attempt a robbery. Jerry escapes, but Rocky is caught and is sentenced to reform school. This starts his life of crime.

After serving his time, Rocky returns to his old neighborhood. Jerry (O'Brien) has since become a Catholic priest in the neighborhood parish. Rocky rents a room in a boarding house run by the mother of Laury Martin (Sheridan). Laury recalls how he bullied her back in their youth and reciprocates with a solid face slap. Rocky likes her spunk.

A group of juvenile delinquents is played by the Dead End Kids and composed of Soapy (Billy Halop), Swing (Bobby Jordan), Bim (Leo Gorcey), Pasty (Gabriel Dell), Crab (Huntz Hall) and Hunky (Bernard Punsly). The boys are dazzled by Rocky's reputation and idolize him, much to the dismay of Father Jerry and Laury.

Rocky forms an alliance with his crooked lawyer Frazier (Bogart) and Mac Keefer (Bancroft) in a gambling casino deal for financial benefits. When Father Jerry launches a campaign to expose corruption in city government, Keefer and Frazier decide to bump off the crusading priest. Rocky learns of the plan and kills them both. He escapes to a nearby warehouse and engages in a shoot-out with police. Father Jerry brings Rocky out alive.

For killing a policeman, Rocky is given the death sentence. Concerned about his negative influence on the boys, Father Jerry implores Rocky to turn "yellow" at the last minute in the death chamber. The gang is disillusioned by this act of cowardice and Father Jerry is heartened that perhaps they have been rescued from a life of crime.

Released in late November, *Angels with Dirty Faces* was a smash hit and ranked among the studio's top-grossing films along with *The Adventures of Robin Hood* and *Four Daughters* (both of which were also directed by Curtiz). Cagney was honored with acting awards from *Photoplay*, the National Board of Review and the New York City Film Critic Circle. He was nominated for an Academy Award, but lost to Spencer Tracy for *Boys Town*. Director Curtiz and writer Brown were also nominated. In 2015, *Angels with Dirty Faces* was voted one of the "100 Best Film Noirs of All Time" by *Slant* magazine. It's considered one of the all-time great gangster films and is required viewing for film buffs. To this day, it remains a compelling, deeply involving motion picture displaying Hollywood craftsmanship at its finest.

There was praise aplenty for the supporting cast with O'Brien and the Dead End Kids receiving the lion's share. For the most part, Sheridan was seen as part of an excellent supporting cast although she garnered mixed reviews. While *Screenland* was disappointed ("Ann Sheridan fails to smoulder much as Cagney's girl"), the *Pittsburgh Press* opined that she "doesn't have much to do, but she makes her part worthwhile." In the end, Sheridan's competent, but less-than-inspired performance did not propel her to stardom despite her association with Cagney and this film.

Despite *Angels'* box office and critical success, Warners executives still believed Sheridan was best utilized as a minor-league actress in "B" films and in an occasional supporting role in an "A" film. She was announced as a strong contender to play the comic strip character Jane Arden in the first film of a proposed series; *The Adventures of Jane Arden* was released in 1939 with Rosella Towne in the title role. Sheridan was also scheduled for *Each Dawn I Die* with Cagney and George Raft, but Jane Bryan assumed that role.

During the "Search for Scarlett O'Hara" frenzy, Sheridan was among the many hopefuls who tested for the coveted role. Louella Parsons wrote,

> Don't be surprised if Ann Sheridan ... nabs the Belle Watling plum. She was on the Selznick lot for a test and George Cukor was very pleased with the idea of Ann playing the role.... In the past year, the Sheridan girl has graduated from unimportant ingénue to girls who know their way around.[24]

Unfortunately for Ann, Jack Warner, who had already consented to Olivia de Havilland's loan-out to play *GWTW*'s Melanie Hamilton, would not let Sheridan off the lot.

In January 1939, columnist Jimmie Fidler proclaimed Sheridan (along with John Garfield, John Payne and Jeffrey Lynn) one of the studio's "Best Bets of 1939" to achieve stardom. Fidler wrote,

> No other studio can list as many promising youngsters of star caliber—most, in fact, haven't a single personality "hot enough" to be considered a major box office threat.... I like the way Lynn, Garfield, Payne, and Sheridan are being developed—a variety of roles designated to give them the most versatile training, but no parts big enough to put them on trial prematurely.[25]

Fidler predicted that Lynn had the best shot for a brilliant film career. While Lynn never quite reached the pinnacle of fame, he had a long and varied career on the screen, television and stage.

After Hedy Lamarr's sensational beauty was spotlighted in her American film debut *Algiers* (1938), moviemakers sought to replicate that movie's box office success with their own forms of glamour and sex appeal. At this juncture, Warners began to emphasize Sheridan's physical allure. One reporter wrote,

> It's a pretty safe bet that a gal is going places when the Hays Office begins to be extra critical of her stills, instead of okaying them in a routine manner. And it's watching Miss Sheridan's these days. This isn't because of intentionally indiscreet posing by the studio photographers on the gamble that some "umph" might get by the censors on an off day.

A Warner Brothers publicity man stated, "She just naturally drapes in scorching poses. And oh, what a time we had with those stills of her in a negligee! They came back from the Hays Office three times to have a little bit added here and there."[26]

The "umph" factor was on full display in Sheridan's next production, *They Made*

Me a Criminal. She appeared opposite one of the studio's red-hot young actors, John Garfield, to whom she took an immediate liking. For a scene involving a passionate kiss, Sheridan and director Busby Berkeley set Garfield up for a gag. Berkeley "instructed" Sheridan to hold the kiss until he yelled "Cut!" As planned, he never gave the command and Sheridan held on for a long, drawn-out kiss that caught Garfield off-guard. Instinctively, Garfield tried to wriggle his way out of the increasingly uncomfortable situation and the two actors fell off the couch and onto the floor. The director and crew roared with laughter. Columnist Sidney Skolsky, perhaps in on the joke, was present on the set that day. He breathlessly informed his readers, "Miss Sheridan is wearing a very low evening gown, which helps her to act sexy and alluring. She leans over and kisses Garfield. And when I say kissing him, I mean just that. You can see that Miss Sheridan is giving the scene all she has."[27]

Despite his tough-guy image, Garfield was embarrassed by such a display on-screen. Sheridan later recalled she found Garfield "a dear man" who appeared to be like the "little guy who brought the apple for the teacher."[28]

The feature was based on the 1933 off–Broadway play *Sucker* by Bertram Millhauser and Beulah Marie Dix; the movie's opening credits give the source as a *novel* by Millhauser and Dix. It was first filmed in 1933 as *The Life of Jimmy Dolan*, with Douglas Fairbanks, Jr., Loretta Young and a young John Wayne in a small role as a nervous boxer! Its director, Berkeley, was the famed musical choreographer responsible for the eye-popping musical numbers in Warners' *42nd Street* (1933), *Dames* (1934) et al. This was his last film for Warners before heading over to MGM. It was also the first starring feature for Garfield, who made a highly favorable impression in Warners' *Four Daughters* the year before.

Sheridan appears briefly in the film's early scenes as Goldie, a "good-time girl" (the Hays Office's version of a prostitute) who catches the fancy of Johnnie (Garfield). Johnnie, a world champion boxer, is falsely implicated in a murder before he is presumed to have been killed in a car accident. Phalen (Claude Rains), a disgraced New York City police detective, is not convinced Johnnie is dead and investigates on his own.

Johnnie (renamed Jack) arrives at Grandma Rafferty's (May Robson) farm, a place where some juvenile delinquents (who else but the Dead End Kids?) and Peggy (Gloria Dickson) live and work. Johnnie ingratiates himself into his new "family" and turns over a new leaf. After Phalen tracks him down, Johnnie surrenders. However, when Phalen realizes how Johnnie has transformed his life, he lets him go.

A box office success, *They Made Me a Criminal* was awarded *Photoplay*'s "Picture of the Month" with Garfield cited for "Best Performance." Most of the other cast members were praised for their excellent work, but it was Garfield who grabbed all of the attention.

Despite her short screen time (roughly five minutes out of 92 minutes), Sheridan got a few favorable comments. The majority of the notices focused on her physical allure rather than acting ability. These comments proved that the executives were correct in pushing Sheridan as a glamorous figure.

Sheridan was assigned to another inconsequential role in a Dick Powell musical comedy, *Always Leave Them Laughing* (apparently a favorite title at Warner Brothers as many musical comedies bore this title early in production). The film was based on the same-name original story by Richard Macaulay and Jerry Wald. By this time,

Powell was tired of trifling stories like this one and decided not to renew his contract after seven years with the studio. When the film wrapped its shoot in mid–December, the executives, out of pure spite, put the film on the shelf with no intention of releasing it.

Sheridan's career took another step forward when she was assigned a supporting role (thus providing "name value" according to the *Motion Picture Herald*) in an Errol Flynn–Olivia de Havilland "super–Western," *Dodge City*. The movie, which began production in early November, was one of the studio's most highly anticipated pictures given Flynn's rising popularity. Directing Robert Buckner's original screenplay was Michael Curtiz, a pro at handling Technicolor spectacles.

Despite the professionalism of all those involved, there were some challenges on the set. Flynn was nervous about appearing in his first Western. As he related in his autobiography, "I felt miscast in Westerns.... It was most frustrating, it stopped my trying to act."[29] Flynn also detested working for Curtiz, whom he considered "a talented man, probably brilliant, but relentless in his demands."[30] The mutual animosity between star and director accounted for much of the tension on the set. Other actors were similarly miserable. Not only was de Havilland weary of fending off her handsome, lovestruck co-star, she had grown tired of playing the dewy-eyed ingénue to the dashing hero. She was simply biding her time until she could report to the Selznick studios for *Gone with the Wind*. Sheridan, who cried so easily in front of bright camera lights, had to contend with the intense lighting used for Technicolor. She recounted to Hagen that the lighting "[a]lmost made me blind."[31] Regarding her role, she confessed to a reporter, "I don't know whether this Ruby has a heart of gold or not.... Everybody on the lot, except me, has read the script. All I know is, she's the gambler's gal, and she sings some songs, and there's a lot of fighting and slapping people."[32] As she eventually learned, this was a role that required visual appeal rather than acting skill.

Sheridan reflected to a *Photoplay* writer, "The way things were before, I took my work as it came. Played through it. You know—it wasn't terrifically important.... Now I regard it with more seriousness."[33] Despite this proclamation, however, she was increasingly annoyed with the studio's low regard for her acting talent. She was further distressed when she realized the public opinion was no different. Columnist Sheilah Graham referred to Sheridan as a "publicity actress" because she "receives lots of ballyhoo, but no roles worth mentioning."[34] Sheridan particularly despised the offensive publicity which continued to focus on her physical attributes: "She's got everything that a screen baggage needs—curves in the right places, a low voice, an eye-catching walk."[35] In an earlier interview, Sheridan conceded to Paul Harrison, "I'm well paid and have a nice husband named Ed Norris, and a nice home, and I like to work in pictures.... Still I wonder if I'd have got along faster if I had gone temperamental and yelled for better parts."[36]

Even if she had yelled, it wouldn't have made much of a difference to the front office. In January, she was handed yet another low-budget picture that emphasized her physical charms: *Indianapolis Speedway*. It was a remake of a popular James Cagney film, *The Crowd Roars* (1932). Not only did the producers utilize much of the original plot and characters, they also liberally lifted footage from the earlier film! This is especially noticeable in the race car scenes, as evidenced in the difference in photographic quality. While in post-production, the editors accidentally mixed up some of these scenes. The racetrack announcer scenes from the 1932 movie appeared in the remake. Even the fiery crash scene involving Frank McHugh (repeating his original role) was lifted right out of *The Crowd Roars*.

Sheridan was next assigned to another low-grade picture, *The Battle Cry of City Hall* (she replaced Jane Wyman) opposite Ronald Reagan. A low-budget attempt to cash in on the success of *Angels with Dirty Faces*, it was soon retitled *The Angels Wash Their Faces*. However, the title and the presence of the Dead End Kids, along with Sheridan, were the only connections to the earlier film. Otherwise, it was a tedious retread of the usual social justice theme, done on a much smaller scale. This was the sixth movie featuring the original Dead End Kids; by this time, Warner Brothers had grown tired of the boys' outrageous antics during production. Sheridan had no trouble with the boys as they fancied themselves in love with her. She used this to her advantage and successfully kept them at arm's length. Reagan was not as lucky. He later recalled that working with the boys was "an experience similar to going over Niagara Falls in a barrel the hard way—upstream."[37] In desperation, the studio hired former football player Ross Saunders to control the boys. At one point, they behaved so badly that Saunders turned a fire hose on them. Eventually, the diminishing box office returns of the Dead End Kids features led to them being dropped from the Warners payroll.

By this time, Sheridan had plenty of reasons to be discouraged after the studio announced yet another standard leading woman role in a low-grade B film, *Escape from Alcatraz* opposite John Litel and Humphrey Bogart. Fortunately, it was a silly, but timely publicity stunt that set her on the trajectory toward stardom.

EIGHT

The Newest Sex Symbol, with Plenty of Oomph

I hated the whole campaign then, but I agreed to it because it gave me a
chance to become known and get the better parts I wanted.[1]

Before there was "Oomph," there was "umph."

The slang word "umph" has been long used to express skepticism or disgust. That changed in late 1936 when some enterprising publicist or entertainment commentator decided to promote a new meaning of the word as a replacement for "It," which in the late 1920s described Clara Bow's on-screen sexual charisma. Before long, newspapers across the country were flooded with picture captions like this one: "Hollywood has a new word for IT. It's 'umph' and here's lots of it—in the highly personable person of Shirley Ross of the films. 'Umph' is personality plus, and what plus takes."[2] This designation did not do much to make the little-known singer more palatable to the moviegoers. Today, Ross is best-known for duetting with Bob Hope on his signature song "Thanks for the Memory."

Walter Winchell has long been credited with popularizing the new meaning. In 1937, "umph" took on a more suggestive connotation. According to Paul Harrison, the word became defined as "a sensual spark, forthright, and elemental. It is sex appeal. It is the intangible something that worries censors but defies specific censure."[3]

The first time Sheridan was linked to "umph" was in late March 1938 when Winchell opined, "That Ann Sheridan, who has many of the late Jean Harlow's charms, including an eye-filling chassis, should be given roles with 'umph,' where she'd have an opportunity to display them. Her flaming red locks should be used to dress a few Technicolor pictures, too."[4] A few months later, Harrison, attuned to her frustration, pointedly noted her desire that "she might have had her dramatic 'umph' recognized faster."[5]

When the "umph" mania failed to make an impact on filmgoers, the publicity angle then leaned toward glamour. Always in the forefront of such matters, Harrison explored the topic of Hollywood glamour in December 1938. He discussed several "Glamour Girls" including Hedy Lamarr (rightfully rated Number 1), Alice Faye and Paulette Goddard. Harrison offered, "Next nearest offering for 1938 in the glamour line is Ann Sheridan, one-time B-picture and utility actress whose earthy quality and physical advantages finally have reminded Warner Brothers that Clara Bow is retired. Miss Sheridan definitely is set for top roles in 1939."[6]

When the glamour angle failed to ignite after a few months, Warner Brothers' publicity department head Bob Taplinger finally struck gold merely by changing the spelling of "umph" to "oomph." He then staged a "contest" to spotlight the Hollywood actresses who best embodied "oomph." The publicity stunt was rigged to crown Sheridan victor and boost publicity coverage for Warners.

Taplinger assembled a panel of 25 judges (including Busby Berkeley, Bob Hope, Earl Carroll, the Earl of Warwick and Hollywood's pre-eminent glamour photographer George Hurrell) to "select" the star most deserving of the coveted "Oomph Girl" title. Each contestant had to submit a photograph to be judged by the committee.

Hurrell was commissioned by Warners to take Sheridan's photographs. For the photo shoot, Sheridan recalled that her outfit "had a roll-back collar and long sleeves. It was a crepe negligee, covered all the way up. Nothing on underneath, of course."[7] Hurrell reminisced that Sheridan "was very good-natured about the whole thing. I played rumba and samba records and she was totally responsive. We laughed a good deal because the beauty mark, courtesy of Perc Westmore, kept sliding down her cheek from the heat of the lights."[8] Years later, Sheridan told Hagen that Hurrell "was the greatest."

Taplinger arranged an award dinner that was held at the Los Angeles Town House on March 16, during which Sheridan was officially declared the winner. Reflecting on that evening years later, she admitted, "It was one of those nerve-wracking things and I actually can't remember very much of it."[9] She received a certificate and a bracelet along with the "Oomph Girl" title. It was revealed in 1945 that Jane Wyman and Margaret Lindsay were also under early consideration for the title.

The publicity department milked the new title for all it was worth. Sheridan loved telling the story that Jack Warner "looked at my picture in the paper and said, 'She'll be dead in six months.'"[10] Much to everyone's surprise, however, the stunt gained traction and Sheridan received more attention from the press than she could have imagined. The publicity ranged from the ingenious to the ridiculous. Typical of the latter was a *Hollywood* magazine ad: In a contest sponsored by *Screen Book* magazine, the ad, promoting a "Glamor Battle!," breathlessly asked:

In early 1939, Sheridan was officially crowned "the Oomph Girl," Hollywood's newest sex symbol. She grew to hate the title because it got in the way of her ambitions as a serious dramatic actress.

"Who is the most glamorous girl in Hollywood? Is it 'Oomph' Sheridan or 'Exstasy' Lamarr?" This was followed by: "Don't miss the detailed statistical chart comparing Hedy's charms with those of Ann!"[11] (While Lamarr was inarguably the most beautiful and glamorous actress ever to grace the silver screen, she couldn't hold a candle to the vivacity and sexual allure of Ann Sheridan.) Another ridiculous bit of promotion was the Nevin-Seymour Company's $1 million insurance policy taken out on Sheridan's "oomph."

Sheridan was surprised to find that she was being sued for $5000 by a radio actress professionally known as Joan Castle for stealing her "Oomph Girl" title. Few people took this seriously, especially Sheridan, who quipped, "An insulting amount in itself. If she had made it $500,000 it would have been worthwhile."[12]

Many of the judges offered up their takes on what "Oomph" meant. Busby Berkeley stated, "Oomph is the quality that drives girls to stardom and men to distraction." The quote from the Earl of Warwick was enough to make Sheridan cringe: "Oomph is a feminine desirability which can be observed with pleasure but cannot be discussed with respectability."[13] Soon the term was being used to denote "a certain indefinable something, something that commands male interest."[14] This was the Code of Decency's sanctioned version of outright sex appeal. It was this connotation that caused Jimmie Fidler to gripe, "Of all the asinine tags ever handed out, this one bestowed on her is absolute tops. Being called an 'Oomph Girl' is enough to blast anyone's dignity to smithereens—the word is one that lends itself to the kind of ridicule that no actress can long survive."[15]

Although Sheridan was initially grateful for the exposure the new moniker brought, she soon became conflicted about its impact on her career and began downplaying it. In an interview, she said, "Sex appeal? I'm not sure what it is, but whatever it is, this much I can tell you—I didn't always have it.... [S]ex appeal is all mixed up with charm and personality, the main ingredients of which are beauty, natural curiosity, and a sense of humor."[16] All of which Sheridan possessed in spades. It has become part of Hollywood folklore that Sheridan once stated, "Oomph ... is what a fat man says when he leans over to tie his shoelace in a telephone booth." She later confessed that the quip was originally dreamed up by a publicist.[17]

Sheridan began to despise the label and complained loudly to anyone within earshot. One day, she was approached by actor Paul Muni in the studio commissary. "Don't be silly," he advised her. "Be smart.... Use it to get parts."[18]

As much as she disliked the tag, Sheridan hated Warners' emphasis on her physical attributes more. Stuart Jerome (a studio employee who later became a television writer) explained, "Though beautiful of face ... and possessing a wonderfully sexy husky voice, Sheridan sorely lacked the mammary endowments deemed necessary to fit her new title." At the time, ample bosom measurements were synonymous with sex appeal, best exemplified by Clara Bow and Jean Harlow's sex symbol status. Warners executives came up with an easy solution. Stuart continued, "Wardrobe was instructed to have one of its experts design a lovely pair of 38s to compensate for nature's mistake. Always outspoken and disdainful of Front Office mentality, Sheridan bitterly resented the deception."[19] At the same time, she was not above using the enhanced "solution" as a source of ribald humor on a set.

The first film to capitalize on Sheridan's new fame was *Dodge City*. Scheduled for national release on April 8, 1939, the feature was heavily marketed as a blockbuster.

Although Sheridan makes what amounts to an enlarged cameo appearance, she was given third billing and was prominently displayed in ads.

To promote the film's April 3 premiere in Dodge City, Warners chartered a special 16-car train that transported film stars, including cast members Errol Flynn, Frank McHugh and Guinn "Big Boy" Williams plus Jack L. Warner from California to Dodge City. A Technicolor film crew was dispatched to film the premiere and much of the footage was incorporated into the theatrical trailer. The event was attended by the president's son, Franklin D. Roosevelt, Jr.; over 70,000 visitors came to the three-day event. Actress Jean Parker recalled the occasion as fun: "We had a great time. I adored [Flynn]! He was fun and had such a sense of humor."[20] Sheridan recalled one memorable episode: "We went to Dodge City where the governor of Kansas had a reception. Errol Flynn had a bottle in his hip pocket and somehow it broke. When he was introduced to the governor, booze was running down his pants and into his cowboy boots, and he smelled like a distillery."[21]

In *Dodge City*, Sheridan plays Ruby, "that most luring and lurid of come-on gals" in the Gay Lady saloon, owned by the corrupt Jeff Surrett (Bruce Cabot).[22] Newcomer Wade Hatton (Flynn) is persuaded to become the new sheriff. Wade and his men undertake a campaign to clean up the town, despite heavy opposition from Surrett and his men. Newspaperman Joe Clemens (McHugh) and Abbie Irving (de Havilland) support Wade's efforts.

When Joe uncovers evidence of Surrett's crooked cattle dealing and his ties to several killings, he is killed. Yancey (Victor Jory), a Surrett henchman, is charged with the murder and the townspeople form a lynch mob. Wade smuggles his prisoner onto a train, in which Abbie rides as a passenger. There's a heart-pounding climax involving a burning railcar and a shootout that leaves the bad guys dead. With Dodge City settled, Wade and Abbie set out for Virginia City (the title of a follow-up film slated for Flynn, de Havilland and Sheridan).

Dodge City became one of the highest-grossing films of the year. Critical comments were generally favorable and the feature was chosen as one of *Photoplay*'s Best Pictures of the Month.

Despite her prominent billing, Sheridan is definitely tucked away in the large supporting cast. She only has a few lines of dialogue and three songs to warble: "I'se Gwine Back to Dixie," "(I Wish I Was in) Dixie's Land" and "Little Brown Jug" (the latter two offering only little snippets). Her overall contribution to *Dodge City* is strictly visual, but certainly not unappreciated.

Next, Warners dusted off *Always Leave Them Laughing*, retitled it *Naughty but Nice* (in reference to Sheridan's new image) and gave top billing to their "Oomph Girl" over their former singing star Dick Powell. Judging by the finished product, the studio really shouldn't have exhumed this one from the vaults.

The nonsensical plot concerns Professor Donald Hardwick (Powell), a staid classical music purist who co-writes the popular song "Hooray for Spinach" with Linda (Gale Page). Its success brings shame to his family and the snooty college music department. Linda sees the commercial viability of Donald's work and, with her music publisher Ed Clark (Ronald Reagan), they write a series of Hit Parade songs.

Their rapid rise attracts the attentions of a pair of music publishers who are not above plagiarizing classical music. Also lurking in the background is Zelda Manion (Sheridan), a glamorous radio singer bent on exploiting the professor's fame to bolster her career. As part of her seduction, she plies the teetotaling professor with spiked lemonade that unleashes his wild side. Before long, the professor is on trial for musical plagiarism. The mess is eventually worked out, but by this time, no one really cares.

Warner Brothers dumped this musical comedy hodgepodge on an uninterested public in June. The publicity department conjured up ridiculous taglines like "The 'Oomph' Girl's Greatest Tri-Oomph." Critics panned the feature and its lack of entertainment value. *Box Office Digest* astutely noted, "There has been quite a publicity build-up for Ann Sheridan as an 'oomph' girl, but we don't think that it is ripe enough yet to sell tickets."

Sheridan is given three solo songs: "Hooray for Spinach," "Corn Pickin'" and "I Don't Believe in Signs." There is a fourth song, "In a Moment of Weakness," a duet between Sheridan and Page, who sings most of it; Sheridan's singing voice in this case was dubbed by Vera Van.

In its July 24 issue, *Life* magazine featured Sheridan on its front cover. "Americans had never had an Oomph Girl before," a writer enthused, "and may never have one again." He went on:

> Upon Clara Lou Sheridan, the effect of becoming the American Oomph Girl has not been altogether salubrious. Physically, she is perfectly equipped for the part. Her red hair, which photographs brown, is less spectacular than Jean Harlow's but this is advantageous because few girls have platinum hair anyway and the spectacle of such a freak makes people nervous. Her low, husky voice is friendly and her Texas drawl has a pleasantly concupiscent quality. Her torso—36 inches around the top, 26 inches around the middle—is highly satisfactory. Standing 5 foot 5 inches and weighing 121 lbs. she does not have to diet.[23]

Once again, Sheridan lamented over the media's focus on her physical attributes rather than her acting talent. As far as any resemblance to the late Jean Harlow, Sheridan was quick to say, "I'll never be another Jean Harlow and there never can be another Harlow."[24]

The first film created to capitalize on the Oomph fame was *Winter Carnival*, which Sheridan made on loan-out to producer Walter Wanger. The feature was originally earmarked for Hedy Lamarr, who appeared in Wanger's *Algiers*. When MGM refused to loan Lamarr, Wanger decided Sheridan would be a worthy substitute. Sheridan recalled in 1951 that Wanger would "have nothing to do with the 'Oomph Girl' ballyhoo. Instead he paid $22,000 for a full-page ad in a national magazine and labeled me 'America's No. 1 woman of allure.' I went back to Warners and the 'Oomph Girl' title and no one ever mentioned the word 'allure' again."[25]

Winter Carnival was based on the short story "Echoes That Old Refrain" by Corey Ford, published in *The Saturday Evening Post* in 1937. It was a project near and dear to Wanger's heart and he invested a substantial amount of money into the production. Wanger was a 1915 graduate of Dartmouth College in Hanover, New Hampshire, then an all-male Ivy League college. He made Dartmouth the film's setting and sent a crew to film scenes on the campus. Wanger then hired F. Scott Fitzgerald, one of the literary giants of the 1920s, to write the screenplay. That's when all the trouble began.

By 1939, Fitzgerald's once notable writing career was in shambles due to acute alcoholism. He moved to Hollywood in 1937 to work as a screenwriter for MGM.

The only screen credit he received there was for *Three Comrades* (1938), a huge critical success for Margaret Sullavan, even though only a third of his original work remained in the final cut. After several more mishaps, MGM fired Fitzgerald. Still eager to prove himself as a screenwriter, he was grateful to Wanger for the job. He promised to remain sober while working on the script.

Wanger recruited Dartmouth alumnus Budd Schulberg (son of former Paramount head B.D. Schulberg) to escort Fitzgerald from California to Hanover. In Los Angeles, Schulberg's father gave them two bottles of champagne as a bon voyage gift. Big mistake. By the time the train reached Hanover, Fitzgerald had fallen off the wagon and was too drunk to write anything. After a prolonged drinking binge, he was fired in a humiliating scene in front of the film crew at the Hanover Inn.

The screenplay was then handed over to Schulberg, Maurice Rapf and Lester Cole, all novice screenwriters. This backstory is far more entertaining than the finished product. *Winter Carnival* is often called one of Sheridan's worst movies, with good reason.

After the initial preview of the movie, Wanger's publicity team went to work to promote Wanger's newest box office success.

> Few actresses of equal years in motion pictures have gone through the rigid training for eventual stardom that Ann Sheridan had experienced.... A natural beauty and enthusiasm for her work helped no little, but only by sheer performance was she able to win consideration for greater opportunities.... Producer Walter Wanger gave her the same opportunity he has given Hedy Lamarr in *Algiers* and Claire Trevor in *Stagecoach*. He saw in Ann Sheridan a composite of Jean Harlow-Clara Bow allure, and a typical American girlishness, giving her more poise and dominance than any role she has had before.[26]

But moviegoers recognized a turkey when they encountered one and this one was the granddaddy of them all.

Sheridan is Jill Baxter, dubbed "America's No. 1 Glamour Girl" by the press courtesy of her highly publicized marriage to (and speedy divorce from) a Russian duke. She finds herself on a train bound for Dartmouth, where she was once the Winter Carnival Queen. She is met at the train station by former flame John Weldon (Richard Carlson), one of Dartmouth's most popular teachers and eligible bachelors. It is not much of a spoiler to report that the former sweethearts bicker, reconcile and bicker some more before falling blissfully into each other's arms at the fade-out.

Released in July, *Winter Carnival* was largely ignored by the public. The feature, ranked by many critics as one of the ten worst films of 1939, recorded a loss of $33,696. Several months later, Sheridan blamed the relentless publicity for the film's failure: "I got blamed; if I hadn't been the 'oomph' girl, nobody would have thought anything about it. So there I am, living in a goldfish bowl without any window shades, all because of that dinner.... [I]t's a case of weighing the good against the bad and if I had to do over again, I'm not sure but I'd rather remain plain."[27]

Bogart once said that Sheridan was "a girl with a well-defined code of honor which few women have in dealing with men—and other women in Hollywood.... [N]one of the Hollywood wives worry that Annie is going to steal a husband. She's not the type!"[28] This proved to be true only in that Sheridan would earn quite a reputation for dating men who were *separated* from their wives. Throughout her lifetime, there were persistent rumors that she had engaged in affairs with married men or while married herself. For the most part, her "honor code" dictated that, while she may not

This lovely photograph, taken for the cover of *Life* magazine, presented a much more natural and appealing version of "the Oomph Girl"—the type that men found hard to resist.

intentionally steal a husband, it was a different matter if he was living apart from his wife.

In one of the earliest published news items, the *Oakland Tribune* reported that Sheridan was named in a divorce suit over an alleged affair with a studio editor, Frank DeWar. Sheridan flatly denied any wrongdoing, stating, "It's perfectly ridiculous."[29] She claimed that DeWar used to call on her secretary Gwyneth Woodford. The fact that Sheridan was often linked to married men leads one to believe that she was not being completely honest about this one.

Warner Brothers' willingness to exploit Sheridan's new fame, while providing her with third-rate vehicles, is best exemplified by *Indianapolis Speedway*, released in August. Sheridan was given top billing in the opening credits and publicity ads over the feature's true star, Pat O'Brien (who received top billing in the end credits). The tiresome plot concerns a champion race car driver, Joe Greer (O'Brien), who is determined to keep his kid brother Eddie (John Payne) away from the dangerous racing business. He also has a hard time trying to keep Eddie from seeing Frankie (Sheridan); Joe regards her as the kind of poison capable of ruining race car drivers' lives.

His interference drives a wedge between the brothers and Eddie signs with a competitive company. Joe's reckless behavior during a competition costs his best friend Spud (McHugh) his life in a fiery crash. Guilt-ridden, Joe quits the business and hits the skids. Eddie rises quickly in the business with his new wife Frankie virtuously standing at his side. Just in time for *the* big race, Joe snaps out of his funk, reunites with his long-suffering sweetheart (Gale Page) and teams with his brother for that all-important win.

The critics were generally hostile, especially when comparing the current feature with the original, *The Crowd Roars*. The most notable aspect of Sheridan's performance was the total emphasis on her physical appearance. She's got that oomph-ish thing going in full throttle: wearing a negligee, taking a shower and sporting a scanty two-piece outfit. Acting skills be damned.

The Angels Wash Their Faces also reached screens in August. Although Sheridan was billed after the Dead End Kids in the opening credits, she is given top billing in the advertisements with her glamorous image prominently displayed.

The plot centers around Gabe (Frankie Thomas), who is released from reform school into his sister's care. Joy (Sheridan) tries valiantly to keep him out of trouble, but he falls in with a local gang, the Beale Street Termites (who else but the Dead End Kids?). One of its members dies in a tenement fire set by sleazy gangster Martino (Eduardo Ciannelli), and Gabe is framed for the crime. Joy is worried sick by this turn of events. Her new boyfriend (Ronald Reagan), the assistant district attorney, works to prove Gabe's innocence. With the aid of the Termites, the bad guys are rounded up and Gabe is cleared.

The Angels Wash Their Faces was ignored by critics and fans alike. With less emphasis on her physical allure and more focus on her acting ability, Sheridan hardly made any kind of impression.

With the "Oomph Girl" campaign reaching a fever pitch, Warners scrambled to keep Sheridan on the screen despite the lackluster reaction to her most recent features. "Now I hear the studio is planning a picture for me to be called *Oomph Girl*," Sheridan fumed. "I just won't stand for it. Maybe the time has come for me to get up and do some fighting. I can stand a suspension or two, but I could never stand a picture like that."[30]

Warner Brothers never went ahead with that project. Instead, Sheridan was scheduled for a supporting role in a James Cagney picture, *The World Moves On*. Given her rising star status, it would have been an insult to toss her into a supporting role with the likes of Priscilla Lane handling the leading lady assignment. The project was released as *The Roaring Twenties* with Gladys George in the supporting role; Lee Patrick and Glenda Farrell had also been considered for it.

It became increasingly clear to people in the business that Warners executives had no idea how to further Sheridan's career without resorting to cheap publicity. As columnist Jimmie Fidler noted:

> Looking at still another magazine cover of Ann Sheridan yesterday, it dawned on me that I've grown weary of reading about the lady. And I'm sure it's because the amazing deluge of publicity she is receiving is not fully justified. I mean, what has she done to rate this flood of magazine covers, interviews, and pictorial lay-outs? Why should she receive more space in public prints than Bette Davis or Jeanette MacDonald or Margaret Sullavan? Those ladies have really done things on the screen; I can understand press praise of their achievements. So far, the best Miss Sheridan has done has been to lend her charms (many, I admit) to a few minor roles in important films and leads in smaller pictures.[31]

Given the current situation, Sheridan had every reason to believe that her film career would flame out once the avalanche of publicity failed to produce the desired box office effect. Very few motion picture careers lasted long when based solely on a catchy label. Something had to be done before it was too late.

NINE

A Star Finally in Alignment

Stardom for me is still a "fur piece away," as we say in Texas.
The "oomph" campaign won't save me if I don't deliver.[1]

Fortunately for Sheridan, something better was in store. For the first time in a long time, she was excited about an acting assignment. As she told *Modern Screen* magazine, "I'm counting an awful lot on what *Years Without Days* will do for me as an actress.... No emphasis on oomph in this one."[2] Of definite assistance to her cause was director Anatole Litvak. Recently divorced from Miriam Hopkins, he was Sheridan's current beau.

The movie was based on the 1932 novel *Twenty Thousand Years in Sing Sing* by Lewis E. Lawes, who served as that prison's warden from 1920 to 1941. An outspoken advocate for prison reform, Lawes wrote several books on the subject. The first film adaptation reached the screen as *20,000 Years in Sing Sing* in 1933 with Spencer Tracy, Bette Davis and Arthur Byron. In the new version, John Garfield, Sheridan and Pat O'Brien recreated the roles.

Garfield was being groomed as a major star by Warner Brothers, but he was tired of being typecast as the criminal and was in constant dispute with producers. However, his character in this new picture was more well-rounded than usual and he consented to the assignment—but only after he secured the producer's promise to leave the original ending and paid an additional $10,000 for his services. One of Warners' cost-cutting measures was to construct the sets to match the ones in the original, so that some 1933 footage could be re-used in the updated version.

After the production wrapped up, the studio further exploited the "Oomph Girl" by sending her on a brief personal appearance tour of various movie houses in Washington, D.C., and New York City from late September to mid–October. She performed a specialty act in which she sang songs including "Hooray for Spinach" and "It Had to Be You." In 1950, Sheridan related her experience in New York City:

So I came into the Strand Theater here for three weeks—five shows most days and six on Saturdays.... I was scared stiff. They had a young lad named Earl Oxford as the master of ceremonies and he was like all these New York kids—poised, glib, taking everything in stride. He had to hold me up onstage, while I shook and tried to sing songs. Then there was Ted Weems' band and a couple of young, un-famous singers named Marilyn Maxwell and Perry Como. They were real pros, and they helped me wonderfully.... I hated the drudgery of it, and personally I doubt that it improved my following at all.[3]

Despite her nervousness, Sheridan made a good impression. The *Washington Post* noted, "Wearing a backless black gown and her copper-colored hair high, Ann looked 'oomphy' enough to meet the most exacting requirements…. Ann is so utterly natural and unaffected that she is instinctively liked. And besides that, the girl can sing." Taking it all in stride, Sheridan recalled, "I don't suppose any girl has been kidded as much as I have. I can take kidding and I do appreciate what oomph did for me."[4]

Years Without Days reached screens as *Castle on the Hudson* in February 1940. Garfield plays Tommy Gordon, a young, cocky crook sent to Sing Sing for armed robbery and assault with a deadly weapon. Warden Long (O'Brien) governs by the principles of rehabilitation instead of punishment. After Tommy is informed that his girlfriend Kay (Sheridan) was critically injured in a car accident, the warden says Tommy can visit her in New York City if he promises to return to Sing Sing.

At Kay's apartment, Tommy learns that his devious lawyer Crowley (Jerome Cowan) has been making unwanted advances on Kay; his actions led her to jump out of his car, sustaining severe injuries. Tommy confronts Crowley and a fight ensues. Fearing for Tommy's life, Kay shoots Crowley. Tommy narrowly escapes the police. Before he dies, Crowley names Tommy as the shooter.

No one believes Kay's accounts and Tommy is convicted of murder. He is scheduled to die in the electric chair. Tommy advises a tearful Kay to move on with her life and marry a decent man, thus sparing her from a life of heartbreak.

After the preview, Louella Parsons reported that there were some unhappy patrons who did not like the downbeat ending. Exiting the theater, one patron complained, "Why doesn't Garfield get Ann Sheridan?" The cynical companion's response: "Maybe Litvak's saving that happy ending for himself."[5] For the record, Litvak didn't get to keep the girl either.

Castle on the Hudson was well-received. The *Motion Picture Herald* termed it an "emotional cocktail" with its vivid depiction of criminality and prison life. The movie's success propelled Garfield to the top level of stardom. While he received the lion's share of the accolades, Sheridan caught many off guard with her strong performance. "The big surprise in the picture," asserted *Showmen's Trade Review*, "is Ann Sheridan, demonstrating rare acting ability in the finest of her screen portrayals, proving the young lady can really act and look pretty too."

Castle on the Hudson gave Sheridan her best role to date. Her next film, *It All Came True*, provided another push into the limelight.

Early in *It All Came True*, Sheridan enters a scene and the effect is *Pow!* For the first time, Sheridan is on in full display with all the beguiling sass, street-smart attitude and plenty of oomph. Fans owe a debt of gratitude to producer Mark Hellinger for his timely intercession on her behalf. His handling of *It All Came True* and her next three films indicated that he understood what Ann Sheridan the Movie Star had to offer.

As a result of their association, Sheridan and Hellinger became friends with a strong emotional connection. She told Hagen, "I adored him."[6] "To her pals," Hellinger wrote a few years later, "she is the most loyal friend in the world…. She claims that her philosophy is to enjoy the present and not worry about the future, and she means exactly what she says."[7] Hellinger was reportedly in love with Sheridan and they had a brief, passionate affair in spite of the fact that he was married. As described ("He had a dark, handsome face, with twinkling blue eyes. The eyes told one and all, at every time, that he wanted to be naughty"), Hellinger would have been irresistible.[8] Reports of an inconsolable Sheridan at Hellinger's 1947 funeral lend credence to the assertion of an affair.

Hellinger, a former newspaper reporter and Broadway columnist, achieved prominence at Warners when he wrote the screenplay for *The Roaring Twenties* (1939). When the James Cagney feature proved exceedingly popular, Hellinger was allowed to produce *It All Came True*. It was based on the short story "Better Than Life" by Louis Bromfield, published in Hearst's *International-Cosmopolitan* magazine in January 1936. Warner Brothers paid $50,000 for the screen rights. The screenplay was offered to, and promptly rejected by, Warners' "Queen," Bette Davis.

According to Sheridan, she had to make a test before the part was hers. The picture was intended to serve as a starring vehicle for George Raft with Sheridan and John Garfield cast in supporting roles. Tired of playing gangster roles, Raft balked, and Humphrey Bogart inherited the part. This casting shift gave Hellinger the opportunity to rewrite the script so Sheridan's character was thrust to the front and center in the starring role. This resulted in Bogart being relegated to the ranks of the supporting cast.

The production began at the end of November 1939 with the studio's utility "B" film director, Lewis Seiler, in charge. During the shoot, Sheridan received a lot of publicity for making her "bow as a full-fledged star."[9] As Louella Parsons reported, this was fortunate as Sheridan "has had more publicity and less opportunity on the screen than any actress in Hollywood."[10]

Another unexpected boost came from a most unlikely place: Harvard University. In February, W. Russell Bowie, Jr., chief editor of the undergraduate humor publication *The Harvard Lampoon*, dubbed *Winter Carnival* one of the ten worst pictures of 1939 and proclaimed Sheridan (along with 20th Century–Fox's Richard Greene) the screen actors "Least Likely to Succeed."[11]

This bit of news might have gone nowhere had the publicity department not smelled a gold mine and launched a "counterattack." An "indignant" Sheridan fumed,

> I wonder what those bozos think is success. Now, I don't mind criticism, but I'd hate to have it come from Harvard.... I met a Harvard man once myself. It was a very sad evening. He could have used a little more oomph. So could the Harvard football team. So could the *Lampoon*.... Look at the *Lampoon*. Why, if it isn't the saddest idea of a magazine, I don't know what is.[12]

Sheridan also pointed out that she was then earning $100,000 a year with her oomph, while the average Harvard graduate made less than $5000.

Bowie played along to the delight of the public, who welcomed the diversion from the depressing European war news. Bowie fired back:

> As a graduate of a remote Texas Kindergarten School, Miss Sheridan is not qualified to offer any intelligent criticism of the *Lampoon*, which caters to a somewhat different class. In view of this, Miss Sheridan's opinion of the *Lampoon* is of supreme indifference to its editors.... If she earns $100,000 a year, it is further proof of public gullibility rather than of Miss Sheridan's success as an actress. We wonder if her brief five-minute orgy in *They Made Me a Criminal* is a sign of success.[13]

Coming to the maligned damsel's defense, Roy S. Fox, Jr., of the rival Yale University's humor magazine *The Yale Record* took aim at Bowie:

> I am glad that there is enough chivalry left in the world for me to cast my glove before J. Russell Bowie and challenge him to a duel to the death. I will not stand for any defamation of Miss Sheridan's honor, beauty and talents. I doubt if Bowie will have the courage to face

me.... Miss Sheridan has always epitomized to me the essence of American womanhood and I resent any and all calumnies directed against her.[14]

As a show of support, Sheridan was invited to Yale's junior prom. She respectfully declined, citing conflict with her busy film schedule.

Just as the "feud" was dying down, a New York–based studio press agent dreamed up the idea of holding the premiere of *It All Came True* on the Harvard campus. This led to another round of publicity, which included tidbits like this: "College officers, frightened by visions of Ann the Oomphy posing for photographers on John Harvard's lap, object to the proposed premiere here on the grounds that it would expose Harvard to a blast of undignified publicity and are applying pressure from all sides to head Warner Brothers off."[15]

A few months later, Sheridan explained how the Sheridan-Harvard "feud" actually did her career some good. "I played in every 'B' picture. Maybe I would still be doing it if the *Harvard Lampoon* hadn't said I had the least chance of any actress of succeeding. It was all a big joke to the boys and they meant no harm."[16]

It All Came True, released in April, was the film that quieted the naysayers once and for all. Ann Sheridan the Star had officially arrived. To emphasize the moment, the theatrical trailer got right to the point: "Oomph! The Girl who gave the world a new word ... now shows you what it really means!" These words scroll by as Sheridan performs a sultry samba.

Sheridan's performance in 1940's *It All Came True* with Humphrey Bogart pushed her to the forefront of important box office stars.

Sarah Jane (Sheridan), an aspiring singer down on her luck, lives in a boarding-house run by her mother Maggie (Una O'Connor) and Nora Taylor (Jessie Bussley). The boardinghouse is on the verge of foreclosure. One night, Nora's son Tommy (Jeffrey Lynn) returns home after an absence of five years with a "friend," who is actually the notorious gangster Chips Maguire (Bogart). Chips, wanted for killing an informant, has managed to concoct enough circumstantial evidence to frame poor Tommy. Chips is introduced as "Mr. Grasselli," a man with a nervous condition in need of total privacy.

Tommy, a struggling composer, has been chasing his dreams for several years without any success. After singing one of his compositions, "Angel in Disguise," Sarah Jane convinces him to team with her. When Sarah Jane recognizes the elusive Mr. Grasselli, she sets out to manipulate Chips into not only paying off the mortgage, but also financing Tommy's and her future. To ensure the financial future of the residence, Chips decides to transform the place into a Gay Nineties night club.

Opening night is a sparkling success and the Tommy–Sarah Jane team seems destined for greater heights. The police arrive to arrest Chips and things look dire for Tommy. Having been transformed by Maggie and Nora's kindness, Chips accepts the blame himself and wishes the couple well.

Most of the critics were enthusiastic about this musical comedy; *Photoplay* made it one of their Best Pictures of the Month. *Silver Screen* magazine was among the many who raved over Sheridan's performance: "For the first time in her young life, pretty Miss Ann Sheridan finds herself in a first rate, corking good picture. Beautifully photographed, and very much at ease in her comedy lines, Ann at last has a chance to live up to her publicity."

With all that the film had going for it entertainment-wise, Sheridan is the big show here and does full justice to her part, whether singing, dancing, delivering wise-cracks or handling the dramatic moments. Her two big numbers, "Angel in Disguise" and "Gaucho Serenade," are well done with Sheridan in total command. *It All Came True* contains the quintessential Ann Sheridan performance and movie that delivers all the goods. In several phases of the film, Sheridan has ample opportunity to display her various screen personas (working class girl, sex symbol, wisecracking dame, entertainer, glamour girl) to full and satisfying effect. If anyone wants to see Sheridan at her best, this is the place to start.

The administrator of "The Bogie Film Blog" was equally enthusiastic in a 2013 post:

> I had one of those Ah-ha! moments with an actor. My whole life I've heard people rant and rave about Ann Sheridan, but for some reason she's never clicked with me. I always figured that I'd just never seen the right movie, and now I have. What a spitfire. From her first entrance to her final song, she was amazing. It makes me want to round up all of her movies that I haven't seen yet and have a marathon.[17]

A wise decision.

Sheridan had star billing above second-billed Lynn and third-billed Bogart. When the feature was reissued in 1945, Bogart was then the studio's top star, while Sheridan was on indefinite suspension. There was no point in promoting a "disobedient star," so Bogart received first billing, Sheridan billed second in the opening credits. The end credits remained the same as in 1940.

As *It All Came True* played around the country and Sheridan was enjoying the positive reviews for her acting, she sat down for an interview with Louella Parsons. Parsons pointedly asked, "How do you like the name 'oomph girl'?"

"Well," Sheridan acknowledged, "I am grateful to Bob Taplinger for it drew attention to me after I had made one bad picture after another, and it made me realize I had to work hard to live up to such a title. Now I would like to have it forgotten as quickly as possible. I hate the word glamour. It's so limiting to any actress who yearns to really do something."[18]

Not long after Sheridan was tagged as the "Oomph Girl," comparisons to former sex symbols Clara Bow and the late Jean Harlow resurfaced. "Not since Clara Bow bounded to fame as the 'It' girl has an actress projected such super-sex appeal as Ann Sheridan," proclaimed *Motion Picture* magazine.[19] On the other hand, Elizabeth Wilson of *Screenland* observed Sheridan's strong resemblance to Harlow in both looks and voice. Furthermore, she noted that Sheridan embodied Harlow's "characteristics which so endeared her to the Hollywood Press—independence, frankness, naturalness, and joie de vivre."[20]

Sheridan's next picture, *Torrid Zone*, was based on an original story by Richard Macauley and Jerry Wald that combined the sexy pre–Code Clark Gable–Jean Harlow classic *Red Dust* (1932) and the breathlessly paced comedy *The Front Page* (1931). Reteamed with both James Cagney (replacing George Raft) and Pat O'Brien, Sheridan enjoyed her association with this production and liked her part. Both O'Brien and Cagney, on the other hand, thought it was a minor effort that would not amount to anything. They couldn't have been more wrong.

Sheridan's Lee Donley, an American singer (she sings "Mi Caballero") and card cheat stranded in Central America, runs afoul of tough-talking banana plantation manager Steve Case (O'Brien), who orders her return to the States. While awaiting deportation in a local jail, Lee befriends a notorious revolutionary, Rosario (George Tobias), the bane of Case's existence because he insists that Plantation No. 7 belongs to him. Tricking the jailer, Rosario manages to escape to renew his efforts to seize that plantation.

On the boat, Lee meets Nick Butler (Cagney) and mutual sparks of attraction fly. Case's interest in Nick's services, however, interferes with Nick's pursuit of romance. Case needs him to manage Plantation No. 7 and Nick, in desperate need of cash, agrees to return to his old job, against his better judgment.

When Nick arrives at the plantation, he finds Lee, now on the lam from the police. He begrudgingly allows her to stay with Gloria Anderson (Helen Vinson) until the next train. Gloria is thrilled to have Nick, an old flame, back and quickly moves in, much to Lee's annoyance. This sets up a bitchy verbal rivalry between the two women and it's frequently funny. One of their best exchanges comes after Gloria carelessly discards her cigarette:

> **LEE:** I believe this is how the Chicago fire got started.
> **GLORIA:** The Chicago fire was started by a cow.
> **LEE:** History repeats itself.

Nick soon has his hands full with fending off the amorous Gloria, the ever-present (but not unwelcome) Lee, and Rosario, who has been busy recruiting Nick's workers. It all comes to an uproarious conclusion with Rosario playing a most unlikely Cupid for Nick and Lee.

Before the kiss at the fade-out, Nick utters, "You and your 14 karat oomph!" Hellinger wrote that line, which Cagney balked at. Hellinger bet Cagney the line would get the biggest laugh of the picture. After the premiere, Cagney sent Hellinger a $100 check.

The rollicking comedy was well-received by critics and moviegoers and, once again, Sheridan was the big news for the mere fact that she held her own among such accomplished actors. According to the *Indianapolis Star*,

> Ann Sheridan, the "oomph" lady, comes into her own as Lee Donley, an amiable tramp in *Torrid Zone*.... Miss Sheridan is Hollywood's nearest thing to Jean Harlow in her prime. Her sumptuous physical appeal, her deep, throaty voice, her underlying honesty and sincerity qualify her admirably for the type of role the platinum blonde used to do.... It is Miss Sheridan's picture as much as Cagney's and O'Brien's."

In the years since its release, *Torrid Zone* has become an almost forgotten feature. Nonetheless, it remains a delightful comedy that ranks among the best that Hollywood had to offer in the late '30s and early '40s. It is Sheridan's magnificent comic portrayal that provides the impetus for serious re-evaluation. Noted film historian and prolific author James Robert Parish observed, "In the annals of post–Production Code Hollywood films, *Torrid Zone* is a landmark of snappy risqué dialog spewn forth by a trio of stars who could slap out a tart line with faultless timing." Of Sheridan, Parish wrote, "Her agility with a wisecrack proved to be as sensational as her curvaceous figure."[21]

According to some sources, the plot of *Torrid Zone* was reworked into the overheated and melodramatic *Blowing Wild* (1953), which starred a dispirited Gary Cooper, Barbara Stanwyck, Anthony Quinn and Ruth Roman. However, the only connection to the previous film lies in Roman's character, Sal Donley, a card dealer stranded in a South American hotel. *Blowing Wild* is really a remake of the George Raft-Ida Lupino-Alan Hale section of Sheridan's next feature, *They Drive by Night*.

In *They Drive by Night*, Sheridan returned to the "working girl down on her luck" characterization. In an interview, she admitted, "I would have liked it better if they had let me play the murderess. But, again there was the bugaboo glamour. Warners decided that a glamour girl

George Raft provided Ann with a love interest in the hard-hitting 1940 melodrama *They Drive by Night*—and off-screen as well.

shouldn't be a murderess. Ida Lupino was given the part, but I must say she is doing a magnificent job."[22]

They Drive by Night is based on the 1938 novel Long Haul by Albert Isaac Bezzerides. The novel only accounts for the first half of the feature. The second half is a partial remake of the 1935 film Bordertown, which starred Paul Muni, Margaret Lindsay and Bette Davis. That feature's only merit is Davis' over-the-top, but always watchable, performance in one of her early showy roles after her unexpected success with RKO's Of Human Bondage (1934).

During the speedy production of They Drive by Night, Sheridan and Raft became romantically involved, much to the annoyance of George Brent (Ann's current fling) and Norma Shearer (who was Raft's).

There was one incident on the set that could have been fatal for Sheridan and her co-stars Raft and Bogart. As Raft recalled,

> In this scene, Humphrey Bogart, Ann Sheridan, and I are highballing down a long hill in an old, beat-up truck. Halfway down, the brakes really went out—a situation that wasn't in the script. Bogart saw me press the pedal and when nothing happened, he began to curse. "We're going to get killed," he yelled. Ann screamed and turned her eyes away from the road as I fought the wheel. I couldn't have been more scared myself. The speedometer hit 80 when I saw a break on the right where a bulldozer had started a new road. I pulled hard on the wheel and the truck went bouncing up the embankment. Thank God—it finally stopped. Ann was too upset to talk, but Bogart said, "Thanks, pal," with definite appreciation. "Don't thank me," I thought to myself, because I didn't have the breath to answer, "write a letter to Owney Madden or Feets Edson [the gangsters who taught Raft how to drive a getaway car]."[23]

Sheridan was shaken up by this near-fatal incident, as it must have brought back memories of the day her stand-in, Marcella Arnold, was killed in a rollover accident during the filming of The Footloose Heiress.

Sheridan is in her cinematic glory as Cassie Hartley, a roadside diner waitress who doesn't put up with nonsense from the ogling customers. The dialogue crackles with sarcasm fast and furiously, much to the audience's amusement. After some suggestive remarks from others regarding her chassis, Cassie asks Joe (Raft), "Anything else?"

> JOE: "Yeah, but it ain't on the menu."
> CASSIE (sharp on the comeback): "And it ain't gonna be. You'd better settle for a hamburger."

A few nights later, Joe and his brother Paul (Bogart) pick up Cassie, now out of a job, on their way to Los Angeles. Joe and Cassie begin a romance.

Life for independent truck drivers is hard and dangerous. One night, Paul falls asleep at the wheel during a long haul and loses his arm in the crash. Joe feels responsible and vows to take care of Paul and his wife Pearl (Gale Page). The plot then switches from its gritty, hard-hitting story to pulsating melodrama, courtesy of Bordertown. From this point on, Lupino takes center stage with an unrelentingly firm grip on the audience.

Joe works for an old friend, Ed Carlson (Alan Hale), who runs his own trucking business. Ed's wife Lana (Lupino), long obsessed with Joe, is awfully glad to have him back in her life. One night, Lana leaves Ed passed out in the garage with the car motor running. The district attorney rules his death an accident and Lana continues to pursue Joe—until she learns of his plans to marry Cassie, "that cheap little red-head." Lana seeks revenge by implicating Joe when she confesses to Ed's murder. If she can't have him, then no one else can.

Joe is placed on trial despite a lack of evidence other than Lana's accusations. During her testimony, Lana suffers from a psychotic break and it's clear that she has gone off the deep end. Joe is cleared of all charges. The film ends with a close-up of a radiantly lovely Sheridan, a sign of her status as a rising box office attraction.

Released in August, *They Drive by Night* emerged as a box office winner, reportedly grossing over $4 million. Performances all around were lauded, with the loudest huzzahs thrown at Lupino (who was awarded a Warner Brothers contract at $2000 weekly). Despite Lupino's showy characterization, Sheridan snagged a few positive notices. *Photoplay* praised her for being "de-oomphed into the good, solid simplicity of a waitress."

Today, this movie deserves to be better known outside of the legions of Ida Lupino fans. "*They Drive by Night* is a fine blend of a message picture with action, romance and spicy dialogue," wrote James Robert Parish.[24] Despite the stiff competition from Lupino's flamboyance, Sheridan more than holds her own and is in her element here as the waitress who has seen too much. This is one of her best understated performances. "I'd pay to see Ann Sheridan watching paint dry, so I'm a little biased," admitted a writer for the Bogart Film Blog. "I can't get enough of Sheridan"[25]

With the success of her recent films, there was talk of Sheridan starring in *Calamity Jane*, but that production didn't reach the screen until 1953, with Doris Day in the title role.

Sheridan was next cast in *City for Conquest*, based on the 1936 novel by Aben Kandel. It was one of Warners' more prestigious productions of the year; all those involved believed they were creating something special. Sheridan's former paramour Anatole Litvak was chosen to direct. His career had recently reached new heights when he directed the critically acclaimed Bette Davis-Charles Boyer weepie *All This, and Heaven Too*.

Early on, there were challenges in adapting the complex novel. As screenwriter John Wexley explained, "The greatest problem was in selecting one central plot. The picture has about six plots, any number of subplots. That is one reason why [the film] is so good. It is rich with plot and characters."

Along with the scripting issues, there were also casting troubles. Cagney couldn't visualize himself in the role of a boxer. "You know he's been throwing grapefruit in women's faces and playing a big shot," Wexley explained, "and this fellow is just a little fellow. No ambition. Doesn't even want to be a prize fighter. Just wants to get along in a small way. I think Cagney was a little scared of it. But once he started, the actor comes out, the real actor, and he's really great in it."[26] After that, Cagney was so enthusiastic about the project that he convinced his brother William to serve as one of the producers.

The producers originally wanted to borrow Ginger Rogers from RKO for the part of Peggy Nash, an aspiring dancer. When Rogers proved unavailable, newly signed Sylvia Sidney (no dancer, but an expert in portraying slum-dwelling heroines) was given the part. Prior to the start of production, however, Sheridan inherited the plum assignment. Although this was her third cinematic pairing with Cagney, this was the first time that both of them were on equal footing (Cagney was the undisputed star in

Angels with Dirty Faces and Sheridan had stolen *Torrid Zone* right out from under his nose). As noted at the time, "Cagney and Sheridan are a perfect screen team—Cagney's hard-boiled pugnacity and straightforwardness being perfectly offset by Miss Sheridan's volatile spirits and colorful vivacity."[27] Sheridan later reflected to Hagen that she was thrilled because "[i]t was a very good part ... [Cagney] sold like wildfire. To be in a picture with him was just the greatest."[28]

After production wrapped, there was considerable editing in the cutting room. Cagney later admitted to disappointment at what had become of a picture that held so much promise.

The film's convoluted narrative focuses on the lives of four New York City tenement dwellers who yearn to escape poverty. Googi (Elia Kazan) takes the dangerous path to become a prominent gambler, while Eddie (Arthur Kennedy, in his screen debut), the brother of Danny (Cagney), pursues his dreams of composing symphonies. Danny is content to work as a truck driver, while his sweetheart Peggy aspires to become a famous dancer.

As Peggy finds success as half of a dance team with Murray Burns (Anthony Quinn), Danny turns to boxing in order to prove himself worthy in Peggy's eyes. Their relationship is continually sidetracked since both of their ambitions get in the way, and they drift apart.

The four storylines weave in and out throughout the film until its tear-jerking conclusion. By the finale, Googi has been murdered, Peggy has abandoned her dancing career, and Danny has been blinded in a rigged boxing match. Only Eddie has emerged triumphant when he performs his seven-minute symphony "Song of the City" (composed by Max Steiner) at Carnegie Hall. Realizing the errors of their ways, Danny and Peggy are reunited at the end.

City for Conquest emerged as a big hit with critics and earned close to $2 million at the box office. The reviewers deemed it as one of Cagney's best films. Regarding the leading lady, the *New York Morning Telegraph* observed, "Sheridan turns on her celebrated 'oomph' at every given opportunity, and, on occasion, even does some fine acting on her own behalf, which is more that you'd expect."[29]

The scenes with Frank Craven, as the tramp who serves as a sort of Greek Chorus, were deleted from the print when the motion picture was re-issued in the mid–1940s. This was the print most frequently shown until it was restored to its original length by Warner Home Video in 2006.

Sheridan had fond memories of this movie and rated it among her favorites because it offered her an acting challenge. She also loved the opportunity to work with one of her favorite co-stars. "Cagney off the screen is exactly like Cagney on it. It was always 'Hi ya, baby,' or 'How are ya, sweetheart?' He's a great guy. He didn't smoke or drink. He could get drunk on two drinks of liquor. And he never made the party scene."[30]

By the end of 1940, Sheridan had established herself as a red-hot box office draw and a major star in the making. After years of bit parts and "B" films, her time had finally come.

TEN

Hollywood's Mystery Man

I have no serious heart interest. I only have fun.[1]

In a 1940 *Modern Screen* article, Sheridan described her ideal man:

He doesn't have to be handsome, but not ugly, either. An older man, preferably, maybe around 35 or 40, ambitious, interesting, and with a sense of humor. Someone who would be a gentleman at all times, would be careful about his appearance and would not take me, or himself, too seriously![2]

Enter George Brent.

It was reported that Brent noticed Sheridan in the Warners' Green Room just as she sat down to eat her meal of ham steak, mashed potatoes with gravy, two side orders and chocolate sundae. From his table, Brent remarked rather loudly to his lunch companion, "Don't tell me that's Ann Sheridan the Oomph Girl.... Delicate little thing, isn't she ... especially her appetite."[3] Sheridan ignored the remark.

After her divorce from Norris, Sheridan wasted little time in joining the dating scene. Among her regular escorts were director Jean Negulesco, Randolph Scott, Bruce Cabot, Franchot Tone, David Niven and Allan Jones—and these were the studio's sanctioned "dates." Sheridan's night club appearances were routinely documented in the gossip columns and several columnists paid close attention to Sheridan's frequent dates with her favorite dancer, Cesar Romero. Romero was the preferred escort of stars Joan Crawford, Ginger Rogers, Lucille Ball and Jane Wyman, among many other Hollywood beauties. It was Sheridan's relationship with Romero that had most observers predicting marriage. However, by January 1940, one columnist predicted, "Cesar is headed for a broken heart—for the first time in his life. He is deeply drawn to Ann Sheridan, but she doesn't return his affections in the same degree."[4] Whatever the true nature of his relationship with Sheridan may have been, it is worth noting that Romero remained a bachelor his entire life, thus fueling the persistent speculation that he was actually a closeted homosexual.

In alignment with Sheridan's surging popularity as the "Oomph Girl," the publicity department orchestrated a date between Sheridan and Brent, which took place on November 1, 1939. What started out as a publicity stunt, however, soon developed into something more serious. Brent was different from the others and both were interested in a new romantic diversion. Their burgeoning romance was a surprise to many as Brent fiercely guarded his privacy, thereby earning the tag "Hollywood's Mystery Man."[5] It wasn't long before Jimmie Fidler alerted his readers: "Keep an eye on George Brent and Ann Sheridan—their romance is more than a rumor."[6] Sheridan was envied for catching the eye of one of filmland's most eligible bachelors.

One of Sheridan's favorite activities was nightclubbing, and her frequent partner was Cesar Romero, long rumored to be in love with her.

Brent was born George Brendan Nolan on March 15, 1904, in Ballinasloe, Ireland, to John and Mary (McGuinness) Nolan. When he was 11, he and his younger sister Kathleen emigrated to New York City to live with their mother, who had previously separated from their father. In early 1921, Brent returned to Ireland and became involved with the Irish Republican Army during the Irish War of Independence; Brent later claimed to have been a courier for guerrilla leader and tactician Michael Collins. With a bounty placed on his head by the British government, Brent escaped to the United States in August 1921.

Brent decided to pursue an acting career and made his Broadway debut as George Nolan in the short-lived play *The Dover Road* in late 1921. During the next decade, Brent performed in numerous plays and even ran his own stock companies. In 1927, he married his co-star Helen Louise Campbell (eight years his senior) in Hartford, Connecticut. The marriage only lasted six months, although Brent did not obtain a divorce until 1930. His last Broadway appearance was in *Love, Honor, and Betray* (1930) with Clark Gable and Alice Brady. By this time, he had adopted the professional name George Brent.

Brent moved to Hollywood and made his film debut in Fox's *Under Suspicion* (1930). He continued in minor supporting roles for Fox, Universal and Mascot until he signed with Warner Brothers in 1931. Enacting a major supporting role in the popular Barbara Stanwyck weepie *So Big!*, Brent was launched as a dependable leading man who could support the studio's top female stars, Bette Davis, Kay Francis and Barbara Stanwyck, without overwhelming their performances and screen presence. Since few other actors on the lot had Brent's sophisticated demeanor, he was steadily employed throughout the 1930s.

In 1932, Brent married co-star Ruth Chatterton (who was being unsuccessfully groomed as Warners' "Queen of the Burbank Lot") after a highly publicized romance. That marriage was dissolved in 1934. He was briefly married for the third time in 1937 to Constance Worth, an Australian actress working in Hollywood.

By 1939, Brent was seriously involved with his frequent leading lady, Bette Davis. Davis recalled that she had "an all-time crush on George" that began when they first worked together in 1932 on *The Rich Are Always with Us.* According to Davis, "[I] had to wait quite a few years before he felt the same way—when we made *Dark Victory.*"[7] Gossip columnists predicted a Davis-Brent union, but by mid–1939, Brent knew the relationship could not survive. With that affair behind him, the time was ripe for the restless actor to indulge in a new romantic adventure.

Early on, Sheridan and Brent were a steady twosome, though non-exclusive. Some in the Hollywood community shook their heads at the unlikely match between the vivacious redhead and "Mr. Gloom." "There's another gay girl gone dreary on us," lamented Elizabeth Wilson of *Screenland* magazine, "how sad Hollywood night life will be without Ann's hearty laugh."[8]

The doubters were proven wrong. Sheridan's lively personality managed to bring out Brent's light-hearted nature. He even started frequenting night clubs with his new love. Brent revealed there were several qualities which drew him to Sheridan: "[She] works hard and enjoys life; she's more fun to be with than any woman I have ever known; I think, on the whole, the quality of excitement which she possesses and generates is what makes her different from the standard glamour girls—that, and her earthy simplicity."[9] Sheridan found Brent intriguingly different from her usual night clubbing escorts. "He's a lot of people—rebel, hard-working artist, playboy, hermit, intellectual, athlete ... and what's most disconcerting, he manages to be a combination of these things all at once. George has an enormous awareness, a flair for being very much alive during every waking hour."[10] While they shared much in common, it was the classic case of opposites attracting.

Sheridan was assigned to appear opposite Gary Cooper in director Frank Capra's *Meet John Doe*; then Barbara Stanwyck, Capra's favorite actress, was cast instead. For Ann's next picture, Warners decided to take an old property out of mothballs, *Goodbye Again*.

The comedy first opened on Broadway on December 28, 1932, and ran for 216 performances. The first film version was released in 1933 with Warren William, Joan Blondell and Genevieve Tobin. The second version had to be considerably laundered to tone down the pre–Code touches. James Stewart (who, incidentally, appeared in a small role in the stage production) was the initial choice for the male lead. However, since Stewart was already busy with *No Time for Comedy* on the Warners lot, it was decided that a Sheridan-Brent teaming would ensure better box office returns.

The picture was shot in a month. By this time, cast and crew members noticed a change in Sheridan's demeanor on the set. It was usually her nature to be friendly and sociable with everyone. Brent, on the other hand, preferred to be left alone and kept to himself. It was apparent to those on the set that Brent was attempting to mold her vibrant personality to fit his secluded lifestyle.

The publicity department went all-out to highlight the Sheridan-Brent romance with the focus on the much-publicized 56.2 second screen kiss they shared. Prior to filming the scene, Sheridan told director Lloyd Bacon, "George may be a little self-conscious, but I'll just hold on if he tries to break."[11] It was breathlessly reported that Brent was visibly shaken after the take. Prior to the film's release, the censors demanded that the producers cut the titillating scene down to 30 seconds.

By the end of the shoot, the producers inexplicably shelved the feature. By this time, Sheridan and Brent had become an exclusive couple, although both denied the rumors of a forthcoming marriage. "I'll put up $10,000 cash, at odds of ten to one," asserted Brent, "that I don't step to the altar for three years. And that's no reflection against Ann. She's a swell girl."[12]

The marriage rumors continued to swirl for the rest of the year, causing Sheridan to joke to columnist Sheilah Graham, "I read that we will be husband and wife before 1941. We keep telling each other. It's getting mighty close now."[13]

By the fall of 1940, not only was Sheridan enjoying her relationship with Brent, but also her fame was approaching its peak. She ranked as the 18th most popular box office draw in 1940 and was one of the studio's top-drawing actresses behind Bette Davis. But her salary was hardly commensurate with her new box office standing. Warners was paying Bette Davis $4000 weekly and Olivia de Havilland $1250 weekly, while Sheridan earned a paltry $500; even her pal Ida Lupino was receiving $2000 per week. Based on the commercial successes of her 1940 features, the studio decreed that Sheridan would be given a raise which would bring her weekly salary up to $600 at her contract renewal on April 1, 1941. To Sheridan, this was no April Fool's Joke. "When I realized that my pictures were making big money at the box office," she explained to *Photoplay*, "it seemed no more than right to me that I should have a better salary, particularly in view of the fact that I had been promised raises several times, but hadn't gotten them."[14] Sheridan was disgruntled by the studio's lowball offer of $600 per week and insisted on $2000 weekly. The studio executives refused to consider her demands. Furthermore, she was fed up with the studio's insistence on capitalizing on her "Oomph Girl" fame. "It's so limiting to any actress who really yearns to do something," she complained to Louella Parsons.[15] Typical of the projects lined up was *Powers' Models*, a high-budget Technicolor musical showcasing beautiful models representing the John Robert Powers agency. This project was eventually made as an independent production with George Murphy and Carole Landis and released through United Artists.

As punishment, Warners assigned Sheridan to a supporting role as the sex object in *The Strawberry Blonde*. A remake of Paramount's *One Sunday Afternoon* (1933) starring Gary Cooper, the new version was announced as a starring vehicle for Brian Donlevy. Sheridan refused the role, stating, "I couldn't do otherwise and keep my self-respect."[16] Rita Hayworth was borrowed from Columbia to support James Cagney and Olivia de Havilland in the revised version. This film, along with 20th Century–Fox's *Blood and Sand*, set Hayworth on the path to Love Goddess stardom.

Watching from the sidelines, Brent was displeased with how Warners was handling Sheridan's career. He gallantly declared to *Photoplay*, "There is no doubt that, if she is given half a chance, she will become one of the foremost screen actresses. She has all the star qualities: beauty, vividness, intelligence, talent and above all, a realness that the cameras capture."[17] Having waged many battles of his own with Warners, Brent encouraged Sheridan to refuse all movie projects until her salary demands were met. Among the films she turned down: *The Bride Came C.O.D.* (replaced by Bette Davis), *Million Dollar Baby* (Priscilla Lane) and *Out of the Fog* (Ida Lupino).

The studio finally forced her hand by placing Sheridan on suspension. Not only would she forfeit her weekly paychecks, but she would also be banned from performing in other entertainment venues like radio. It was a common practice used by the studios to put a rebellious actor in their place. What Jack Warner did not count on was Sheridan's Texas-born fighting spirit.

ELEVEN

Return from Exile

Hollywood does a double shift and suddenly you see people exactly as they are. You see, oh, so clearly, the ones who've been friendly just because you've had a name.[1]

During the long period of Sheridan's suspension, the studio decided that they had milked the Sheridan-Brent publicity enough and that they shouldn't keep Sheridan out of the public eye for too long. So they finally released *Honeymoon for Three* in January 1941.

Sheridan is Anne Rogers, the efficient and well-groomed secretary to popular romance novelist Kenneth Bixby (Brent). Anne has her hands full arranging his promotional book tours and keeping her boss out of romantic entanglements with overly ardent fans. Although Ken has professed his love for Anne, he cannot help being swept up by the spontaneous moments of passion with his lady fans. One such diversion comes in the form of Julie Wilson (Osa Massen), a former college sweetheart. She is convinced that she is the inspiration for the character Miriam in his latest best-seller and is only too willing to trade in her older, suspicious husband (Charles Ruggles) for Ken. A series of trifling incidents are paraded out until the long, drawn-out conclusion in which Anne forgives Ken and the two end in a clinch.

The one bright spot in all this nonsense is Sheridan, who demonstrates real charm. Her chic appearance illustrates the studio's attempt to give the "Oomph Girl" a shiny veneer of sophistication. The critics were sour on the lame comedy, but it managed a decent return at the box office due to the Sheridan-Brent romance and the moviegoers' desire to escape from the grim reality of the war in Europe.

While *Honeymoon for Three* played in movie houses, Sheridan continued to live in exile as neither Warners executives nor Sheridan were willing to concede to the other. Sheridan later admitted that this period proved a lonely one; she was dismayed by the cold shoulder treatment she received from members of the film community. Too many of them were afraid to risk the wrath of the all-powerful studio executives. In the days when the studios were in control of the entertainment industry, an actor could not afford to get on the bad side of a studio head like Jack Warner or Louis B. Mayer. Too many careers have been ruined. John Gilbert and Kay Francis remain the saddest examples of dirty studio politics.

Fortunately for Sheridan, she had much in her favor. She was young, attractive and a rising box office draw with whom much more money could be made. She was also glamorous enough to give serious competition to the other glamour girls

(Veronica Lake of Paramount, Hedy Lamarr of MGM, Rita Hayworth of Columbia *et al.*). Warners would have been foolish to kick her to the curb before they finished profiting off of her.

During this time, Sheridan found solace with staunch friends James Cagney (still the studio's top-drawing star), Pat O'Brien (who had just left Warners for Columbia) and Ida Lupino (Warners' best threat against the feisty Bette Davis). Brent remained her main support and source of encouragement. While a *Photoplay* writer was under the impression that the two were no longer together, Sheridan set the record straight. "We just didn't go around to night clubs and such, where we were seen. Until this salary business was settled, I preferred not to be on parade."[2]

During her early years at Warners, Sheridan was only too willing to accept any roles that was tossed her way. Stuart Jerome asserted that while Sheridan "[lacked] the ruthless ambition of others, she seldom complained about her unimportant, thankless roles."[3] Now that she was recognized as a real actress by major critics and a box office draw, she was no longer willing to settle. As she recalled to John Kobal, "Of course, at Warners everybody seemed to have to fight. Cagney and Davis. That's the only way it was done. A knock-down, drag-out fight. You didn't always win, but it let them know you were alive."[4]

Sheridan ended her eight months' suspension when she learned of a film project based on Henry Bellamann's controversial bestseller *Kings Row*. Bogart told Sheridan that Warners had bought the screen rights to the novel (reportedly as a vehicle for Cagney, Bette Davis and Pat O'Brien). "I think you ought to have it," Bogart told Sheridan, "I think you'd be wonderful as Randy Monaghan. Read it, fight for it, do anything you can."[5] Desperate to play the role, Sheridan swallowed her pride and extended an olive branch to Warners. Years later, she recalled, "Reading the book, I knew that this was just the kind of girl I wanted to portray—a kid born on the wrong side of the tracks, but with a character and spirit which everybody must admire."[6]

Not surprisingly, Warners executives had not even considered casting her in the highly coveted part. Producer Hal B. Wallis originally wanted to send the script to Ginger Rogers, who had exemplified the poor, working class girl in the 1940 films *Primrose Path* and *Kitty Foyle*. As Sheridan told Kobal, "I would never have gotten the role of Randy Monaghan in *Kings Row* if I hadn't fought for it."[7] The executives finally relented, but only if she would make a musical comedy, *Navy Blues* (a project Sheridan previously turned down). She would then have the opportunity to play Randy. She agreed. The suspension was over and Sheridan's contract was renegotiated to set her weekly salary at $650. However, the studio offered her another pay raise if she was cooperative during the filming of *Navy Blues*; they also agreed to cast her in a maximum of four pictures per year.

In his column, Jimmie Fidler had harsh words for the actress:

"Most rising starlets become so greedy the moment they taste a little fame that they attempt to stick the boss for enormous pay increases—or else. On the other hand, the boss usually signs a beginner on such low terms that, should he become a star, the studio will have him safely bound for many years at a fraction of its true value. Somewhere between the two evils there must be a middle ground."[8]

Navy Blues was patterned after the peacetime draft comedies of the pre–Pearl Harbor days. It bears a strong resemblance to Universal's *In the Navy*, which starred the popular comedy team of Bud Abbott and Lou Costello. *Navy Blues* was budgeted at $1.2 million with Mark Hellinger initially chosen as associate producer and Sam Wood as director. Early on, the studio considered making the film in Technicolor.

The publicity department worked overtime to make *Navy Blues* a profitable venture. Servicemen were solicited to choose six beautiful women from a group of 150 to make up the "Navy Blues Sextet"; among those chosen were future stars Marguerite Chapman and Alexis Smith (who was reassigned to a more prestigious role as Errol Flynn's leading lady in *Dive Bomber*). *Navy Blues* posters were incorporated into scenes of two Warner films, *Affectionately Yours* (released in May) and *Manpower* (August) before its own release in September.

With a screenplay by four writers, direction by the ever-efficient Lloyd Bacon and a cast of seasoned comic performers including Jack Oakie, Jack Haley and Martha Raye, *Navy Blues* began production in mid–April. "It was a horrible film, but I had such fun making it," Sheridan recalled in 1966.[9] The source of fun, according to Stuart Jerome, was the continual drinking parties in Sheridan's dressing room with Oakie and Jackie Gleason (making his film debut). By this time, Sheridan's penchant for alcohol and her masculine sense of humor were well-known on the studio lot. Jerome revealed,

> Ann Sheridan's genuine warmth and earthy good humor endeared her to scores of visitors. On one occasion, welcoming a group of vacationing school teachers, she served her favorite libation, a glass of milk liberally spiked with Scotch. It was a warm day and the refreshing drinks were quickly downed. The messenger who took them around said the teachers did a lot of giggling and staggering as they left the lot.[10]

The movie's premise is simple, but its comic energy keeps things interesting. Cake O'Hare (Oakie) and Powerhouse Bolton (Haley) are sailors on leave in Honolulu. They are met by Powerhouse's ex-wife Lilibelle (Raye), who demands that he make good on her alimony payments. Easier said than done, as Powerhouse is always broke.

Cake and Powerhouse hatch a scheme that involves recruiting a sharpshooter, Homer Matthews (Herbert Anderson, a replacement for Eddie Albert), to transfer to their ship and win the gunnery contest. When they learn that Homer has no intention to re-enlist, Cake and Powerhouse convince Lilibelle's friend, night club singer Margie (Sheridan), to romance him into staying in the Navy. Of course, Homer falls head over heels in love with Margie and wants to return to his family farm with her as his wife. Cake and Powerhouse's schemes continue to go haywire until the chaotic conclusion when it is discovered that Margie does indeed love Homer.

Well-received by moviegoers, the musical comedy had a worldwide gross of $1.8 million. The critics focused mainly on Sheridan's physical charms. With patronizing reviews, it's no wonder Sheridan later lamented, "[F]or every good part I got, they would put me into two turkeys like *Honeymoon for Three* and *Navy Blues*."[11] Sheridan does look fetching in two numbers, "Navy Blues" and a hula routine. Inexplicably, her singing voice was dubbed. As the top-billed star, she has the least to do, but is lovely to look at and should be given credit for surviving the antics of Oakie, Haley and Raye with her "name value" intact.

By early fall, the Sheridan-Brent romance continued to baffle Hollywood insiders and gossip columnists. Some predicted nuptials, while others foresaw the relationship's demise. In a *Photoplay* article tantalizingly titled "George Tells Why, 'Ann Sheridan and I Won't Marry,'" Brent pointed out that the combination of two film careers and marriage rarely succeed. He offered as proof his three failed marriages and Sheridan's own marriage to Norris. "We're very happy as it is," he said. "We are perfectly congenial and we have fun together, so why risk clouding a grand friendship by assuming new responsibilities?"[12] Maude Cheatham told her readers, "This romance has steadied Ann: she's gained poise and assurance from George's strength and masculinity." Cheatham also noticed a difference in Brent as he was "more approachable, laughs easily and often, and the old hurts seem to have faded away."[13]

As the Sheridan-Brent romance was dissected in the gossip columns, Sheridan finally began preparations for her dream role: Randy Monaghan in *Kings Row*, the best role of her

"The Oomph Girl" meets "Hollywood's Mystery Man" (George Brent). **This most unlikely match resulted in marriage.**

career. It would also provide the clearest rebuttal to those who had downplayed her dramatic abilities.

The novel *Kings Row* was an uncompromising and controversial observation on small-town hypocrisy. Author Bellamann had drawn upon his own experiences as a German-American child whose family members were social outcasts in the small Missouri city of Fulton. After the novel was published in 1940, many Hollywood studios vied for the screen rights. 20th Century–Fox wanted the property for Henry Fonda, but Warners prevailed with a $35,000 bid. Producer David O. Selznick offered the studio $75,000 to sell him the screen rights, but the executives had already earmarked this project as one of their prestigious offerings for 1942.

From the beginning, the production was fraught with casting issues. For the showy role of Cassandra Tower, there were many contenders, among them Marsha Hunt, Joan Leslie, Laraine Day, Priscilla Lane and Gene Tierney. Warners' top feminine stars Ida Lupino and Olivia de Havilland were offered the part but turned it down. The Queen (Bette Davis) wanted the role, but Hal B. Wallis astutely knew that such casting would throw the film completely off-balance. Davis reportedly suggested Betty Field, who was eventually cast in the role.

John Garfield was considered for the role of Drake McHugh, before the studio's resident "B" film leading man, Ronald Reagan, got the part that proved to be the best of his film career. Philip Reed, Rex Downing and Tyrone Power were all considered for the role of Parris, before Wallis borrowed Robert Cummings from Universal. Other important roles were filled by veteran character actors Claude Rains, Judith Anderson, Charles Coburn and Maria Ouspenskaya.

Bellamann's novel presented seemingly insurmountable problems given the Production Code restrictions. In a memo to Wallis, Wolfgang Reinhardt declined the offer to produce the project; he wrote, "As far as plot is concerned, the material in *Kings Row* is for the most part either censorable or too gruesome and depressing to be used. The hero finding out that his girl has been carrying on incestuous relations with her father ... people dying from cancer, suicides—these are the principal elements of the story."[14] After several screenplay drafts were submitted to Joseph Breen, Warners finally got the green light. With director Sam Wood at the helm, *Kings Row* began production in mid–July 1941. Sheridan later told Hagen, "I loved it. I worked so hard, I worshipped the part."[15] Sheridan appreciated the high level of care that went into all of the technical aspects of the production. It was a filmmaking experience that she did not often experience, unless cast in a Cagney feature.

In 1946, Sheridan revealed in the *Life* magazine article "The Role I Liked Best":

> Before I played my favorite role—Randy Monaghan in *Kings Row*—I appeared mostly in musical and B pictures, and I was fed up with the monotony of dozens of the same kind of parts. Everything combined to make the *Kings Row* role so pleasant that it hardly seemed like work. Sam Wood's directing was a wonderful experience for me; few directors are so painstaking and at the same time so patient.... All of the cast got along very well with one another, and there never was a gayer, friendlier set between scenes. Then, too, most of my scenes were with Ronald Reagan and Bob Cummings, both of whom I had known for a long time—a condition which helped greatly to put me at ease. All in all, I couldn't have asked for a more favorable and gratifying opportunity that Randy brought me.[16]

Her joy did not last long. Early in the shoot, the executives decided that Sheridan, while still working on *Kings Row*, would be cast in a new production, *The Man Who Came to Dinner*, from the Moss Hart–George S. Kaufman play. While she was tempted to refuse the role, she knew such action could have a negative impact on her participation in *Kings Row*. So, once again, she swallowed her pride and did what she was told. Luckily, the new project proved almost as rewarding. "I was happy with my role in *The Man Who Came to Dinner*," she told John Kobal; the only problem was that she was not paid for her work in the second film. "They couldn't make you do that now," she said. "They'd have to pay you for two pictures. But at that time they'd often cast me in two pictures simultaneously, and I'd be running from one set to the other."[17]

Another bright spot was that she got to work with Bette Davis, her "favorite actress now and for a long time back ... because I admire her courage—there is a stronger word for it—in playing the most difficult roles, and in making them seem honest and reasonable. Only a great actress could do the things with her roles that Bette manages every time."[18] To another interviewer, Sheridan mused, "What I most want to do is to be a good actress. If I can be a quarter as good as Bette Davis, I'll be happy."[19] Davis reportedly admired Sheridan's screen work as well.

The Man Who Came to Dinner opened on Broadway in late 1939 and became a hit (739 performances). The main character, Sheridan Whiteside, was reportedly based on Alexander Woollcott, *The New Yorker*'s acid-tongued drama critic. The stage production made a star out of Monty Woolley, a one-time Yale professor and minor character actor in several MGM films.

Acting on Bette Davis' recommendations, Warners paid $250,000 for the screen rights to the play as a vehicle for their Queen. She desperately wanted to play opposite John Barrymore, an early contender for the Whiteside role. At her insistence, Barrymore was tested but his deteriorating health and inability to remember lines eliminated him from the running. A disappointed Davis later recalled, "I've always said I'd rather take Barrymore's adlibbing than make the film with anyone else."[20]

Despite Woolley's Broadway success, Warners was not keen on the idea of having him reprise his role for the screen. One of the key issues was Woolley's lack of box office standing. Several well-known stars, including Fredric March and Charles Laughton, made screen tests. Lesser-known actors Robert Benchley, Orson Welles and Laird Cregar (who appeared in the West Coast stage production) were likewise unsuccessful. At one point, Cary Grant was signed to play Whiteside (an unlikely casting choice, but a strong box office draw); Bette Davis objected loudly and he was diverted to *Arsenic and Old Lace*. It wasn't until Wallis had secured Davis and Sheridan (second-billed) to head the cast (providing the necessary box office pull) that Woolley was finally given the role. This, however, did not please Jack Warner, who believed that Woolley's homosexual mannerisms would be glaringly obvious on the screen.

Despite her misgivings over Woolley's casting, Davis welcomed the role of Maggie, Whiteside's long-suffering secretary, as a respite from her usual melodramatic roles. She was also thrilled that her "discovery," Richard Travis, was cast as the romantic male lead. Despite all of this, however, Davis was miserable on the set. She later revealed, "I felt the film was not directed in a very imaginative way. For me it was not a happy film to make—that it was a success, of course, did make me happy. I guess I never got over my disappointment in not working with the great John Barrymore."[21]

Ever on the lookout for newsworthy stories, the publicity department attempted to manufacture a feud between Davis and Sheridan. The feud never happened because Sheridan lacked the kind of ego needed for a clash of temperaments. "Annie just didn't rub her wrong," director William Keighley marveled; "in fact, flattered her by asking advice on the timing of her lines and like that. Davis ate it up; she loved playing God."[22] As Sheridan described the situation to Ray Hagen, "I think she was conditioned at the time to remain angry with Miriam Hopkins and think that anybody on the set was going to fight with her." Sheridan even made it a point to agree with everything Davis said. It worked like a charm and Davis quickly relaxed and enjoyed their association on this film. "[T]oday we're very friendly," she told Hagen. "She was just— temperamental? Who wasn't temperamental? ... All of us had the greatest admiration for her. She was the queen. One of my greatest, greatest favorites."[23]

Upon the completion of both features, Sheridan barely had enough time to close her makeup kit before assuming a role previously turned down by Ida Lupino. The new project *Juke Girl* was based on a Theodore Pratt story, "Jook Girl," which, in turn, was based on Pratt's *Saturday Evening Post* article "Land of the Jook." Her *Kings Row* co-star Reagan was her leading man. It is worth noting that, based on his performance in *Kings Row*, Reagan's weekly salary rose from $1000 to $3500; Sheridan's weekly salary, on the other hand, remained at $650 despite her ranking as the studio's third most popular actress.

The film crew was sent to Florida to shoot location scenes. Reagan recalled *Juke Girl* as a "back-breaker" of a picture, because the exterior night scenes were filmed from dusk to sunrise for 38 nights with temperatures at the freezing mark.[24] "Ann Sheridan was wonderful, a real trouper," director Curtis Bernhardt enthused. "She kept up the mood of the whole company—and that wasn't easy under such grueling shooting conditions."[25]

In late November, Sheridan suddenly broke off her secret engagement to Brent and returned the ring. She then went into seclusion at her Encino ranch, which afforded her needed respites and privacy, away from the hectic Hollywood hub of activity.

Then, the unimaginable happened. On December 7, 1941, the Pearl Harbor, Hawaii, naval base was attacked by Imperial Japan. After two years of neutrality while the war in Europe raged, the United States could no longer remain uninvolved. The country declared war on Japan on December 8. Three days later, the U.S. government declared war on Germany and Italy.

On Christmas Day, Sheridan visited Brent and gave him a model of his former yacht, *South Wind*, as a present. Touched by her gesture, Brent convinced her to take back the engagement ring. Swept up in the chaos and uncertainty of the looming global war, the long-time "friends" decided it was time to get married.

TWELVE

No Room for George

"We tried very hard, but as I see it now, we simply had too many odds against us."[1]

The surprise wedding took place on January 5, 1942. The couple took the train to Palm Springs, Florida, without attracting notice from the press. A New Year's Eve wedding was originally planned, but delayed due to rainy weather. The ceremony was conducted at the home of Brent's sister Kathleen, the widow of Broadway producer Sam H. Harris. George's nephew Patrick Watson served as best man and William Cain gave the bride away. Judge Richard Robbins presided; former actress Constance Talmadge was in attendance. Sheridan was dressed in a champagne-colored dinner gown. She also wore a white mantilla, a gift from Brent, and carried white orchids. Her wedding ring was a double diamond band linked by pear-shaped diamonds. As a prophetic sign, it rained prior to and during the wedding day.

Afterwards, Brent told reporters that they would honeymoon for several days on his private yacht before returning to Hollywood. Both were expected to report to the sets of new productions, Sheridan to *Wings for the Eagle*, Brent to *The Gay Sisters* (as Barbara Stanwyck's love interest).

The fan magazine writers were in a dither over the unexpected wedding. Fredda Dudley of *Modern Screen* asked, "Can these two high-voltage personalities blend?"[2] Going by early reports, everything was just lovely. Brent called her "Tex" and "Piyute," while she called him "Keoki" (Hawaiian for George). To complete the image of domestic tranquility, Ida Zeitlin of *Screenland* reported that Sheridan was busy "knitting in a corner of the sofa with the lamplight on her hair." "If I'd known it was going to be like this," the bride gushed, "I'd have done it long ago."[3] Hollywood insiders didn't buy this fabricated bit of malarkey and began waiting for things to unravel.

Sheridan and Dennis Morgan were scheduled to be teamed in *Across the Pacific* (1942). Producer Robert Lord wanted to replace Morgan with Bogart. The leading female role was eventually played by Mary Astor, who had appeared opposite Bogart in *The Maltese Falcon* (1941). Sheridan, Morgan and Jack Carson (a last-minute replacement for Ronald Reagan) were then cast in *Wings for the Eagle*. This highly propagandistic feature was shot in five weeks in response to the Pearl Harbor attack. The producers received special permission to film scenes at the Lockheed plant in Burbank, California, with additional footage filmed at the Curtiss-Wright Aircraft Company in Buffalo, New York. For security reasons, the film crew and actors were instructed to keep a birth certificate on them at all times. Sheridan told Hagen that she found the finished product "dreadful."[4] After the shoot, Sheridan, Morgan and

Carson went on war bond tours together. Sheridan also embarked on a tour of military camps in Kansas, Missouri and Wyoming. She proved very popular and it was no surprise that she was crowned "Queen Jeep" by the doughboys in Wyoming.

The Man Who Came to Dinner had its New York premiere on New Year's Day 1942 and was released nationwide on January 24. The comedy was a success with critics and moviegoers alike; it became the studio's sixth-highest grossing film of the year, earning $2 million at the box office.

Woolley, billed third, takes his place front and center as the irascible and overbearing radio personality Sheridan Whiteside, injured on the icy steps of the Stanleys' (Grant Mitchell and Billie Burke) Ohio residence. The self-absorbed and obnoxious Whiteside proceeds to turn the family's life upside down as he demands that every whim, no matter how small, be met to his exact specifications.

On the sidelines to

The Sheridan-Brent marriage lasted exactly one year. They were unable to live under the same roof.

smooth his ruffled feathers is his efficient secretary Maggie Cutler (Davis). When she falls in love with a local reporter, Bert Jefferson (Richard Travis), Whiteside fears that she will leave him and he schemes to break up the budding romance. Whiteside uses Bert's unpublished play to lure temperamental actress Lorraine Sheldon (Sheridan in the role inspired by Gertrude Lawrence) to Ohio. Catching sight of the handsome young man, Lorraine is only too willing to help Bert get his play produced with her headlining the cast.

Suspicious, Maggie warns Whiteside that he'd better not interfere with her happiness. She also implores a mutual friend, actor-turned-playwright Beverly Carlton (Reginald Gardiner), to lure Lorraine away by imitating her titled millionaire boyfriend Lord Bottomley on the telephone. Furious at being played, Lorraine vows vengeance by stealing Bert from Maggie.

Whiteside realizes that he has made a royal mess of things with the heartbroken Maggie, who plans to leave him immediately. He concocts a new scheme to get Lorraine out of the way for good. He enlists the aid of his friend, Hollywood comedian

Banjo (Jimmy Durante, who in a delightful ad-lib refers to Lorraine as "The Oomph Girl"). They trap Lorraine in an Egyptian sarcophagus and ship her off by air mail to Nova Scotia. Maggie reclaims her man and Whiteside, who had faked the seriousness of his injuries all along, falls down the steps on his way out.

Reviewers cheered the performances of the entire cast. Woolley was the undisputed critics' darling with his star-making turn and was nominated for a New York Film Critics Circle Award for Best Actor. After this success, he went on to appear in *The Pied Piper* (1942) and *Since You Went Away* (1944) and received Academy Award nominations for Best Actor and Best Supporting Actor, respectively.

There was also plenty of praise for Sheridan and other members of the large supporting cast. The *Pittsburgh Press* critic was among the many who opined that Sheridan brought to the role "all her celebrated oomph and surprising acting ability." After 80 years, *The Man Who Come to Dinner* remains a fresh and hilarious comedy. One of Moss Hart and George S. Kaufman's most popular plays, it was also adapted for television, including a 1954 *Best of Broadway* production with Woolley and Reginald Gardiner reprising their roles, Merle Oberon as Maggie, Joan Bennett as Lorraine and Buster Keaton as Dr. Bradley. In 1967, a musical version entitled *Sherry!* proved a disappointment with its 72-performance run on Broadway. The PBS television production of the Broadway revival in 2000 with Nathan Lane and Jean Smart is the latest film adaptation.

Sheridan was next suggested for *The Hard Way* when Ida Lupino became ill due to nervous exhaustion after one week of filming. Jack Warner refused to consider Sheridan with the astute observation that film audiences would not accept her as the manipulative, unsympathetic main character. The director shot around Lupino until she was sufficiently recovered and returned to the set. Lupino's mesmerizing portrayal earned her a New York Film Critics Circle Award for Best Actress. In 1957, Sheridan appeared in the *Lux Video Theatre* presentation "The Hard Way" in the Lupino role. A *Variety* TV critic noted that Sheridan displayed "some flashes of thespic adeptness." It's safe to assume that her performance did not erase memories of Lupino's *tour de force*.

After its New York premiere on February 2, the highly anticipated *Kings Row* was released on April 18, 1942, with the original running time of two hours and 36 minutes edited down to two hours and seven minutes. With the promotional tagline "The screen brings you a vivid, living drama from the pages of a powerful novel," it could not fail—and it didn't.

The dark drama follows the lives of five children in Kings Row into early adulthood at the turn of the twentieth century: Parris Mitchell (Cummings), who aspires to study psychiatry in Vienna; "Cassie" Tower (Field), the strange daughter of Dr. Tower (Claude Rains); wealthy orphan Drake McHugh (Reagan); Louise Gordon (Nancy Coleman), the daughter of sadistic Dr. Gordon (Charles Coburn), who performs needless operations without anesthesia; and Randy Monaghan (Sheridan), a girl from the "other side of the tracks."

During the first hour, the viewer is subjected to an awful lot of angst. While absorbing, the picture threatens to wear thin. Fortunately, Sheridan finally arrives on the scene and injects much-needed life and energy into the plot. That rascal Drake, hurt by Louise's refusal to disobey her parents, decides to court Randy to make Louise jealous. Randy is different from other girls in Kings Row and proves to be Drake's ideal mate.

Drake is shocked to learn that his life savings has been stolen by an unscrupulous bank officer. Broke and shunned by the upper class, Drake is taken in by Randy's family and gets a job with the railroad company. One night, he is hurt in an accident. Dr. Gordon, having long harbored hatred toward Drake, needlessly amputates his legs. After Drake and Randy marry, he becomes increasingly despondent and confined to his bed.

Desperate, Randy writes to Parris for help. He takes a leave of absence from his studies to return to Kings Row. It is hoped that Parris will remain in town to replace the recently deceased Dr. Gordon. Mrs. Gordon summons Parris to examine her daughter for possible mental issues. Parris is stunned when Louise reveals that her father amputated Drake's legs because he believed it was his moral obligation to punish wickedness. After this is confirmed by Randy's father, Randy implores Parris to keep this information from Drake. After wrestling with his conscience, Parris tells Drake the truth. To his surprise, Drake bursts out laughing. Drake finally comes to terms with his circumstances. A brighter future looms for Drake and Randy.

Kings Row was met with diverse critical reactions; the *New York Times* found it "gloomy and ponderous," while *Variety* called it as "impressive and occasionally inspiring." *Motion Picture Herald* marveled, "*Kings Row* comes to the screen as a star-studded, superbly mounted Warners production which has an emotional impact

Sheridan's performance as Randy Monaghan in 1942's *Kings Row* (with Ronald Reagan) has often been cited as one of her finest, and it remained one of her favorite roles.

few pictures have ever had." It emerged as the studio's third highest grossing movie that year. With box office returns of over $5 million, the feature ranks today as Sheridan's most financially successful film.

Performances from top to bottom received excellent reviews. Dependable actors Rains, Coburn and Anderson garnered their usual fine notices. It was the younger actors, however, who caught the critics off guard. The biggest surprise of all was Sheridan. *Motion Picture Herald* effusively noted, "Miss Sheridan may now be forgotten as the 'oomph girl' and be billed as a top flight actress because of her characterization of Randy." *Variety* was likewise impressed: "Miss Sheridan rises admirably to the emotional demands of the later scenes and gives one of her most effective performances thus far." *Photoplay* called her portrayal one of the month's best and the National Board of Review cited it as one of the best of the year. Sheridan's Randy Monaghan rightfully remains one of her best dramatic performances. *Kings Row* received Oscar nominations for Best Picture, Best Director and Best Cinematography, Black-and-White (James Wong Howe).

Encouraged by the success of both the novel and the film, Henry Bellamann began writing a sequel, but died of a heart attack in June 1945 with the novel uncompleted. His wife Katherine, a novelist and poet, finished the work; *Parris Mitchell of Kings Row* was published in 1948.

Warner Brothers planned a remake in 1955 for Montgomery Clift, Frank Sinatra, Eva Marie Saint and Ronald Reagan (reprising his original role), but it was not made. Instead, a new version surfaced on the small screen. *Kings Row* was one of three hour-long, rotating TV series shown on ABC's *Warner Brothers Presents* (1955-56); the others were *Casablanca* and *Cheyenne*. *Kings Row* starred Jack Kelly (Parris), Nan Leslie (Randy) and Robert Horton (Drake). Future stars Natalie Wood and Dennis Hopper appeared in small parts. With the episodes focusing primarily on Parris' psychiatric practice in his hometown, *Kings Row* was the least successful among the three shows and canceled after seven episodes.

After the box office success of *Kings Row* and *The Man Who Came to Dinner* along with positive critical plaudits, Warners raised Sheridan's weekly salary to $1000. At last, she was happy with the direction her career was taking. She believed that she had begun to shed the "Oomph Girl" label and looked forward to more acting challenges. The only fly in the ointment was her marriage to Brent.

Since their impromptu wedding, the couple had little time to settle into married life. Compounding the situation was that they both continued to live in separate residences. In 1941, Sheridan bought four acres and an Encino ranch house that she dearly loved. George was still living in the small Toluca Lake house that he rented from screenwriter Charles Kenyon. Plans to build a new home together were scrapped due to wartime restrictions on building materials. Sheridan tried to compromise by moving into Brent's bachelor pad, but found it too small for the two of them. Brent refused to move into her ranch, so they maintained their separate residences. This arrangement kept the gossip columnists' tongues wagging as it seemed that the time had finally come when opposites no longer attracted. A messy breakup was surely in the works. According to Lawrence J. Quirk, "George Brent was an erratic fellow, disdainful and sharp-tongued. He seemed to have a realistic approach to women and made them dance to his tune rather than the reverse." Brent once told producer Hal Wallis, "No woman will ever own me, I own myself!."[5] Sheridan was too free-spirited and independent to put up with his attitude for long. Despite the growing tensions, the couple still managed to ward off the inevitable by immersing themselves into their careers and wartime activities.

With the completion of Warners' *You Can't Escape Forever*, Brent decided to call it quits with the studio and become a freelance actor. He wanted to enlist in the armed services, but was denied because of his age and physical condition. As an accomplished pilot, however, he served as a Civilian Flight Instructor for the Civilian Pilot Training Program. He later became a pilot for the Coast Guard.

Doing her part for the war effort, Sheridan went on war bond tours and entertained troops in local camps. She became a popular pin-up girl along with Betty Grable, Rita Hayworth and Hedy Lamarr.

At the end of May, *Juke Girl* was released. If Sheridan thought that the studio finally had some respect for her acting talents, her hopes were dashed by promotional taglines like this one: "Shapely Ann Sheridan is starred with Ronald Reagan in the story of a dime-a-dance girl who discovers her veneer of hardness is not so solid as she had thought."[6]

The plot is concerned with the plight of low-wage Florida farm workers who struggle to combat the strong-arm tactics of unscrupulous packing plant owner Henry Madden (Gene Lockhart). Danny (Richard Whorf) decides to work for Madden, while his pal Steve (Reagan) takes the side of independent farmer Nick (George Tobias). Steve befriends a hard-bitten and cautious "Juke Girl" (read that as "tramp"), Lola (Sheridan), who even warbles the cynical "I Hates Love" to prove her point. Lola is sympathetic to the underdog Nick and shows her heart of gold. A romance blossoms.

With Steve's guidance, Nick becomes a prosperous farmer, much to Madden's annoyance. One night, Madden accidentally kills a drunken Nick. He tries to cover up his crime by placing the blame on Steve and Lola. Danny suspects that Madden is responsible. Madden's last-minute confession prevents a vigilante mob from lynching Steve and Lola. The couple make plans for a future running Nick's farming business.

Despite its downbeat social theme, *Juke Girl*, with its fast-paced action and fight scenes, proved a popular feature with wartime audiences, grossing $1 million. Critical opinions were mixed, but Sheridan garnered some positive notices.

With the continued financial success of Sheridan's features, Warners was anxious to capitalize on her popularity. Several movie projects were offered and promptly turned down by the frustrated actress: *The Man I Love* (which emerged as an Ida Lupino vehicle in 1947); *Gentleman Jim* (1942, with Alexis Smith opposite Errol Flynn); *Saratoga Trunk* (1945, with Ingrid Bergman opposite Gary Cooper), and *Casablanca* (initially proposed as a reteaming with Humphrey Bogart). One project that Sheridan desperately wanted was a biopic based on Texas Guinan's life, because she felt the role was tailor-made for her. The screenplay was owned by Paramount; Warners was willing to loan Sheridan out in exchange for Fred MacMurray's appearance in *Princess O'Rourke* opposite Olivia de Havilland. The deal fell through, most likely due to Warners' asking price for Sheridan's services. Betty Hutton, Paramount's "Blonde Bombshell," appeared as Guinan in *Incendiary Blonde* (1945), much to Sheridan's bitter disappointment. The seeds of deeply rooted resentment were sown, and she never forgot that the studio had cost her this opportunity.

By early summer, the Sheridan-Brent union was in serious trouble. Sheridan had grown tired of Brent's secluded lifestyle. In an interview with *Screenland* magazine, she disclosed, "George suffers from a shyness that is out of this world.... I used to think he was pretending when he said he didn't like people, but after I married him I discovered it was really a phobia."[7] Brent cancelled many social engagements at the last minute and the couple stayed home. Even while Brent was occupied in the Civilian Air Force full-time, he expected his restless wife to remain at home during the evenings. Fed up with this hermitic lifestyle, Sheridan began to frequent night clubs and attend social functions with old friends like Cesar Romero. By this time, Brent had become suspicious of other men—including her newest co-star, Jack Benny.

Sheridan (a replacement for Olivia de Havilland) and Benny were paired in a comedy called *George Washington Slept Here.* Brent was not the only jealous spouse. As Benny's wife, Mary Livingston, later wrote,

> Over the years, I still have to admit that, once in a while, immature jealousy reared its impetuous head. I'll never forget 1942 ... Jack was making a picture co-starring with Ann Sheridan, the 'Oomph Girl.' It was a film called *George Washington Slept Here.*... I could tell from things Jack said that he liked Ann. It upset me. Then George Brent called to say that he knew that Jack had sent Ann flowers. My husband was always sending people flowers, but this time I wasn't thinking about Jack's perpetual generosity. I got mad.[8]

Although she had no reason to suspect Jack, Livingston nonetheless did: "Being very good looking, he was completely charming and captivating.... Women were enchanted by him—and I'm talking about some of the greatest beauties of the world like Ann Sheridan, Barbara Stanwyck, Irene Dunne, Claudette Colbert, Marilyn Monroe."[9]

Livingston, who had never before visited Benny at the studio, paid a visit to the *George Washington* set to check out the situation. Benny warmly greeted his wife and introduced her to Sheridan. Livingston was polite, but cold, in the brief interaction. Several weeks later, Livingston invited Sheridan to a dinner party. During the evening, Livingston approached Sheridan privately. "Miss Sheridan, I don't know whether you like Jack, or if he likes you.... But you are making a picture together.... I wanted to remind you of something. Jack wouldn't give my little finger for your whole body! Now, have a good time."[10] With that, Livingston just walked away. Given Sheridan's sexual escapades which were only too well-known within the Hollywood community, Livingston's behavior was perhaps understandable. For many Hollywood wives, Sheridan was viewed as a threat to their domestic happiness.

The following day, Sheridan and Benny talked about her conversation. Benny confronted his wife that night. "Mary, that was an awful thing you said to Ann Sheridan." Livingston replied, "I know it was awful ... but I meant it." After staring at his wife for a few seconds, Benny broke into a smile. "Well, you were right, doll, you never have to worry about me."[11]

George Washington Slept Here was based on a hit Broadway comedy that ran for 173 performances during the 1940–41 season. Playwrights George S. Kaufman and Moss Hart based the plot on their own experiences after they each bought an old farmhouse in Bucks County, Pennsylvania. The Broadway production starred Ernest Truex, Jean Dixon, Dudley Digges and Percy Kilbride. After Benny saw the play, he insisted that Kilbride be hired to recreate his stage role. Once filming began, however, Benny and Sheridan found Kilbride's deadpan delivery so hilarious that they could not get through a scene without doubling over with laughter. These constant interruptions slowed the production down and caused the film to go over budget. Benny resolved this by not sleeping at night, so he would be too tired to laugh at Kilbride's antics.

The screenplay was revised to fit the popular Jack Benny radio persona. In the play, the husband is the idealistic dreamer and the wife handled the sarcastic lines. Screenwriter Everett Freeman switched the two characters and their lines. Sheridan felt the revamped part of the wife wasn't all that great, but she still enjoyed the opportunity to work with Benny. He also proved his gallantry when he protected Sheridan from serious injury by pushing her out of the way of a falling tree on the set.

Wings for the Eagle reached the screens in mid–July. With its opening dedication ("To our airplane factory workers, whose magnificent efforts will enable the United Nations to preserve a free way of life, this motion picture is respectfully dedicated"), the audience was primed for a patriotic, flag-waving propaganda film and they were not disappointed.

The timeworn love triangle (an unhappily married couple and the handsome friend of the family) is exploited in this outing. Sheridan is Roma, whose unemployed husband Brad (Carson) squandered their savings on a scam. A college friend, Corky (Morgan), moves in despite Roma's objections. The usual tiresome plot contrivances arise when Roma leaves Brad, and Corky immediately moves in on his friend's wife. It is all resolved in the end when the lazy husband redeems himself and the draft-dodging friend becomes a pilot who shoots down enemy planes.

Much more interesting is a secondary storyline which becomes the feature's emotional centerpiece: German immigrant Jake (George Tobias), a supervisor at Lockheed, is portrayed in a sympathetic fashion that was quite rare for a propaganda film of the early war years. Tobias' skillful acting highlights the film's most interesting character and he demonstrates once again what a fine performer he was.

Many critics, perhaps swept up by the theme of flag-waving sentiments, viewed the feature favorably. With a box office take of $1.1 million, *Wings for the Eagle* proved a profitable venture for Warners.

By mid–August, Sheridan was on location filming another wartime propaganda film, *Edge of Darkness,* opposite pal Errol Flynn. This situation did not sit well with Brent as rumors quickly circulated about a torrid affair between the two stars. Reportedly, Brent once discovered the two in bed and received a sound beating by Flynn for his untimely interruption.

Brent made one final attempt at a reconciliation. Sheridan recalled to *Screenland* that Brent hadn't spoken to her for a month. One Sunday, he drove down from Oxnard (where he was stationed) and arrived at Sheridan's Encino ranch in the late afternoon. The couple spent several hours talking things over. "George very frankly told me what was wrong with me," Sheridan groused, "and that took some time." His main complaint: She was more concerned about her career than their marriage. After Brent had finished, Sheridan accepted the futility of the situation and simply stated, "Well, George, it looks like this is it."[12] It was decided that Sheridan would contact Alex Evelove, the head of Warners' publicity department, early Monday morning and give him a statement for the newspapers.

The next morning, however, Sheridan was surprised to learn from Louella Parsons that Brent had wasted little time contacting newspaper reporters with his own exclusive. Brent painted himself in a sympathetic light by declaring to Parsons, "Ann wants her freedom. It is the last thing in the world I wanted. But I don't see what I can do about it. Ann wants her freedom and she is going to issue a statement explaining that our marriage is finished." In the same column, Parsons quoted Sheridan's response: "George said he wanted his freedom, and so I am going to give it to him."[13]

Brent's play for sympathy fooled no one; the Hollywood community was familiar with his "moroseness, his defeatism, and a gloomy fatalistic attitude toward life."[14] It was Sheridan the reporters flocked to for an honest scoop. "George and I didn't part the best of friends," she revealed to *Hollywood* magazine. "I see no reflection on George by my being honest about our separation, and I'm certain the public is tired of hearing the same old refrain every time two movie people decide it's best to end their marriage."[15] She acknowledged their likes and dislikes were too different for a compatible marriage. She even told *Screenland*, "I'm sure the fact that we had two homes had much to do with the failure of our marriage."[16]

With all the depressing war news, moviegoers were in the mood to laugh and *George Washington Slept Here*, released in late November, proved to be another moneymaker. During the course of its 93-minute running time, there are a series of comedy episodes which undoubtedly pleased Jack Benny fans.

When Bill Fuller (Benny) and his wife Connie (Sheridan) are faced with eviction from their New York City apartment, Connie impulsively buys a dilapidated Pennsylvania farmhouse without Bill's knowledge. Once they move in, the farmhouse falls apart. Adding spark to the standard comical situation is the local handyman, Mr. Kimber (Kilbride), hired to make the house livable.

After several months, the farmhouse is finally updated but the Fullers, broke due to the cost of renovation, can't pay the mortgage. They are saved from foreclosure when their dog (played by "Toto" from *The Wizard of Oz*) discovers a letter written by George Washington. The letter is valuable enough to cover the cost of the mortgage and all ends well—except for the swarm of locusts arriving on the scene.

The reviews were mostly positive and all members of the cast were praised. The comedy earned $1.3 million, which made it Sheridan's third most popular film for 1942. It was nominated for an Oscar for Best Art Direction for Max Parker, Mark-Lee Kirk and Casey Roberts. *Photoplay* called it one of the "Best Pictures of the Month." It provided the inspiration for *Mr. Blandings Builds His Dream House* (1948) and *The Money Pit* (1986), and was officially remade as a Greek TV movie, *Bam kai kato* (1996).

Next, Sheridan filmed a musical sequence, "Love Isn't Born (It's Made)" for Warners' all-star musical revue *Thank Your Lucky Stars* as a favor to producer Mark Hellinger.

In late December, Sheridan traveled to Mexico for a divorce decree. She was granted her freedom on January 5, 1943, by Civil Judge Acuna Pardo in Cuernavaca. She had been married to Brent for exactly one year. She still maintained a friendly relationship with her ex, Norris, but Sheridan never resumed her friendship with Brent and they rarely spoke well of each other in private. Sheridan often referred to their marriage as a mistake. Once, near the end of her life, she publicly admitted, "I can't stand my ex-husband."[17]

For his part, Brent chose to remain tight-lipped about his four former wives. When Don Stanke interviewed him in the 1970s for the book *The Debonairs*, Brent took the opportunity to reflect on Sheridan's passing: "What a waste of what could have been a good life."[18]

THIRTEEN

Waging Battles of Her Own

[Jack Warner] has his side to fight for and I have mine.[1]

Although the Sheridan-Brent union lay in ruins, Sheridan made it clear that she was not through with love: "[E]ven now I have no disillusionment about marriage, and I look forward to having eventually the kind of life that belongs naturally to a woman."[2] Hollywood insiders assumed she was referring to a possible marriage to her *Edge of Darkness* co-star Errol Flynn.

Edge of Darkness was based on the novel *The Edge of Darkness* by William Woods. In January 1942, prior to the novel's publication, Warners bought the film rights for $30,000. Lewis Milestone, who helmed the Oscar-winning anti-war classic *All Quiet on the Western Front,* was hired to direct. During the shoot, Milestone told the *New York Times*:

> It is 12 years now since I made *All Quiet on the Western Front.* That film embodied the retrospective disillusionment toward another war. In *Edge of Darkness* we are making a picture that has done away with disillusionment. We know the enemy we are fighting and we are facing the stern realities of the present war. The moral in *Edge of Darkness* is that "united we stand, divided we fall." That is the keystone for victory in all the democracies.[3]

Sheridan and Bogart were initially announced for the leading roles, but Bogart opted out and Flynn stepped in. The supporting cast included a number of noted stage actors: Walter Huston, Judith Anderson, Charles Dingle and Ruth Gordon. Warners contract players Nancy Coleman and Helmut Dantine assumed important roles. From the start, the production was plagued with problems, including a fog that had settled in the Monterey area where outdoor filming took place. This caused delays in the shoot for several weeks.

Flynn was insecure about his acting skills in a part that called for a realistic approach to playing his character. He was also self-conscious about the fact that, although he appeared the picture of health and vitality on the screen, he was unable to enlist in any branch of the armed service. Among his health issues (apart from excessive drinking) was a heart condition, malaria, tuberculosis and back problems. When he said he needed to recuperate from a sinus infection, Warners gave him two weeks. However, it was soon reported that Flynn instead traveled down to Mexico City with a friend for a hunting trip. Realizing that Flynn was in no hurry to return to the set, the studio tried to pressure him by announcing his pal Bruce Cabot as a replacement. Flynn eventually returned to the studio after signing a new four-films-per-year contract with the option of producing his own pictures.

But Flynn still doubted that he could play the role. Milestone later recalled,

"Flynn kept underrating himself. If you wanted to embarrass him, all you had to do was to tell him how great he was in a scene he'd just finished playing: he'd blush like a young girl and, muttering 'I'm not an actor,' would go away somewhere and sit down."

Much more challenging was the statutory rape charges leveled against Flynn midway through the production. The scandal and the trial received intense press coverage and public scrutiny. Although Flynn was acquitted of all charges in February 1943, this sordid affair took a toll on his mental well-being and likely aggravated his drinking problem.

Despite *Edge of Darkness*' grim story, Milestone later told an interviewer that it "had some interesting things in it. An extremely mixed cast gave some damned good performances."[4]

Sheridan had fond memories of this production as she enjoyed the professional interplay between the actors. She recalled to Hagen that working with Flynn "was always strictly fun. Never any trouble. I adored him."[5]

Sheridan went south of the border in December for her divorce. There she discovered a new love: Mexico City. "My secret dream is to build a home in a picturesque suburb of Mexico City," she revealed, "and fly to Hollywood whenever I have a motion picture commitment." She added:

I find everything about the country appeals to me. I love the temperament of the people, especially their leisurely way of living. Unlike Americans, they are never too busy to live! I love the warmth and courtesy one meets from everybody.... I love fragrances of semi-tropical flowers and fruits; the thrill of the bull fights; the laughter; the pomp and ceremony of the many festivals. All this means the ideal life to me.[6]

Once in Mexico City, Sheridan was seen with Flynn, who coincidentally happened to be in the city at the same time. The gossip columns began to overheat with rumors of an impending marriage. Cornered by reporters, Flynn dismissed the rumors. "Sure, I saw Ann," he declared. "We are pals. We have laughs together. We laughed about

Sheridan and Errol Flynn on the set of *Edge of Darkness* (1943). Despite their on-and-off romantic relationship, they remained great friends until his death.

everything. We'd probably laugh right in the middle of a kiss. That's why we couldn't get serious about each other."[7]

Sheridan had this to say: "Flynn is just not my kind of guy. I liked him, but I wasn't thinking about marrying him." She went on: "[The] only way a girl in the movies could keep out of such stories would be to live in a hermit's cave, without the hermit.... I can't go out any place with anyone, without having somebody say it is a romance."[8]

The Flynn-Sheridan rumors persisted until *Edge of Darkness* was released in April 1943. Louella Parsons wrote:

> Ann has emphatically denied that she is even remotely interested in the dashing Flynn and was so vehement in her desire not to have her name linked with the Warner actor that she refused to go to Mexico City on the same plane. But, maybe the lady protested too much. Until their friendship was so widely publicized, there is little doubt that Annie did like Errol.... The love scenes in [*Edge of Darkness*] indicate there was no turning of the cheek for the love-making is very ardent, to put it mildly. While Ann was in Mexico City, she made it a point to appear in public with Oscar Brooks, head of the Warner film exchange there. Those who saw them together felt they were too obvious in the attractions to each other to make it ring true. Apparently Ann was not averse to giving the impression that she had "fallen" for the Warner film man. I, nor any one writer nor columnists, can say that when the oomph girl is legally free she will wed Errol Flynn. I am not sure she would marry him no matter what her feelings are. Ann has come up the hard way in movies and she isn't likely to do anything to harm her career, and if she feels marrying Flynn would not be wise, you can wager she won't marry him. On the other hand, if she feels she can marry him without any criticism she may become Mrs. Flynn. She has bought a house in Mexico City and it was through this same Brooks that the deal was made. Errol shared her enthusiasm over the "south of the border" country and oh, well, anything can happen down there—or here.[9]

Next came rumors that Sheridan was linked to Brooks, the wealthy Mexican in charge of Warners' interests in Mexico. Apparently, it was Brooks who provided the heart-pounding reasons for her frequent trips to Mexico, not Flynn. This romance proved to be short-lived as, according to Harrison Carroll, the "[c]hief reason keeping him and Ann from the altar is that he can't leave his job, and her career ties her to Hollywood."[10]

Despite the merry-go-round of eligible men in and out of Sheridan's romantic life, her personal conduct did not bother the front office much as these stories were in perfect alignment with the "Oomph Girl" image. But there were also rumors of extramarital affairs, many of which the studio hid from the public eye with the help of complicit gossip columnists.

Louella Parsons reported that the "romantic 'dark horse' in Ann Sheridan's life is Tony Averill ... a Latin type, good looking and attractive" and "reported to be at Miss Sheridan's house all of his leisure moments."[11] Averill, an one-time Warner Brothers contract player who appeared in *Mystery House* and *Broadway Musketeers*, was a married man. Parsons, confronted by angry Warners executives, quickly engaged in damage control. She began her "mea culpa column" with "Tony Averill is happily married to Linda Cross and has been for two years," and continued:

> The misinformation printed that Tony was devoting himself to Ann Sheridan is regrettable, especially since he and his wife are Ann's closest friends. The friendship between Ann, Linda and Tony has extended over several years.... So apologies are offered to Ann, Tony and Linda.[12]

The studio could not afford to let salacious rumors affect the box office draw of one of their most popular stars.

Edge of Darkness premiered in New York City on April 9 and was released nationally a few weeks later; audiences flocked to watch their matinee idol Flynn in a rousing war drama. The tense tale begins with Nazis discovering that all the Nazi soldiers in a German-occupied Norwegian fishing village have been killed. Flashbacks reveal that the residents formed a resistance group to reclaim their town. This group is headed by fisherman Gunnar Brogge (Flynn) and his sweetheart Karen Stensgard (Sheridan). Karen's father (Huston), the village's highly respected doctor, is neutral, but becomes conflicted as the Nazis place more restrictions on the villagers.

A shipment of arms is secretly delivered to the villagers and they wait for the right moment. The arrival of Karen's brother Johann (John Beal), known Nazi sympathizer and traitor, threatens to disrupt their plans. After Dr. Stensgard kills a German soldier, the resistance leaders are sentenced to die by firing squad. On the morning of the executions, the townsfolk arrive fully armed and begin their assault. After a bloody battle, the townsfolk reclaim their village.

The film returns to the present day as Gunner, Karen, Dr. Stensgard and the surviving resistance members hide out in the hills, knowing that their work is not done. During the closing minutes, President Roosevelt's voice is heard on the soundtrack: "[I]f there is anyone who doubts of the democratic will to win, again I say, let him look to Norway."

Edge of Darkness was met with respectable reviews. Yet another Hollywood war drama set in Nazi-occupied Norway (*Commandos Strike at Dawn* and *The Moon Is Down* preceded it), the Warners feature rated more favorable reviews due to its high quality of craftsmanship. While the supporting players received accolades, both Flynn and Sheridan received mixed notices for their uncharacteristic portrayals. *Edge of Darkness* was banned in Buenos Aires in 1943 because of its anti–Nazi sentiments. In 2001, it was one of 400 movies nominated for the American Film Institute's Top 100 Most Heart-Pounding American Movies.

Sheridan was next assigned to a movie that was stymied at every turn on its way to the big screen. The tangled tale begins with Warners assigning Olivia de Havilland and Dennis Morgan to *One More Tomorrow*, a screen adaptation of Philip Barry's Broadway hit *The Animal Kingdom*. De Havilland refused the role and was placed on suspension for the fifth time in three years. Next, Sheridan got the *One More Tomorrow* assignment; the film was to be directed by Irving Rapper, co-director of the play. Others in the cast were Alexis Smith, Jack Carson and Dane Clark. After five weeks of shooting, Jack Warner discovered that his company had neglected to get the script approved by the Johnston Office. Without this approval, the film would not receive its seal of approval for release. Warner shut the production down until this situation was rectified. The screenplay was hastily rewritten to meet the strict specifications of the Johnston Office. One casualty of the revised screenplay was Clark, whose character was written out of the script.

With *One More Tomorrow* temporarily halted, the studio wasted little time in shuffling Sheridan, Morgan and Carson into *Shine On Harvest Moon*, a musical based on the life of Nora Bayes, a popular entertainer and songwriter in vaudeville and on Broadway in the early 1900s. Since Bayes was known for her deep singing voice and dynamic style in putting over a crowd-pleasing song, such as the World War I favorite

"Over There," the role seemed a perfect showcase for Sheridan. Four writers fashioned a script that skirted some aspects of Bayes' life. Sheridan later called the picture "the worst thing I've ever seen on the screen. It was supposed to be the life story of Nora Bayes, but after they cut out her five marriages there wasn't a story to tell."[13]

The screenwriters narrowed down the script's focus to Bayes' relationship and marriage to Jack Norworth (played by Morgan). After a few weeks of filming in color, the producer decided to make the feature in black-and-white as a cost-saving measure.

Thank Your Lucky Stars, released in late September, was Warners' entry to the all-star revue film genre that was popular as morale-boosting entertainment during the war years. Paramount had revived this genre with *Star Spangled Rhythm* in 1942; most of the other studios followed suit with MGM's *Thousands Cheer* proving a big financial success. The crowd-pleasing *Thank Your Lucky Stars* became Warners' third-highest grossing film for the year.

There really isn't much of a plot: Eddie Cantor plays a dual role as an egotistical version of himself and a look-alike who helps an unknown radio singer (Dennis Morgan) break into the movies. But this was enough to allow for a steady stream of the studio's biggest stars to perform in musical numbers and comedy sketches with varying degrees of success. The big surprises were Alexis Smith, proving herself an elegant and graceful dancer, and Bette Davis, relishing the opportunity to croak out the Oscar-nominated "They're Either Too Young or Too Old." Meanwhile, Errol Flynn, Olivia de Havilland and Ida Lupino really should have spared the audiences from their cringe-worthy and misguided efforts. Sheridan's appearance is one of the few highlights and many critics recognized it as such.

Filming finally resumed on *One More Tomorrow* with a new director, Peter Godfrey. After a few weeks, production wrapped and the picture was put on the shelf for two and a half years.

In an interview conducted by Alyce Canfield, Sheridan made it clear that she was not through with love. Taking a thinly veiled swipe at George Brent, Sheridan said that her ideal man was "not possessive or jealous or overly critical.... He does have a sense of humor, great adaptability. He's a little nuts, same like me, and he thinks life can be fun.... I'd go more than halfway toward making our marriage a success. Sure, I intend to be married again someday."[14]

Without knowing it, she was describing the man many close friends and associates considered to be her one true love: Steve Hannagan.

Stephen Jerome Hannagan was born in 1899 in the "Irish Ghetto" of Lafayette, Indiana. An ambitious young man, he began his career as a correspondent for United Press. His first public relations job was promoting the Indianapolis 500. Early financial successes led to the formation of his own agency, Steve Hannagan and Associates, located in New York City. From that point on, there was nothing Hannagan could not achieve without glittering success. "Hannagan's career typifies our typical American Dream," reminisced one reporter after Hannagan's death. "Here, anyone can make his mark and enjoy the laurels of his achievements."[15] Along with Hannagan's phenomenally successful advertising campaign to promote the newly developed Sun Valley, Idaho, another of Hannagan's most notable achievements was the widespread popularity of "cheesecake pictures" in national publication. At the peak of his career, Hannagan was nicknamed the Prince of Press Agents. He has been described as "a loud-shouting, belligerent, whip-smart press agent, who has never been known to pull a phony or a double cross."[16] In short, he was the ideal match for Sheridan.

Sheridan met Hannagan in October 1943 and, by Christmas, they were a steady item. According to Louella Parsons, "She loved him from the moment she laid eyes on him—affable, charming, blue-eyed Irishman—and he loved Ann. He recognized in her that forthright, sincere quality that is so much a part of her personality."[17]

Shine On Harvest Moon was released in April 1944. The standard musical comedy plot follows the up-and-down careers of singers Nora Bayes (Sheridan) and Jack Norworth (Morgan) as they engage in romance while pursuing their dreams of success in vaudeville. Their stint as a successful husband-and-wife team comes to an end when a spurned former lover of Nora's interferes with their efforts in getting theater bookings. In a self-sacrificing mood, Nora leaves Jack so he can pursue success on his own. Of course, Jack instead hits the skids. The two are reunited by the end and his song "Shine On Harvest Moon" propels them to long-deserved fame; with this number, the movie bursts into Technicolor for the finale.

With taglines promoting the musical as "The Biggest, Brightest, Happiest Hit of the Season!," *Shine On Harvest Moon* could not fail to draw wartime moviegoers and it made over $3.7 million. The critics, however, were none too thrilled with Warner Brother's lame attempt to cash in on 20th Century–Fox's successful Betty Grable Technicolor musicals. Sheridan received some positive comments here and there, with critics and fans unaware that her singing voice was dubbed by Lynn Martin.

The next project under consideration for Sheridan was director Howard Hawks' *To Have or Have Not*. Screen newcomer Lauren Bacall snared the role along with star Humphrey Bogart's heart (she soon became his fourth wife). A film role that did not come Sheridan's way was Fanny Skeffington in Warners' *Mr. Skeffington*. The director, Vincent Sherman, believed that the film "could have been greater with Ann Sheridan in the lead. That's who I wanted. The part of the most beautiful woman of her day would have suited Ann but Bette [Davis] heard of it and demanded it and she was box office at the time."[18] This was exactly the kind of challenging role that Sheridan was clamoring for, but did not get because everything was offered to the Queen first. Sheridan was not enthusiastic about her next assignment, *The Doughgirls*. Warners paid $250,000 for the screen rights to the 1942 Broadway hit, which ran 671 performances with Virginia Field, Natalie Schafer and Arlene Francis. James V. Kern and Sam Hellman were commissioned to adapt the play by toning down or, in some cases, eliminating the plot's more risqué elements. The original source material, with its emphasis on extramarital sex, would not have passed the Breen Office. When Sheridan saw the play in New York, she felt it would be an impossible task to transfer the stage material to the screen. As she told Hagen, "I hated it ... there wasn't one single part that I could play with any honesty."[19] The executives, however, were dead set on Sheridan's appearance in this film as they needed her "name value" to help sell this comedy to the public. Sheridan put up a fuss, but eventually conceded as a favor to her friend Mark Hellinger.

Despite her dissatisfaction with the project, Sheridan remained professional on the set—and the cast and crew loved her for it. According to Humphrey Bogart, it was that "good, old, down-home touch which she has never lost that makes her universally liked."[20] Vincent Sherman agreed: "She was bright, lively, opinionated, sheer joy, had terrible trouble with the men in her life.... She had this wicked humor the screen couldn't capture…. Jack [Warner] said she was the studio vixen and that was that."[21] No one was surprised when Sheridan received the Golden Apple award from the Hollywood Women's Press Club for the most cooperative female star in 1943 and 1944. Sheridan quipped, "You can call me 'Apple Annie' now."[22]

At this time, Sheridan expressed her admiration for the First Lady, Eleanor Roosevelt: "I envy her ability to meet all kinds of people, every possible kind of person—in a warm and friendly manner. In pictures, we meet people constantly—on the set, on tour, everywhere. There never seems to be time to make friends, to find out about people—and I like people!"[23] Some of her closest friends included Jane Wyman, Ronald Reagan, Dennis Morgan, Ann Sothern, Lucille Ball, Desi Arnaz, Hedy Lamarr, director James V. Kern and Jack Carson.

What made the *Doughgirls* shoot fun for Sheridan was working with Alexis Smith and Jack Carson. She was also thrilled to act with Jane Wyman, one of her best friends since the early days on the Burbank lot. Even though Sheridan was enjoying a red-hot film career while Wyman was stymied by Warners' refusal to see her as a serious dramatic actress, Wyman had no hard feelings. It has been rumored that Sheridan was one of several women who had a sexual relationship with Reagan during his bachelor days, but Wyman (then Mrs. Reagan) did not seem to be bothered by this in the least.

When Wyman was assigned the scatterbrain character in *The Doughgirls*, she was willing to go on suspension rather than play the part. Sheridan told Lawrence J. Quirk,

> She was a real pro. I know she hated the parts they often handed her before her break-through [*Johnny Belinda*, 1948], but she was always game to make the most of them, and actually, given the dialogue and situations they inflicted on her in that earlier period, became a wiz at making something out of nothing.[24]

Sheridan often visited the Reagans' home. "I'd go there because Jane was such a good cook. On one occasion, Ronnie, a baseball nut, had heard a game on radio and he gave us a play-by-play account. After the fourth inning, Jane said, 'Ronnie, please stop, Annie doesn't care about baseball.' But he went on for all nine innings."[25] Wyman delighted in telling friends that Reagan was such a talker, he even made speeches in his sleep. Perhaps this was all in preparation to cement his reputation as an eloquent speaker as the fortieth president of the United States.

Upon the completion of *The Doughgirls*, Sheridan turned down *The Conspirators*. Hedy Lamarr was borrowed from MGM to play opposite Paul Henreid. Sheridan also refused *Hollywood Canteen* and was promptly placed on suspension. She begged to be taken off suspension so she could go on an overseas tour sponsored by the USO and Hollywood Victory Committee. After much haggling with the executives, she received permission. The publicity from this patriotic duty would do much good.

Sheridan was scheduled for a three-month tour of the China-Burma-India (CBI) region during the summer of 1944. Prior to embarking on the tour, Bob Hope advised Sheridan to keep the servicemen a priority as the troupe would be undoubtedly courted by the officers and their wives. Sheridan heeded his advice. Other members of the CBI troupe included comedian Ben Blue, Mary Linda, Ruth Denas and Jackie Miles. Sheridan's act consisted of singing a couple of songs and playing the straight girl in one of Blue's comedy skits; Miles served as the emcee; Linda danced several numbers, and Denas played the accordion. In June, the company arrived in New York

City to rehearse their routines prior to going overseas. The CBI tour officially began its 35,000-mile trip on July 19.

Conditions were difficult. There was the strain of traveling through uneven terrain, and sleeping in makeshift beds (usually bucket seats or the floors of planes). Sheridan took it all in stride. As one pilot's daughter recounted, "Dad ferried her between performances ... 'She was one tough broad!' he used to say, largely because she was tough enough to pee in a funnel at 20,000 feet without the courtesy curtain they offered her. 'Don't worry about it, boys.' It made an impression on Dad!"[26]

The weather certainly did not help matters. "At one place in China," the actress later told a newspaper reporter, "it was pouring rain when the show was given, on a roofless log stage. GIs appeared with a huge tarpaulin and held it over the heads of the performers for an hour and a half, the length of the show, and wouldn't change places with any of the others, either." In India, the troupe was caught in a four-day monsoon. Even with the rain, the jungles were unbearably hot. Sheridan recalled that she never knew she "could sweat so much in as much rain." As far as the food was concerned, she described the canned corned beef and wieners as tasteless; worst of all was the rice bread, which was black, hard and heavy. "You could break a window with a roll," she claimed.[27] Water had to be boiled and drank steaming.

One of the unexpected highlights of the tour came from the men of the 491st Bombardment Squadron, 341st Bombardment Group. Technical Sergeant Francis E. Strotman was assigned to paint Sheridan's likeness on a B-25 aircraft. Given the lack of painting supplies, Strotman used house paint and a frayed rope on a stick for a brush. "I had no photo of Ann Sheridan," he recalled, "but

During the CBI tour in the summer of 1944 Sheridan made one memorable stop, where she saw the B-25 aircraft that bore her likeness. Also pictured are fellow performers Mary Linda (left) and Ruth Denas (right).

I knew she was a sexy redhead and my paint job emphasized that hair.... As the jeep passed by ... there she was, in all her glory—an unkempt dishwater blonde."[28]

Warner Brothers executives were unhappy that Sheridan remained on tour longer than the period to which they had agreed. The studio sent her wires and cables ordering her to return immediately.

Sheridan arrived in New York in early September and spoke about her experiences with reporters. She told Louis Reid of *Silver Screen*, "I would have regretted it all my days if I couldn't have had a part in bringing a bit of happiness and cheer to our fighting men. Every actor and actress should visit the war theaters.... If the boys can take it for months on end, we can do so for a few short weeks."[29] While proud to have done her patriotic duty, she was nonetheless honest: "I never want to go back to the CBI Theater. Spare me that, please."[30]

A few years later, Sheridan again talked about her wartime efforts: "It's nothing to shout about. A lot of Hollywood people did much more than I.... But one thing I know—a lot has happened that I'll never forget."[31]

Sheridan's initial comments about the tough conditions overseas sparked an unexpected firestorm from the U.S. Army. The *CBI Roundup* newspaper called out Hollywood stars Joel McCrea, Joe E. Brown, Al Jolson and Sheridan for failing to complete scheduled entertainment tours in the CBI region. Officer Darrell Berrigan, editor of the *CBI Roundup*, minced no words in his vitriolic attack.

> We are of a mind to win this war and it does not seem to us that that cause will be served by a public brawl between an Army newspaper and some moving picture performers. We—which means the armed forces of the CBI—have admiration, respect, and love for people who cross oceans and incur personal danger and discomfort to give us a few hours' respite from what is at best a tedious and unpleasant task. For quitters and phonies, in or out of the Army, we have another name.

Berrigan refuted Sheridan's comments that she endured harsh conditions. "Miss Sheridan and her company had the very best food available everywhere they went. If and when they ate K or C rations, which was seldom, it was because everyone else was eating it. As to latrines: Everywhere Sheridan played, a latrine was cleared in advance and reserved for the use of girl troupers and guarded." To emphasize the point that the army shouldn't expect women to "stand up under strenuous conditions," Berrigan offered, "Army nurses seem to manage all right."[32]

These were fightin' words and Sheridan was not inclined to let them pass:

> Being from Texas, I know what roundup means, and I also know they give the steer as much chance as the rider. So having read your recent gripe on Hollywood entertainers, I thought you'd like to give this little doggie her chance at your readers. In the first place, I don't blame any G.I. or even an officer, if you want to treat them as equals, for bellyaching about a show he's been promised and which he doesn't get to see. But who promises them the shows? Certainly not us. We sign on and some guy in uniform does the rest, and brother, that rest is no bed of roses.... I have no defense to make about anybody who is displeased with me as an actress. I'll join and get my mother to help if necessary in any criticism, but I'll fight boy fashion, no holds barred, with anybody who thinks I or any of the gang I accompanied dogged it in the overseas theater. We traveled 60,000 miles in a few days less than 60 and we tried to play two shows a day each and every day.... The United Press quoted me accurately when it said: "Sheridan is anxious to return again to overseas entertaining, but does not wish to return to the CBI—it's too tough." I say that again.... I'd like to hear your comments from the GIs in the places we played. We spent most of our

time with them, even over the protest of special service officers, whose noses went out of joint because we didn't play the officers' clubs in the rice paddy league ... [T]he trip was worth the effort from my standpoint—even if you didn't like it—because of the joy we were able to bring to specific, previously unknown to us, mothers, wives, sisters and sweethearts in direct messages from their G.I.s in the CBI. At worst, there are two sides to the problem and I had to get my side off my heaving chest. Show folks are supposed to be inarticulate in their defense, but remember, I studied to be an old school teacher.[33]

The lengthy letter was signed "G.I. Annie."

The initial responses from the G.I.s were against the Hollywood celebrities. According to Sergeant Robert Finkle, an ex-screenwriter and assistant director, it was not the actress' fault:

I see the affair [with] Ann Sheridan has caused quite a sensation in theatrical circles. The general opinion over here is that the stars are completely at fault. After careful thought, I am of a different opinion. These old-timers here are beat from the word go, they're hyper-critical and will take it out on anybody. And it is rough and rugged in the CBI. It is the ruggedest spot in the world, so how can we expect a woman to fly direct from the softness of the Hollywood life and drop here into a mosquito-infested, wet, miserable dirty hole and stick it out for more than a few days. And they do show after show, fly in all kinds of conditions, etc. Hell, we trained 18 months to do the same thing expected of them overnight. No, the actors, in my opinion, are not at fault.[34]

While the Sheridan-CBI feud played out in the papers for several months, *The Doughgirls* was released during the Thanksgiving holiday. The plot involved newlyweds Arthur and Vivian (Carson and Wyman), who have reservations for a honeymoon suite in a luxurious Washington, D.C., hotel. But, with the overcrowded wartime conditions, they are not the only people in need of accommodations. Compounding the stressful situation is that Vivian is unable to get rid of her old friends Edna (Sheridan) and Nan (Smith).

The comic situations pile on top of one another at lightning speed as it is revealed that two of the couples may not be legally married and the third couple has lost their marriage

During World War II, Sheridan contributed to the war effort as an entertainer and a pin-up girl.

license. It all comes to a head where everything is worked out for all the couples. Smith and on-screen husband Craig Stevens married after completing the film's shoot.

The wartime comedy with its timely theme fared well at the box office despite the mixed critical notices. For the most part, Sheridan was complemented for her chic appearance rather than her wry comic portrayal.

At this point, Sheridan was disheartened by Warners' habit of assigning her films that continued to capitalize on her drawing power rather than building her as a serious dramatic actress. One of the several projects Warners tossed her way was a light musical comedy trifle called *The Time, the Place and the Girl*, which would have reunited her with Dennis Morgan and Jack Carson. The feature was released in 1946 with Janis Paige in Ann's place.

One project that Sheridan regretted turning down was *Mildred Pierce*, the film that handed Joan Crawford the Oscar for her career-rejuvenating performance. Its critical and box office success established Crawford as Warners' most likely successor to the "Queen of the Burbank Lot" title. Bette Davis' long reign was nearing its end as evident by the dwindling box office returns of her most recent films. The realization that Crawford would likely edge her out must have irked Sheridan, who was hoping to get better film assignments. In retrospect, Sheridan would not have had the success that Crawford had with *Mildred Pierce* as the movie greatly benefited from Crawford's surreal, ultra-glamorous persona—the qualities Sheridan lacked given her no-nonsense, natural approach to film acting.

After Sheridan refused *When Old New York Was Young*, Warners threatened to place her on suspension yet again. On the advice of Hannagan, she went on strike, refusing all projects until her new demands were met: better scripts, a pay raise, and two or three pictures a year. Her contract was up for renewal and she wanted the upper hand for a change. Many Hollywood insiders predicted a quick resolution as she was still one of the studio's top-drawing female stars.

This time, her self-imposed exile lasted 18 months.

FOURTEEN

On Her Own Terms

I'm too old to be an "Oomph" girl anymore. I just want to be an actress.[1]

In January 1945, Louella Parsons informed her readers that Sheridan's strike was nearing its end. "I knew the little spat wouldn't last long," she declared.[2] According to Parsons, Sheridan would have the lead opposite Claude Rains in *The Man Who Died Twice.* Unfortunately, Parsons was either misinformed or purposely led astray as Sheridan had no intention of going back to the Burbank lot any time soon. While in exile, Sheridan spent much of her time in her new Mexico City home. The bucolic life was the perfect respite from the grim realities of the war.

After Sheridan and Hannagan bought a New York City apartment, rumors again circulated about their impending marriage and her retirement from acting. Columnist Walter Winchell wrote that not only was Sheridan through with motion pictures, but all she wanted to do was to marry Hannagan, who had unofficially assumed the role of her manager.

Acting on Hannagan's advice, Sheridan was close-mouthed with reporters. This did not sit well with some news-hungry newshawks, as evident in sexist comments like this one: "I still can't get over Ann Sheridan making $340,000 in 1944. That is some figure. But come to think of it, Ann is some figure any way you look at it."[3]

With World War II officially over in early September 1945, moviegoers were interested in resuming their pre-war lives. Warner Brothers was particularly interested in bringing Sheridan back to the studio, as her fans were clamoring to see their beloved Annie on the screen. The studio persisted, but Sheridan held firm.

In November it was reported that a new contract was in the works, and by December, Sheridan had finally signed a new contract: a three-year deal with two pictures per year, a pay raise and script approval.

The first project awaiting Sheridan's approval was *The Man Who Died Twice* (this time without Claude Rains). Director Vincent Sherman had bought the story (reportedly based on an actual insurance case) by Paul Webster with the intention of producing it independently. Warners bought the story from him, assigned him as director and requested that the story be revised into a vehicle for Sheridan. But she was not interested. Instead, she tried convincing executives that she should play the title role in *Anna Lucasta.* That movie was later made by Paramount with Paulette Goddard.

Sherman was dispatched to New York City to persuade Sheridan that *The Man Who Died Twice* was the vehicle in which to return to the screen. His no-nonsense approach and sincerity put both Sheridan and Hannagan at ease, so she agreed to the project.

Sheridan is pictured here with comedian Ben Blue (right) and long-time lover Steve Hannagan. Many believed that she was the true love of his life.

From that first meeting, Sheridan's friendship with Sherman was one of the most rewarding professional relationships either one of them enjoyed in Hollywood. Sheridan found him to be a good director, wonderful to work with. As for Sherman, he had nothing but praise:

> She became one of the most skillful comediennes in Hollywood.... She knew how to toss away a line, underplay it with a wry quality, and get a full measure of the laugh therein. She could also play a dramatic role with the best of them. But because she came up from the ranks, her skill was underrated. And what a joy to work with. She was genuine, no affectations and no bullshit; she loved to laugh and have fun and could, when provoked, curse like a sailor on a stormy night.... [T]o me she was so honest, so lacking in feminine guile, so down to earth, that I came to think of her not as a sexy female but as a good friend or as a sister.

In describing her off-screen allure, Sherman said, "Many men made passes at her and tried to seduce her, her bedroom eyes causing all kinds of fantasies."[4] Unlike many other Hollywood wives who were threatened by Sheridan's working relationship with their husbands, Sherman's wife Hedda found Sheridan a warm and natural person without an actor's ego.

Once Sheridan was back at Warners, reporters swooped in. Columnist Bob Thomas reported, "Ann confided that she was happy to get back to work and all that.... I asked if she obtained her contractual demands. 'Certainly,' she said. 'Otherwise I would not have come back.' She declined to discuss the new terms, however."[5] She told her old friend, Sheilah Graham: "In [my next film], I play a night club singer, but it's not a musical. It's a comedy drama and I have a wonderful leading man—Kent Smith. He's like a taller Laurence Olivier with a voice like an American Ronald Colman.... He'll be a sensation."[6]

Director Sherman spent much time during the three months' shoot of *Nora Prentiss* (the movie's eventual title) revising the script to meet the executives' demands of spotlighting Sheridan's character at the expense of Smith's. Sherman recalled that he worked hard to make Nora (Sheridan) and the doctor (Smith) "real people, not merely stock characters for the melodrama." During the shoot, Sheridan had an ear infection, so the final scenes had to be photographed from one side with Sheridan wearing an oversized (and unfashionable, one may add) hood.

According to Sherman, "the first two-thirds of the picture became a moving human drama, while the last third seemed, by comparison, phony." Nonetheless, he was pleased with the performances, which he found to be excellent. As for Sheridan, Sherman noted, "She had played this kind of role before, so it was no stretch for her, but she brought it to life."[7]

In early March 1946, *Cinderella Jones*, starring Joan Leslie and Robert Alda, was released. In this film, Sheridan made an uncredited appearance as a Red Cross nurse.

After the completion of *Nora Prentiss*, Warners executives were anxious to get Sheridan into another film project before she had a chance to escape to New York City or Mexico City. The chosen project was a screen adaptation of James M. Cain's controversial 1937 novel *Serenade.* The studio had bought the screen rights in February 1944 and attempted to film it with Dennis Morgan and Sheridan. Familiar with the sordid plot of the novel, Vincent Sherman knew that it would not make it past the censors. The plot focused on a male singer made famous by his manager, an older homosexual man. After being sexually intimate, the singer loses the masculine tone in his voice and runs off to Mexico. There, he has a sexual encounter with a hooker who "restores his manhood."

Producer Jerry Wald was enthusiastic about *Serenade*, but Jack Warner shot it down after he realized that it was too scandalous. The project eventually reached the screen in 1956 in a much-revised and watered-down form with Mario Lanza and Joan Fontaine (as a wealthy socialite in place of a homosexual manager).

After collecting dust on the shelf for two and a half years, *One More Tomorrow* was released in June 1946. The plot concerned the romantic adventures of wealthy Tom Collier (Dennis Morgan), who is bored by the sedate life of the rich. After he meets commercial photographer Christie (Sheridan), he purchases a failing liberal activist magazine so he can spend more time with her. Christie, however, turns down his marriage proposal and leaves for Mexico to further her photography career.

On the rebound, Tom marries glamorous Cecelia (Alexis Smith), who turns out to be an ambitious gold-digger desirous of the things Tom's wealth can provide. Christie returns from Mexico, realizing that she has made a mistake, and tries to reconcile with Tom. Despite her best efforts, Cecelia eventually loses Tom to Christie.

If Warner Brothers was worried about the box office viability of this feature, they need not have been. The postwar audience flocked to theaters to see the all-star cast, and *One More Tomorrow* earned $3 million. The cast, playing within familiar lines, earned mixed reviews.

As Sheridan was enjoying a career resurgence, Hollywood insiders wondered about her relationship with Hannagan (whom she nicknamed "O'Toole"). Many gossip columnists noted that, although the couple spent a lot of time between Hollywood and New York City, there were no plans for marriage. When Sheridan was asked by Louella Parsons if she was already married to Hannagan, she joked, "No, I'm not. I've never been able to corner him." Then she became serious: "I love him and he loves me, and we've had three very happy years, but we have no plans to marry." Parsons referred to the Sheridan-Hannagan relationship as an "adult romance," whereas her two previous marriages were "juvenile."[8]

The highly anticipated *Nora Prentiss* reached the screens in February 1947, with tantalizing taglines such as "A mouth like hers is just for kissing, not for telling.... If you were Nora Prentiss would you keep your mouth shut?"[9] It was this kind of lurid advertisement that drew in the paying customers. *Nora Prentiss* raked in $2.4 million, making it the studio's seventh highest grossing film for the year.

The film begins promisingly in the classic film noir style. A prisoner, believed to have killed the well-respected Dr. Talbot, is under intense police questioning. As the man reflects on what has led to this moment, the movie goes into flashbacks.

Stuffy, middle-aged Dr. Talbot (Smith) has a wife who values her social obligations more than him. Even his children have little time for him. The unhappy doctor meets and falls in love with night club singer Nora Prentiss (Sheridan). The hard-boiled Nora tries to keep him at arm's length, but she ends up falling for him. However, she has no desire to break up his marriage and leaves for New York City.

Through a rather improbable plot contrivance, Talbot is assumed dead in a car accident. He joins Nora and they continue their affair. The plot then spins wildly out of control and ends in melodramatic foam and overheated froth. It is a rather disappointing end to a drama that held a great deal of promise and intrigue.

In the movie, Nora sings two songs, "Would You Like a Souvenir" and "Who Cares What People Say." Sheridan's sexy performance earned her some of the best reviews in a long time despite the fact that a few critics were less than charmed. "Ann Sheridan won't be winning any Academy Award as Nora that's for sure," declared the *Cedar Rapids Gazette*, "but she is still the best part of the picture."

Sheridan's next movie afforded a meaty dramatic role previously played by the likes of Jeanne Eagels and Bette Davis: a murderess who kills her lover in an updated version of Somerset Maugham's *The Letter.* Sherman was commissioned once again by the studio to revamp the screenplay and serve as director. With the start date delayed due to a strike, Sherman had only two weeks to put this feature in production. Even though the script was not yet complete, he managed to convince the cast to trust in his instincts as a director. The actors were only told that the general plot followed *The Letter* with a change in location (from Malaya to Los Angeles) with a topical commentary on wartime divorce. The actors were handed their lines at the beginning of each day's shoot. Although Sheridan played an adulteress who goes unpunished (not in accordance with the strict Production Code), the final script was approved due to the message that divorce is highly objectionable in post–World War II America.

Both Sheridan and Sherman enjoyed associating on their second film together. Sherman later reflected:

It is not easy to know what people are like inside since most of us tend to hide our true feelings, but I've always felt that Ann was not driven to become a big movie star. It slipped up on her, and she went along with it. She was no intellectual but she had good sense and a keen instinct about people and events.... I always felt that she would have preferred being a housewife with a loving husband and children. She was a grand girl, talented, and a joy to know and work with.[10]

On the set of *The Unfaithful*, Sheridan told Louella Parsons, "[F]or the first time in my life, I've liked my last two pictures." Regarding her lesser Warners pictures of the past, Sheridan said, "[I]n the beginning, it was all right for me to do stories of that kind, but I feel I must have benefitted by my experience or I wouldn't still be on the screen after all these years—so now I want to act."[11]

The Unfaithful tells the harrowing story of a young wife, Chris Hunter (Sheridan), who claims to have killed an unknown intruder in self-defense. With the support of her husband Bob (Zachary Scott) and counsel of their lawyer friend Larry (Lew Ayres), she tells her story to the police and is believed. While the gossips' tongues wag, Bob and Chris attempt to return to their normal lives.

However, facts soon emerge suggesting a more sordid story than the one Chris told. She eventually confesses to Larry that she once had an affair with the dead man and implores Larry to help her. When Bob learns the truth, he is devastated. The dead man's wife goes to the police and Chris is arrested for murder. With the ensuing scandal and trial, Bob finds it difficult to forgive Chris. After she is acquitted, Larry encourages the couple to reconsider getting a divorce and reconcile. The movie ends on a hopeful note as the couple takes the first step toward healing.

Upon its release in July, *The Unfaithful* proved popular among female moviegoers and raked in $2.25 million. Critics called the acting, screenplay and direction above average. Sheridan's portrayal was praised as one of her finest. *Movieland* magazine pronounced, "At long last Ann Sheridan has a picture worthy of her talents.... [Her] performance will wring your heart."

Even in her early 30s, Sheridan was still a potent symbol of sexuality and glamour.

By the beginning of 1948, it was clear that Bette Davis had lost favor with both the studio and her fans. Her swift career demise was soon accelerated by the release of two truly awful features, *Winter Meeting* (1948) and *Beyond the Forest* (1949). Joan Crawford then assumed the position of "Queen" with the box office success of her films *Humoresque* (1946) and *Possessed* (1947). As for Sheridan, her "dramatic actress" ambitions continued to be thwarted by the executives' steadfast belief that moviegoers were primarily interested in the "Oomph Girl" rather than her acting talent. Crawford was able to blend her megawatt persona as a glamour girl and her dramatic talents into a viable box office attraction. Sheridan was not. While her last three features were profitable, the box office revenues paled in comparison to the Crawford pictures' profits.

Next up for Ann was a project that held much promise, *Silver River*. Veteran director Raoul Walsh, who had helmed many successful Warners features, was assigned to bring Stephen Longstreet's novel to the screen. Sheridan was assigned to play the leading lady to her friend Errol Flynn. At the time, Flynn was still a potent draw and she stood to benefit from her association with this film. Sheridan told Ray Hagen, "I thought that it might turn into a good picture."[12] Unfortunately for all concerned, it didn't.

The main problem was that Flynn's drinking had gotten out of control and his personal life was in shambles. Compounding this situation was Flynn's lack of confidence in his acting skills. "Errol was a strange person," recalled Ronald Reagan, "terribly unsure of himself and needlessly so. He was a beautiful piece of machinery, likable, with great charm, and yet convinced he lacked ability as an actor."[13]

Longstreet, who was hired to adapt his novel into a screenplay, noted that Flynn was not the only drinker on the set: "[Sheridan] too, as a director told me, was 'lapping up the sauce.' … Raoul Walsh … came to me and said, 'Kid, write it fast. They're not drinking, they promised Jack Warner that, but you never know.'"[14] Sure enough, it was soon discovered that the pitchers of "iced water" that both Sheridan and Flynn drank from on the set actually contained pure 90-proof vodka. Sheridan had also learned from Flynn the trick of injecting vodka into oranges, which she ate on the set. According to Longstreet, "The stars' behavior resulted in delays, which led to cost overruns, which forced the studio heads to declare *Silver River* finished. It is the only major studio film I know of for which there is no ending."[15]

Despite all of the problems, both stars enjoyed working together and took delight in outdoing each other with outrageous behavior in front of set visitors. The studio's publicity department did a masterful job creating the impression that it was all fun and games on the movie set. According to *Photoplay*, "Working with Annie is like having old happy days here again, says old-timer director Walsh…. She makes work play, as it should be, and sparks the spontaneity in everyone."[16] What the writer tactfully failed to report was Sheridan's ability to outdrink and out-swear her co-star off-camera.

With all of Sheridan's prankishness and sense of fun, those who worked closely with her on the set adored her. Myrtle Giddings, her wardrobe woman, had glowing praise: "If you're under the impression Annie is just a female Good Time Charlie, let me set you straight … generosity is such an integral part of her personality. You can't know the real Sheridan without knowing about her many kindnesses."[17]

Released in May 1948 *Silver River* was a talky psychological drama dressed in Western clothes. Flynn plays the embittered Mike McComb, a former Civil War officer who decides to play by his own rules in his quest for success and riches. While setting up a gambling hall and saloon in Silver City, he meets Georgia Moore (Sheridan), the beautiful wife of his competitor. Mike and Georgia form an uneasy business alliance that should have benefited all those involved.

The convoluted plot follows the typical psychological dramas of the late 1940s when her husband dies in an ambush believed to have been a setup. Mike wastes little time in making Georgia his bride, ignoring the gossips. He also makes shady deals in a bold attempt to become the richest man in the mining town. As with many morality tales, Mike gets his comeuppance through financial ruin, and Georgia leaves him. Realizing the error of his ways, Mike decides to start over with Georgia once again at his side at the finale.

While receiving mostly negative notices, particularly for Flynn and Sheridan's performances, *Silver River* had a worldwide gross of $3.5 million and ranked as the studio's eighth most popular film that year. Despite the respectable grosses, however, it was a far cry from Flynn's most popular features. With the diminishing returns of his recent films, Flynn's days on the lot were numbered.

During the making of *Silver River*, Sheridan and director John Huston, who was simultaneously shooting *The Treasure of the Sierra Madre*, schemed to play a practical joke on *Sierra Madre* star Humphrey Bogart. In a scene set in a Mexican town, Bogart is followed by an old prostitute making indecent proposals. When Bogart turned to rebuff her, he was shocked to find Sheridan in the woman's place. "Sheridan, you wench!" Bogart shrieked as the entire set broke out in laughter.[18]

Warners hoped to star Sheridan in *Flamingo Road* with Vincent Sherman directing. Sheridan felt the screenplay was neither good nor faithful to the original novel and turned it down. Joan Crawford starred in the production, which was released in 1949.

Still dissatisfied with the scripts offered, Sheridan became interested in a loanout to RKO for director Leo McCarey's *Good Sam* opposite Gary Cooper. McCarey originally wanted to cast Jean Arthur, but she had already committed to Billy Wilder's *A Foreign Affair* at Paramount. Arthur reportedly suggested he should cast Sheridan. A chance meeting at the Kentucky Derby convinced McCarey that Sheridan would be perfect for the role of Cooper's wife. He sent her the script and Sheridan loved it so much that she offered to do it for nothing. It was the kind of part (a mother of two) that offered something different from the usual "Oomph Girl" roles. According to McCarey, the "Oomph Girl" label "served its purpose but it always embarrassed Annie. She has deserved a better title for many years,".[19] He was successful in convincing Jack Warner to loan Sheridan. It could be surmised that Warner's consent was an indication of Sheridan's declining star status on the lot. Sheridan was thrilled by the project: "McCarey's one of my idols, when I was a stock girl at Paramount he was a big shot there, and I'd always yearned to work with him."[20]

Production began in August 1947 and lasted two and a half months. The cast and crew had a great time making this comedy, which came from an original idea of McCarey's. He was pleased with Sheridan's work: "[S]he turned in far and away the finest performance of her life ... we had an immense amount of fun."[21] Sheridan felt the same way about making the movie: "It was a delight to work with Leo and Gary."[22]

Cooper plays Sam Clayton, a department store manager whose propensity for helping others constantly gets him into trouble with his wife Lu (Sheridan). His acts of kindness extend to anyone in need: a lazy brother-in-law who refuses to get a job, neighbors in need of Sam's only car so they can go on vacation, a despondent salesgirl with no place to stay. He even loans $5000 (money he and Lu saved to buy a house) to a couple that wants to build a gas station business.

Many of these selfless acts backfire and Sam eventually becomes frustrated because his generosity has gone unreciprocated. Lu is likewise fed up and contemplates leaving him. When another financial calamity falls on Sam, he goes on a drinking binge. It takes the intervention of the Salvation Army to bring Sam and his family back together on Christmas Day. A few last-minute "miracles" paint a brighter future for the family.

A September 1948 release, the overlong comedy got mixed reviews. While a few questioned the wisdom of casting the sexy "Oomph Girl" as a mother, many astute critics hailed her comic portrayal. The *New York Times* noted, "[I]t is the lovely and willful sarcasm in her approach—the non–Pollyannaism—that keys the whole purpose of the film." *Photoplay* deemed Sheridan and Cooper's performances among the best of the month. Columnist Hedda Hopper was likewise enthusiastic after seeing Ann's comic turn: "If ... she isn't right up in Ingrid Bergman's league, I'm set to munch some of those hats Annie and Steve are always sending me."[23]

Good Sam turned out to be a real crowd-pleaser and ranked as RKO's third most popular film of 1948. But Sheridan was not fond of the finished movie. "Gary and I did not have the spark we should have had together," she told Hagen.[24]

Back on the Burbank lot, Sheridan continued to turn down project after project, like *Caged* (released in 1950 with Eleanor Parker). Despite feeling overlooked, she lacked the drive to fight for better roles. "I want to enjoy what I do," she told McCarey. "I don't care what kind of parts or what kind of pictures I make but I do want good stories."[25]

At this time, Warner Brothers was building up younger actresses Eleanor Parker, Doris Day and Patricia Neal. Even established stars Jane Wyman and Joan Crawford continued to draw better vehicles than Sheridan. She should have been unnerved by the studio's shabby treatment of Bette Davis and considered moving on while she was still a viable screen commodity. Sheridan's option with the studio was up on January 8, 1949. With only six months left on her contract, she paid Warners $35,000 to end her contract. "What really burned me," she later recalled, "was that Stanwyck was given her freedom from Warners right afterward without paying a cent."[26]

As the news made headlines, reporters flocked to the departing star for some quotes. Sheridan calmly responded in her usual direct fashion. "I've been with Warner Brothers 13 years, and that's long enough, don't you think?"[27] It was time to venture out on her own.

FIFTEEN

Freelancing

There have been three phases of my career—and the present one, playing comedy and to hell with the oomph, is by far the most satisfying.[1]

Now that Sheridan was no longer under contract to Warner Brothers, gossip columnists speculated on the likelihood of Sheridan-Hannagan nuptials. This, they feared, might result in her retirement from the screen. Leo McCarey said, "I don't know why they don't get married.... They're a grand pair."[2] Hedda Hopper asked Sheridan outright why there were no plans to marry. "Why marry and spoil a perfect friendship?" Sheridan replied. "Maybe it's something I can't explain, but I've had two tries at marriage and two unhappy experiences. Maybe marriage isn't for me. Why try again and risk spoiling the best friendship I've ever known?"[3]

By late 1948, however, that special friendship was in a rut with no foreseeable resolution. Hannagan had been pressuring Sheridan to give up her acting career and move to the East Coast. There was also the occasional rumor that Hannagan had become jealous of her friendships with several handsome, younger men. All of the expensive gifts could not buy her faithfulness, even though he professed a willingness to overlook her indiscretions.

Hannagan headed the nation's top publicity agency; its biggest client was the Union Pacific Railroad. Although he was in a financial situation to support both of their lavish lifestyles, she was not ready to entertain the notion of giving up her career. "I'd like another five years in pictures with good stories," she said.[4]

Since Hannagan was a devout Roman Catholic, Sheridan consulted a priest about converting to Roman Catholicism. The priest informed her that she couldn't marry a divorced man (Hannagan had been married twice) and be a newly baptized Catholic convert in good standing with the church. "And what the priest told me was the last straw," Sheridan said.[5] After this unpleasant encounter, Sheridan gave up on organized religion altogether.

In the end, it was officially stated that, with two high-powered careers and a steadfast religious doctrine, there was nothing for the couple to do except part ways while maintaining a close friendship.

Sheridan wasted little time in playing the field with the likes of Bill Cagney (James' brother), Franchot Tone, Cesar Romero and Bruce Cabot. She was at the peak of her beauty and had little trouble attracting men. Rex Harrison was one of many who found her enchanting. "I was struck by her extraordinary magnetism and directness," Harrison said. "[Her] distinctive quality of earthiness that never transcends to blatant sexiness."[6]

Sheilah Graham took a rather perverse interest in chronicling the star's romantic escapades in the gossip columns and magazine features, including one called "Annie, Get Your Guy" for *Modern Screen*.[7] When asked by Graham if she ever intended to re-marry and settle down, Sheridan replied, "I am too busy to settle down. And why must I get married? A woman can have an enduring friendship with a man and not be married to him, I hope. I like being single because I have so many things to do."[8]

The most persistent suitor was set designer Jacques Mapes, who met Sheridan on the *Good Sam* set. Sheridan enjoyed Mapes' sense of humor and good looks. Mapes said he found Ann's sense of humor "one of her most remarkable qualities. That, and her complete honest sincerity about people and everything she does."[9] Mapes was a bisexual in a long-term relationship with Sheridan's friend Ross Hunter, then a struggling actor. He went on to become a renowned producer of lush "woman weepies" of the 1950s and 1960s, including the 1954 *Magnificent Obsession* and the 1959 *Imitation of Life*. The Mapes-Hunter relationship was one of Hollywood's longest, 40-plus years. In the late 1950s, Sheridan and Hunter had a well-publicized falling-out that lasted for a few years. It is likely that Sheridan's on-and-off romantic relationship with Mapes ignited this feud.

Sheridan was offered many movie deals from other studios. One was Fidelity Pictures Corporation's *Montana Belle* with Brian Donlevy as her leading man. Filmed in 1948, the film instead starred Jane Russell and Sheridan's ex-husband George Brent. Early in September, Sheilah Graham reported that Sheridan was offered *Ricochet*. Sheridan finally signed a two-picture contract with 20th Century–Fox.

Her first Fox feature turned out to be the screwball comedy classic *I Was a Male War Bride*. It was based on the real-life experiences of Roger H. Charlier, a Belgian resistance fighter during World War II and a member of the prosecuting team for the Belgian and Luxembourg delegation to the Nuremberg trials. His wife was American army nurse Marie Helen Glennon. This marriage was unusual, since most American soldiers married European women. When the couple requested permission to go to the United States, the American consul in Frankfurt suggested to Charlier that "spouse" could refer to a groom as well as a bride. Under the pen name of Henri Rochard, his story was first published as "Male War Bride Trial to Army" in *The Baltimore Sun* in September 1947. A condensed version appeared in the November 1947 issue of *Reader's Digest* under the title "I Was a Male War Bride." In 1955, Charlier expanded it into a book.

20th Century–Fox snatched up the screen rights almost immediately. Early candidates for the male lead included Rex Harrison and Louis Jourdan before Cary Grant was cast. For the role of Catherine, MGM's Ava Gardner was briefly considered, but director Howard Hawks doubted that she was right for the part. With Sheridan's release from her Warners contract, Hawks knew he had the perfect leading lady. "Oh, she was quick and good and everything," recalled Hawks. "And when we made *Male War Bride*, she wasn't so young. She'd been through the mill by that time. But if you're going to make a good picture with Cary Grant, you'd better have somebody who's pretty damn good along with him."[10] Sheridan jumped at the chance to work with Hawks. "I would have taken anything of Howard Hawks', and with Cary Grant in it, sight unseen."[11]

Production began in late September 1948 with exterior scenes in the German cities Heidelberg, Manheim and Frankfurt. During the three-month shoot in

Germany, the cast and crew had to contend with an unbearably cold winter. The production crew then moved to Shepperton Studios in London to film interiors. There, many cast and crew members became ill, starting with Sheridan: "I came down with intestinal flu, pleurisy and pneumonia—in that order."[12] Her condition was serious enough to warrant newspaper coverage in the United States:

> Movie actress Ann Sheridan is so seriously ill with pleurisy at her Savoy hotel suite that she cannot be moved to a hospital. Miss Ann Sheridan collapsed on the set during the filming of *I Was a Male War Bride* 10 days ago and x-rays showed she was suffering from pleurisy with complications in one lung.[13]

The actress was bedridden for three weeks. After two weeks of a production shutdown, she recovered and returned to the set. Others who became sick included cast member Randy Stuart and screenwriter Charles Lederer. As a favor, Lederer's friend Orson Welles (who was filming *The Third Man* in London) wrote part of a short chase scene. Hawks himself came down with a mysterious rash from head to toe. Despite the various illnesses, filming continued. Then Grant became ill. As Sheridan recalled to John Kobal:

> We were doing a scene in a haystack—you know, the scene where his motorcycle crashes into it and we have this love scene. It's 4:00 in the afternoon, the fog is coming in under the door, and I am sitting there and praying, "Oh, God, I hope he doesn't get my cold [or] pneumonia," because I could barely breathe as it was, loaded down with penicillin and all that nonsense, when suddenly Cary, who had just rewritten this scene with Howard, says, "You know, Howard, I don't like this scene." And Howard said, "But, Cary, you just wrote it." And Cary said, "I don't care, it's bloody awful. I don't like it." And it isn't like him at all, and I looked at him and felt his forehead and it was awfully hot....[14]

Grant, diagnosed with jaundice and infectious hepatitis, was taken to the hospital for treatment. His girlfriend Betsy Drake nursed him back to health and he regained some of the 37 pounds he lost during his long illness.

While Grant recuperated, the production was shut down in early February 1949. The delay had pushed the budget over $2 million, so the crew returned to the 20th Century–Fox studios in Hollywood and waited for Grant to recover. After six months of recuperation and rest, Grant was healthy enough to return to the movie. Filming resumed in early May 1949 for three more weeks, and the feature was finally completed. There were, however, some scenes that had to be reshot after a preview. The biggest unintentional laugh was garnered by the haystack scene. "It was filmed in Germany," Jacques Mapes recalled. "Then Cary became very ill, and when the next scene was shown, filmed in Hollywood, there was 20 pounds less of him. 'He visibly melted right in my arms,' [Sheridan] laughed, and so did the preview audiences."[15]

In an interview, Sheridan quipped, "[T]he picture has everything except a horse. Only two things vie with a nag for spectator interest—dogs and babies. There isn't any competition of that kind in this movie, so maybe I stand a pretty good chance of having the audience look my way at least half the time."[16] Despite all the trouble during the shoot, Sheridan later admitted that she enjoyed working with Grant and wished they could have reteamed in another vehicle. The closest they came was a *Lux Radio Theatre* version of *I Was a Male War Bride,* but the broadcast was cancelled because Charlier failed to release his radio rights to the story.

While the Hawks feature was in post-production, Sheridan had reasons to be optimistic about her future. Prior to the making of *Male War Bride*, Louella Parsons announced that Sheridan had signed with Polan Banks to star in an independent film to be released through RKO, based on his novel *Carriage Entrance*. Sheridan looked forward to making this movie with Robert Young as her co-star. But studio politics made this feature more of a challenge than she expected.

Earlier in 1948, eccentric millionaire Howard Hughes gained control of RKO, which at the time was struggling financially. Within weeks of the acquisition, Hughes dismissed hundreds of employees and cut back on the number of features produced. Hughes learned that RKO production chief Dore Schary, who recently left for MGM, had okayed the purchase of Banks' novel. Schary also engineered a deal in which Banks was given a three-picture, independent producer contract with RKO. Hughes terminated the original deal, then offered Banks a one-film deal as producer. Studio insiders speculated that Hughes objected to the deal because the project was conceived as an expensive period piece. The truth proved to be much more complicated.

For Hughes, the biggest bone of contention was Sheridan's casting. Her agent had brokered a sweetheart deal with Banks: a $150,000 salary and ten percent of the profits, plus script, director and male lead approval. For some unknown reason, Hughes had an intense dislike of Sheridan (most likely financially driven) and conspired to get rid of her.

Robert Young dropped out weeks ahead of the production's start date. Studio insiders believed that the actor was bought off by Hughes. Sheridan provided Hughes with a list of five actors she considered to be a suitable replacement: Richard Conte, Franchot Tone, Charles Boyer, John Lund and Robert Mitchum. The criteria for her choices was based on the notion that the role "called for a man with 'good physique who could portray weakness."[17] Of these, Sheridan wanted Mitchum, who was already under contract with RKO, but Hughes refused her request. Production delays continued while Hughes made no effort to appease his angry star. The two butted heads continually over the Mitchum casting.

In August, Hughes unexpectedly fired Sheridan from the film. The incident made national news: "Ann Sheridan out of Picture at RKO" was a *New York Times* headline.[18] Two weeks after Sheridan was let go, Hughes borrowed his former lover, Ava Gardner, from MGM to play opposite Robert Mitchum.

As Sheridan and her agent pondered their next move, *I Was a Male War Bride* was released at the end of August and proved to be a smash hit. The comedy begins in postwar Allied-occupied Heidelberg. French Army Captain Henri Rochard (Grant), on the eve of retirement, is assigned to locate a highly skilled lens maker named Schindler. He is annoyed when American Lt. Catherine Gates (Sheridan) joins him on his mission (they had previously worked together on missions that were fraught with hostility). By the end of their operation, with all of its comical mishaps, they discover to their surprise that they actually love each other and decide to marry. But since Henri is foreign-born, he and Catherine are required to follow Army procedures in order to secure entry into the United States. Given the unusual circumstances, Henri is forced to apply as a "war bride." This leads to further complications for the newlyweds, who want nothing more than to consummate their marriage.

I Was a Male War Bride was well received by critics, with Hawks and the two stars receiving the lion's share of enthusiastic notices. The *Pittsburgh Press* noted, "[W]ith Ann Sheridan providing a well-played and sex-appealing foil, the two principals manage to eke out enough entertainment to repay audiences for their attention." Earning $4.5 million at the box office, the comedy was 20th Century–Fox's top-grossing film of the year. It remains a hilarious classic to this day.

As Sheridan was basking in the success of the Hawks comedy, *Carriage Entrance* was plagued with problems. As a result, the production fell behind schedule. Once completed, the feature did not test well with preview audiences, necessitating the filming of retakes. It was then that Sheridan and her lawyer filed a lawsuit against Hughes and RKO. She sued for $350,000, claiming that RKO had "arbitrarily, wrongfully and unreasonably" violated the terms of her contract.[19] The studio filed a countersuit alleging it was Sheridan who failed to honor her contract.

In January 1950, the judge dismissed Sheridan's claim to a share in the film's profits. He also denied the defense motion to dismiss the claim for the $150,000 in salary. Hughes and RKO's lawyers continued to fight Sheridan in court for another year before she proved victorious in State Federal Court. In February 1951, a jury awarded the actress $55,162.42 in monetary compensation ($50,000 was the minimum amount she would have earned had she worked on the film from April to August 1949, plus $5162 for additional costs). In addition, she was entitled to a new deal with RKO at the salary of $150,000 for one motion picture with her approval. "I'm very happy," Sheridan told the reporters. "The jury acquitted me on running out on a contract, which I didn't do."[20]

Carriage Entrance was released as *My Forbidden Past* in April 1951 (a delay in release that most likely was caused by Sheridan's lawsuit). It proved to be both a critical and financial failure, losing $700,000.

While *Carriage Entrance* was undergoing its legal battles, Sheridan made her television debut on *The Ed Wynn Show* on February 11, 1950. Her friend Lucille Ball, who also made her TV debut on that show, may have convinced Sheridan that the new form of entertainment would provide her a new career. The *Variety* TV critic reported favorably on Sheridan's brief appearance: "Ann Sheridan, one of the top-billed film stars yet to appear on television ... proved again the old adage that a talented performer in any part of show business will show well on tv."

Sheridan sports the chic new hairstyle she adopted for *I Was a Male War Bride* (1949). The look signaled the end of her sex symbol status and fans turned away.

For Sheridan's second film of her two-picture deal with 20th Century–Fox, she was cast in a quirky dark comedy, *Stella*, opposite Victor Mature. The studio purchased the 1949 novel *Family Skeleton* by Doris Miles Disney for $10,000. It was originally announced as a vehicle for their top female star, Susan Hayward, but she went on suspension rather than take the assignment.

Stella was a reunion of sorts for Sheridan and director Claude Binyon, as he was one of the screenplay writers for her motion picture debut, *Search for Beauty*. She gratefully acknowledged his help on her first feature.

A sad event occurred during the shoot. Longtime character actor Hobart Cavanaugh (who appeared in a few of Sheridan's programmers in the 1930s) was suffering from terminal stomach cancer. He valiantly tried to complete all of his scenes, but collapsed twice on set. He died on April 26, 1950, while the feature was still in production.

Stella was released in August 1950. The film opens with a family burying their Uncle Joe, who died accidentally. The family keeps this secret from Stella (Sheridan), who provides for the family by virtue of the fact she is the only one who works at a regular job. She is engaged to her boss, Fred Anderson (Leif Erickson), but does not really love him.

Enter Jeff De Marco (Mature), a claims adjuster whose presence unnerves the skittish family and irks Stella, who rebuffs him as a suitor. When Stella is told about Uncle Joe's death, she must keep Jeff at arm's length to protect her shiftless family. Next the family has to dig up Uncle Joe's body in order to collect on his life insurance policy. The problem is that they can't remember where they buried him. Stella sensibly opts to leave town with Jeff.

With its dark humor, *Stella* was either praised or dismissed by the reviewers. Relying solely on Sheridan and Mature's star status, the comedy failed to make a profit. Supporting players David Wayne and Frank Fontaine garnered most of the praise; Sheridan and Mature were not well served by their straight man roles.

Sheridan admitted to Hagen she was initially enthusiastic about the script, but disliked the finished film: "[I]t was a dreadful mistake.... It was dreary, and it shouldn't have been."[21] Furthermore, while Sheridan admired Mature, she felt there was no chemistry between them, and that was apparent on the screen.

Although much of Sheridan's personal life was often fodder for gossip-hungry fans, many were taken aback by the newest revelation: "Ann Sheridan Is Skid Row Club Angel." It turned out that Sheridan had been secretly sponsoring a "Skid Row" boys club in the Los Angeles area since 1947! She had donated money, food, clothes, television sets and her own time in support of policeman Mickey Finn's Youth Clubs. Finn told reporters,

> When we first started, we had nothin'. Then Annie heard about it. She said she'd like to come down. I didn't pay any attention to that. I'd heard it from those movie stars before. But darned if she doesn't show up. Not in mink and satin like those others. She had on a skirt and sweater. Then she started talking to the kids—in their own language.... And the kids are crazy about her. They know she really cares about 'em. We've had other movie stars down there. They make big promises—but that's the last we ever hear of 'em.

For years, her press agents tried to convince Sheridan to go public about her mission, but instead they had strict orders to keep it under wraps. "I finally convinced her she had to talk about it," Finn disclosed. "The boys need the donations her name would bring in." Sheridan conceded, "We're broke. All this news about teenage attacks had chopped off our donations. Nobody wants to give money to boys they think are sneaking up on people in the dark."

Not surprisingly, Sheridan was dubbed the "queen" of the toughest district in town. "When she came down to Bunker Hill to shoot scenes for *Woman on the Run*," Finn grinned, "all the gangs showed up to take care of her. Plenty of women get robbed and beaten up down there—but the boys make sure nothing happens to Annie."[22]

While on the *Woman on the Run* set, Sheridan expounded on her personal life with columnist Bob Thomas. Asked about marriage, she didn't mince words: "I tried it twice with Edward Norris and George Brent. I'm happier the way I am. I'll think it over very carefully before I try it again."[23] Although Jacques Mapes remained high on the list of marital prospects, Steve Hannagan was never completely out of the picture. To the astonishment of many, they maintained their close friendship and continued to socialize in a highly publicized manner at various New York City and Hollywood night clubs, fueling speculations they would rekindle their romance. Not so, said Sheridan. "I have known him seven years, to be exact," she told Sheilah Graham, "and it has been a wonderful friendship. But I have known other men as long and even longer, one of them 17 years, and those are good friendships, too. And yet, all I have to do is go out to dinner with one of them and the rumors start again that we are a 'thing' or an 'item,' and that Sheridan is going to get married at any minute."[24]

Still, the rumors of a Sheridan-Hannagan nuptials persisted. In 1952, Louella Parsons pointedly asked Sheridan about her relationship with Hannagan. "I'm not thinking of marriage. I've always listened to Steve's advice and it's always been good," Sheridan responded before skillfully pre-empting a follow-up question from the nosey columnist. "When I left Warner Brothers…, I wondered if I was doing the right thing. Now I know that it was right for me and that it's right for any actress to freelance and not tie herself up to a studio except for a limited number of pictures."[25]

Woman on the Run was the second independent feature produced for the short-lived Fidelity Pictures; their other movies include *House by the River* (1950), *The Groom Wore Spurs* (1951) and *Rancho Notorious* (1952). Sheridan not only starred in *Woman on the Run* but also served as a silent co-producer with Howard Welsch.

The movie was based on the short story "Man on the Run" by Sylvia Tate, published in *American Magazine* in April 1948. Actor-turned-director and former Orson Welles protégé Norman Foster was given the task of directing the feature. The producers originally wanted New Orleans to serve as the movie's background, but financial constraints forced the crew to shoot in the more affordable location of San Francisco. The budget was kept in check throughout the shoot, so improvisations were a common occurrence. Even the script was constantly revised due to Sheridan and co-star Dennis O'Keefe's inclination to ad-lib many of their lines.

Woman on the Run was released in November 1950. A classic film noir, this motion picture remains a superior example of the genre. The thrills begin early and tension steadily builds until its nail-biting climax.

While out on a walk with his dog, Frank Johnson (Ross Elliott) witnesses a murder, thereby making himself the killer's next target. Johnson eludes the police, so Inspector Ferris (Robert Keith) solicits the help of Johnson's wife Eleanor (Sheridan), who proves surprisingly reluctant to help them. It turns out that this couple has a lot of unresolved issues and are on the brink of separation.

Knowing that her husband has a weak heart and needs his medication, Eleanor sets out on her own to find Frank. She is joined in her search by reporter Danny Leggett (O'Keefe), who helps her elude the police. The identity of the killer is revealed at the midway point and suspense builds as Eleanor and the police race against time to find Frank before the killer does.

The *Buffalo Courier-Express* praised the Universal-International release as a "suspense melodrama with a novel twist…. Its plot idea is clever, excitement builds well, and entertainment values are good…. Miss Sheridan scores in straight role." Unfortunately, the movie failed to live up to its box office potential due to the misguided advertising campaign that touted it as a woman's picture with taglines like "a probing study of the failure of modern marriage."

In 1953, writers Manuel Seff and Paul Yawitz sued Fidelity Pictures, producer Howard Welsch and Universal-International for $75,000. They alleged that their unpublished story "Pay the Piper" was the inspiration for the film. The matter was settled out of court.

Many years ago, the feature entered the public domain when the original copyright holder failed to renew its copyright. This resulted in the proliferation of poor copies televised and released in digital versions. Compounding this situation was that the only known pristine print of this film was destroyed in a fire in June 2008. Fortunately, through the intervention of Eddie Muller, host of Turner Classic Movies' *Noir Alley* series, a 35mm print was discovered at the British Film Institute. It was preserved by the UCLA Film and Television Archive with financial help from the Film Noir Foundation and the Hollywood Foreign Press Association's Charitable Trust. Today, *Woman on the Run* remains a worthwhile film noir just for the fact that the main character is a woman who indulges in detective work.

During the first half of 1951, Sheridan was mainly off the big screen. With the exception of a poorly photographed appearance on TV's *The Ken Murray Show*, there were not many acting offers. This inactivity was an indication that there was no room for aging sex symbols like Sheridan (now 36), with the public clamoring for newer, younger, sexier actresses like Marilyn Monroe. Sheridan later had words of advice for Monroe. Her words were remarkably astute and eerily prophetic:

> All the publicity helps, of course, but the big test comes after that. Then the public starts saying, "Let's see you act." Marilyn's lucky that they didn't give her a tag, but she'll still have a tough time convincing people that she can be so beautiful, and an actress, too. And the critics probably will give her a bad time as well, said Annie. They're bound to pick on her. She's too big. She'll have to work hard to overcome a sort of resentment that comes with all the publicity. Boy, it's a tough road.[26]

Sheridan's professional situation was not lost on Hollywood insiders and there were many syndicated columnists who lent a helping hand. Sheilah Graham reported, "Ann Sheridan is searching madly for a movie to make."[27] Sheridan told Louella Parsons, "I have owned a comedy, 'It Must Be Love,' for two years and I have been planning to make it myself."[28] Erskine Johnson got right to the point when he posed this question to his readers: "Ann Sheridan ho-hum about her movie career?":

The accusing finger has been pointed at Ann, but she slipped it to me that she's still ga-ga about sound stages, cameras, and movie razzle-dazzle. "I can understand people saying that I've lost interest," husky-voiced Ann said. "I've said no to so many movies offered to me. But the rumor's not true. I wouldn't be happy at all unless I could make pictures. I'm not knocking a good drama if one can be found, but I'm doing the comedy stuff that I like to do. We're in for a laugh time. People want to laugh."

Johnson also reported that Sheridan, "a high favorite with Latin Americans," was offered a film contract from Uruguay; she would get her normal Hollywood salary as well as a percentage of the film's profits.[29] Nothing came of this.

By the early summer of 1951, Sheridan had dismissed her agents in an effort to rejuvenate her fading film career. The switch proved to be lucky as she then signed a three-picture contract with one picture a year for Universal-International producer William Goetz. The first screenplay offered was a Technicolor drama, *Steel Town*, and her co-star would be Jeff Chandler.

Universal-International's biggest male star, Chandler had made a terrific impression with his Oscar-nominated (Best Supporting Actor) performance in *Broken Arrow* (1950). He was ruggedly good-looking, a man's man—just the type for the always romantically inclined actress. Despite Chandler being a married man and father to two daughters (aged two and four), he and Sheridan began a passionate affair. Since Sheridan did not have a publicity department like Warner Brothers to keep her name out of tawdry headlines, newspaper coverage was expansive and damaging. While her reputation suffered, Chandler's remained unaffected as it only added to his mystique. The U-I publicity department made it clear that Chandler was already living in a separate residence prior to this affair, but Hollywood insiders knew better.

Erskine Johnson approached Chandler and asked him point-blank about his relationship with Sheridan: "Rugged Jeff Chandler answering the $64 question: Will he and Ann Sheridan rush to the altar after Mrs. Chandler obtains her divorce from the stone-faced, graying actor?" Chandler gracefully dodged the question. "Ann Sheridan? I'm very fond of her. Who can help it? She, on the other hand, has her own setup. We both have our own problems. She's a wonderful girl. I guess it will have to be friendship."[30] A skeptical Dorothy Kilgallen was not convinced about the "friendship" part. "Jeff Chandler and Ann Sheridan look like a four-star romance," she asserted, and then wistfully added, "[B]ut she must still have a soft spot in her heart for Steve Hannagan."[31] Tne gossip columnist reported that Chandler spent a lot of time with Joan Crawford when Hannagan was in California. "The merry-go-round of Joan Crawford having quiet dinners at her home with Jeff Chandler, who dates Annie Sheridan at the night spots and big parties." Chandler lamented he could not see Sheridan because "the big man's in town."[32]

A sympathetic report came from *Modern Screen*. "When you ask him about his impending divorce, he says, 'I'm willing to do anything to make Marge [Marjorie Hoshelle, his wife] happy,'" the interviewer wrote. "If she insists on a divorce, okay. I guess there's no sense in quarreling all the time. Sometimes, people just get on one another's nerves. There's nothing anyone can do about it. She's a very fine person and a very fine actress, and I'm sorry it had to end this way." It was further noted that "Since Jeff has stopped living at home and the divorce announcement has been made, he's been seen on and off with Ann Sheridan. Both he and Sheridan insist that there's 'nothing serious between us.'"[33]

With the high-profile romance and intense public scrutiny on Sheridan's conduct, it was just a matter of time before the Chandler-Sheridan passion fizzled out. After the affair ended, Chandler reconciled with his wife …for a little while, anyway.

After the Sheridan-Chandler affair ended, Sheridan made an ironic guest appearance on *The Kate Smith Evening Hour*, playing a woman who averts an extramarital affair by sending the philandering heel back to his wife! Either this was all tongue-in-cheek satire or Universal was engaging in damage control on behalf of the careers of Sheridan and Chandler.

Once again, Sheridan found solace in Hannagan's company and it wasn't long before Sheilah Graham reported that Sheridan was wearing an expensive jeweled clip from Hannagan to celebrate eight years of their friendship.

Production on *Steel Town* began in September 1951, with John Lund in Chandler's place and Howard Duff (Ida Lupino's husband) as the third member of the romantic triangle. Scenes were filmed at the Kaiser Steel Plant in Fontana, California. A number of mill workers were hired as extras, and four were given speaking roles. Charles P. Boyle, the director of photography, had shot the highly regarded Technicolor short *Steel: Man's Servant* for the U.S. Steel Company in 1938. The scenes shot in the mill gave a documentary feel to the new feature. Sheridan enjoyed her time making this movie and had much to say about leading man Lund. "He's such a fine

actor, so intelligent and so nice to work with. He never loses his temper and is always so helpful."[34] She agreed to appear with Lund in a romantic comedy, *Just Across the Street*, as her second film for Universal-International.

In *Steel Town*, Sheridan's "Red" McNamara runs a restaurant located near the Kostane steel plant. Her boyfriend Jim (Duff) gets into a fistfight with a stranger over a steak dinner. The stranger turns out to be Steve Kostane (Lund), nephew of the steel company's owner and heir to the business. He remains undercover so he can learn the business before taking control.

Steve becomes part of Jim's crew, proves to be a skilled worker and earns the respect of the other men. Red falls in love with Steve but isn't sure they can overcome

As shown in a publicity pose for *Steel Town* (1952), the years of heavy drinking and smoking took a toll on Sheridan's appearance.

their class differences. It isn't until Steve saves her father from an accident at the plant that she decides he's a keeper and accepts his marriage proposal.

Steel Town world-premiered in Birmingham, Alabama, on March 20, 1952, with Sheridan, Lund and Duff making a five-city personal appearance tour that weekend. One reporter had the audacity to compare this hyped-up premiere to that of *Gone with the Wind* at Atlanta in 1939. The critics were generally dismissive.

With Sheridan's appearance in *Steel Town*, viewers could not help notice that the once glamorous "Oomph Girl" looked a little wan in the face and stouter in the figure. All the years of excessive drinking and chain-smoking were taking a toll on her physical allure. As a result, her popularity continued to wane and film offers dwindled further. Such is the fate of an aging Hollywood sex symbol.

Louella Parsons continued to champion Sheridan's cause. She even went so far as to declare that Sheridan was

> more successful now than when she checked in at Warner Brothers studio some years ago.... One reason Ann gets better each year is because everyone adores her on the set and works hard to make her pictures good. She's a pal to everyone, from the grips to the top executives. She never has taken herself too seriously and she has an almost wicked sense of humor.[35]

Nice try, Louella, but Sheridan's days were numbered.

Just Across the Street (the working title was *The Girl Across the Street*) had a short shooting schedule. During the shoot, Sheridan's third film under the Universal-International contract was announced: She would star opposite former paramour Jeff Chandler in Ross Hunter's production of *Vermillion O'Toole*, based on Richard Morris' story "Flame of the Timberline." Since that project was earmarked as an expensive "A" production, it took some time to get it ready.

While *Vermillion O'Toole* was still in the planning stages, another project was offered in which she would play a role inspired by the real-life Texan bullfighter Patricia McCormick. "I'd do it just to wear the gorgeous costumes," Sheridan said. "But they'll never get me close to one of those bulls. No thank you."[36]

Just Across the Street reached theaters in June 1952. The paper-thin romantic comedy deals with that staple of romantic comedy plots: mistaken identities. It all begins when working girl Henrietta Smith (Sheridan) assumes the identity of the daughter of a rich family to deceive a plumber. The plumber, Fred Newcombe (Lund), hires her as a secretary, believing that it will be good experience for the rich young woman to earn her own money. When Fred insists on dropping her off at her house, Henrietta continues the ruse because she fears Fred will not love her if he finds out she's poor. The mistaken identity scheme leads the rich couple to suspect each other of carrying on an affair (with the husband "romancing" Henrietta and his wife "seeing" Fred on the side). It all works out when Henrietta finally tells Fred the truth and they declare their love for each other.

A lightweight effort, it failed to make a profit. The screenplay was recycled for a 1957 *Lux Video Theatre* TV presentation starring Julie Adams, Jack Kelly and Cecil Kellaway repeating his role as "Pops" Smith.

After a lengthy delay, *Vermillion O'Toole* was ready for production in early October 1952. The feature was Ross Hunter's first motion picture as a producer. When working as an actor earlier in his career, Hunter had failed to make an impact.

Determined to make good, he found work as a drama teacher and dialogue director on films such as *The Jackie Robinson Story* and *Woman on the Run*. He recalled Sheridan's timely intervention: "When I was a complete flop as an actor, she kept getting me into her pictures. When there wasn't any part for me in them, then she'd get me put on as dialogue director the way she did with *Good Sam*.... She would always stop to say something kind to me, make a joke." Sheridan suggested that he try his hand at producing, so he spent his spare time learning the various facets of moviemaking. After he was offered the job of producing *Vermillion O'Toole* (retitled *Take Me to Town*), Sheridan agreed to star in the film. As a favor to her friend, she waived her salary of $475,000 and instead accepted $100,000. Years later, after Hunter had become a successful producer, he acknowledged, "It was Annie who really gave me my first break. She was a very great lady."[37]

To play the role of a dance hall singer, Sheridan got herself in shape by dieting. She even took singing lessons from radio singer Harriet Lee, who had served as vocal coach to major stars like Dorothy Lamour, Ava Gardner and Ginger Rogers. Sheridan enjoyed her experience on the set and proclaimed to Erskine Johnson, "It's real corn—vintage 1870 and wonderfully bawdy. And I've never been photographed so well in my life."[38]

Hunter was so enthusiastic about the project that he wanted to produce a TV series entitled *The Life and Loves of Vermillion O'Toole* (purported to be a continuation of *Take Me to Town*). The idea was dropped after the movie failed to recover its costs. In the late 1950s, Hunter entertained the idea of adapting the film into a Broadway musical with Sheridan as the star. That project also fell through.

Upon the completion of her Universal-International deal, Sheridan entertained other film offers. While former co-stars James Cagney, Humphrey Bogart and Cary Grant continued to be active in the business, film work for aging actresses was scarce. A sympathetic columnist noted that in the case of Rosalind Russell, Loretta Young and Sheridan: "It's ability, not age, that matters. If the youngsters in the industry have the talent, then they, too, can comfortably say: 'Grow old along with me; the best is yet to come.'"[39] Young moved on to three Emmy Awards as the host of TV's *The Loretta Young Show* and Russell likewise found renewed success as the irrepressible *Auntie Mame* on both Broadway and the big screen. No such luck for the "Oomph Girl."

Within a short period of time, Sheridan decided a change of location would be the answer to her career doldrums. In early 1953, it was announced that she was moving to Mexico to organize her own film company. Sheridan was ready to take measures to revitalize her career before it was too late.

SIXTEEN

Uncertain Times

*I've begged for years to be allowed to play character parts. But they
told me I was a glamor girl and a clotheshorse and that nobody would
believe in me. Now we'll see.*[1]

Even in the early 1950s, Sheridan had failed to recognize (perhaps intentionally)
that moviegoers were not interested in Ann Sheridan, the *actress*. That was reserved
for performers who delivered the dramatic goods in flamboyant fashion; superstars
like Bette Davis, Joan Crawford and Rosalind Russell come to mind. In Sheridan's
case, the fans wanted more of the "Oomph Girl" of the 1940s they recalled so fondly
and, if they didn't get it, they simply looked elsewhere. Compounding the issue was
the state of the Studio Star System. The era of major studios developing and nurtur-
ing their actors into box office stars was on the decline. The emergence of television
as a popular alternative form of entertainment added to the changing culture in Hollywood. Sheridan's career downturn continued and she spent more of her days occu-
pying her time with men and alcohol.

Then, tragedy struck and turned her world upside down.

In January 1953, Steve Hannagan was on a trip promoting Coca-Cola products
in several countries in Europe and Africa. After his arrival in Nairobi on February
2, he cancelled a dinner engagement with famed author Robert Ruark. Hannagan
explained that he felt tired and was experiencing uncomfortable pressure in his
chest. Ruark arranged for him to see a local doctor. After an examination, the doctor
prescribed bed rest. The next morning, Hannagan was found on the bathroom floor,
dead at the age of 53.

His body was wrapped like a mummy in preparation to be flown to New York
City. A funeral mass, held at St. Patrick's Cathedral, was attended by over 1500
mourners, including film and stage personalities, presidents of major corporations,
business associates and close friends. Afterwards, his body was taken to his hometown of Lafayette, Indiana, where he was laid to rest next to his mother in St. Mary's
Cemetery.

When Sheridan learned of Hannagan's death, she was devastated. After a few
days, she mustered up the strength to issue a statement for the press:

Once in a while the world is blessed with a man born with great understanding. This is
attested to by the number of true friends he gathers during his life. Such a man was Steve
Hannagan. My personal loss and feelings, which are extremely deep, must therefore be
shared by many others around the world by those who knew, loved and were influenced by
the greatness of this man.[2]

In the days following Hannagan's death, Louella Parsons wrote extensively on the Sheridan-Hannagan relationship, which she described as one of "Hollywood's greatest love stories."[3] "They would have been married," Parsons authoritatively reported, "but there was a little matter of Steve's church, which was very close to his heart, and a little matter of their two independent careers." One of the more painful disclosures Parsons made must have stoked Sheridan's guilt: "A friend of mine who took Steve to the plane the night he left said he was very unhappy and disturbed. 'Ann can't see why I won't give up everything and go to Hollywood and live, and I can't see why she won't give up her career and become just Mrs. Steve Hannagan.'" Parsons described the grieving Sheridan as "strangely calm with that calmness that comes with a hurt that is so deep you can't give vent to your feelings."[4]

As Sheridan mourned, she was shocked when his business associates filed a lawsuit against her. The lawsuit claimed that she had failed to repay a $40,000 loan from Hannagan. Sheridan had borrowed the money to purchase two film properties she hoped to either produce or sell to a studio. The understanding between the two was that she would pay him back from the sale of the screenplays. Although Hannagan had instructed one of his associates to destroy the promissory note in the event of his death, the business associates claimed that Hannagan did not follow the proper protocol. To settle the matter, Sheridan paid $15,000 for the two scripts. When the affairs of Hannagan's estate was settled in 1955, it was reported that Hannagan left Sheridan $218,399. Even in death, Hannagan was still taking care of his great love.

In March, the producers of *This Is Your Life* planned to spotlight Sheridan's nearly 20-year career. This was the popular program in which a famous figure was "ambushed" (taken by surprise) and honored with a tribute. Sheridan somehow got wind of the upcoming episode and, at the last minute, the producers cancelled it. A repeat episode featuring Lillian Roth was aired in its place.

In April, it was reported that Sheridan, unhappy with her career progress, had switched agents. The move produced no worthwhile offers. It was not long before Harrison Carroll revealed, "Ann Sheridan is going to sell her Hollywood home and move to Mexico. She is currently renting an apartment there and will spend much of her time there when not filmmaking."[5] Since the 1940s, Sheridan had maintained a separate residence in Mexico. "I fell in love with Mexico long ago," she later elaborated to Bob Thomas. "I like the people and like the living. It's a much easier life, although it is changing somewhat.... It's not quite the gentle place it used to be, but it's still a lot more restful than the way of life up here."[6]

There was talk that Sheridan would launch her own production company in Mexico. Since she was fluent in Spanish, Sheridan would star in both English- and Spanish-speaking features. "I think the Mexican film industry is just hitting its stride," Sheridan told Bob Thomas. "They're going to be doing great things down there. I'm sure it's going to rank next to Hollywood in importance as a film capital."[7] However, she made it clear that she was not through with Hollywood "[i]f there is a television series in Hollywood I can't resist, or a film role that's attractive."[8] One project that interested her was MGM's *Why Should I Cry?* (released as *Torch Song* with Joan Crawford). A more exciting prospect was 20th Century–Fox's *King Solomon and the Queen of Sheba*. The film was released as *Solomon and Sheba* in 1959 with Gina Lollobrigida and Yul Brynner (a replacement for Tyrone Power, who suffered a heart attack on the set and later died).

The movie that brought her back to Hollywood, however, was anything but enticing. RKO had sent scripts in accordance with the court ruling that she was owed one film, but none appealed to her. The latest screenplay, *Rage of the Jungle*, was not any better. "I was tired of fighting," Sheridan recalled to Hagen, "and thought it was just about time to call everything off…. So I consulted the lawyer and he told me to do it if I thought the script was worth it, and I said, 'Oh well, it may never be, I don't know.' … Never saw it. I heard it was an absolute horror."[9]

Under Jacques Tourneur's direction, production began in mid–May with Glenn Ford and Zachary Scott in the main male roles. At first, Sheridan enjoyed the challenges of a role that downplayed her glamorous image. She told Erskine Johnson, "I couldn't bear being one of those dolls who go through Hades with every strand of hair in place. Why try to look beautiful when the script says you look like the devil? The audience only laughs. The trick is to strike a balance, to retain a little glamor and still look beat up. Katharine Hepburn did it perfectly in *The African Queen*."[10]

She enjoyed reuniting with Scott, but found Ford difficult to work with. According to Johnson, "Reports of Ford's scene-stealing and interfering with Ann's close-up; production titled *Rage of the Jungle* should be renamed *Rage of the Sound Stage*. Ann says, 'They warned he was realistic in the clinches with his leading ladies. Realistic nothing. He's just rough.'"[11] Cal York of *Photoplay* reported: "Action in *Rage of the Jungle* has nothing on the 'rage' Ann Sheridan and Glenn Ford felt for each other. Glenn, it seems, claims that Annie's tardiness on the set

Sheridan lent a helping hand to first-time producer Ross Hunter when she agreed to star in *Take Me to Town* (1953) with Phillip Reed (left) and Sterling Hayden.

held up production. She contends he was always afraid someone might take one foot of film away from him!"[12]

A pleasant diversion on the tumultuous set came in the manly form of Mexican actor Rodolfo Acosta, who was cast as a villain. Sheridan was attracted to the swarthy, handsome actor and the pair soon became involved in a romantic relationship. After the completion of the production, Sheridan and Acosta shared an apartment in Mexico City, despite the fact he was married and a father of two young girls. Away from the prying eyes of Hollywood gossip columnists, they carried on their affair without attracting attention.

The musical comedy *Take Me to Town,* released in June 1953, emerged as an enjoyable family-friendly comedy with Sheridan appearing to advantage as Vermillion O'Toole, the streetwise saloon singer on the lam from the police. She finds the perfect hideout when she aligns herself with a logger-preacher (Sterling Hayden). A widower with three young boys, the preacher believes that Vermillion would make the perfect mother for the family. Much of the comedy results from the jaded entertainer adjusting to a rugged pioneer life far removed from anything she has known and eluding her crooked partner (Phillip Reed) who wants her help in a new scheme. Through her practical, no-nonsense manner, Vermillion wins over the conservative-minded townspeople and marries her preacher suitor.

This lightweight feature was generally well received as wholesome family entertainment by the critics, but the moviegoers, looking for more adult and sturdier cinematic fare, stayed away in droves even though the fabled "Oomph Girl" was on full and enticing display. The sad truth of the matter was that she had become passé. Both Sheridan and Hunter were disappointed with the poor box office reception.

Released in October, *Appointment in Honduras* fared poorly with the critics. The confused, muddled plot concerns Sylvia Sheppard (second-billed Sheridan), the disillusioned, unfaithful wife of wealthy but weak-willed Harry Sheppard (Scott). There is a violent revolution in Honduras and the couple is taken hostage by Jim Corbett (Ford), a fellow traveler on the steamboat. Corbett is actually an American hired to secretly transport a large sum of money to the deposed political leader. Accompanied by several criminals, Corbett and the couple journey through the danger-filled jungle. Despite herself, Sylvia falls in love with Corbett, much to her husband's annoyance. Corbett reaches his destination and reveals his mission to Sylvia. During a fierce gun battle, Harry is conveniently killed off. Corbett and Sylvia are free to marry.

The critics mercilessly skewered this half-baked melodrama and the performers. Sheridan received many swipes for her unrealistically glamorous appearance as a woman who endures the trials and tribulations of jungle travel.

Early in 1954, it was reported that producer Raymond Strauss wanted Sheridan for his remake of the 1947 Italian film *Furia*; it was eventually released in 1957 as *Wild Is the Wind* with Anna Magnani and Anthony Quinn.

With no worthwhile Hollywood film offers coming her way, Sheridan again entertained the idea of a TV film project in Mexico. "Ann has a picture cooking south of the border," Hedda Hopper reported, "for which she'll serve as both star and co-producer. 'But the money backing the film is coming from private sources, and I can't go into details yet.'"[13]

When that film project failed to materialize, Sheridan turned her eyes toward television. Unfortunately, the pickings were slim on that front as well. Sheridan told an interviewer,

> Television is in a childish copycat rut. Every week, agents come to me with TV ideas and say 'This is something like *The Lucy Show*' or 'This is something like *The Ann Sothern Show.*' ...There's no use trying to top someone else. But when I argue that I won't follow somebody, the agents shrug their shoulders and say 'Well, that's all they'll try.' It's really crazy.[14]

In mid–1954, Parsons informed her readers,

> Ann Sheridan may not spend as much time in the future in Mexico as she's been doing. She's going to star in a new TV series.... Paul McNamara and Jack Chertok, who created Ann Sothern's now famous *Private Secretary* series, will produce the Sheridan show, which starts soon. Says Paul, "We believe that Ann Sheridan has a good chance of becoming very successful in the series."[15]

In the proposed show, originally entitled *Assignment in Las Vegas*, Sheridan would play a press agent in a Las Vegas hotel. Filming was set to start in late August. However, the shoot was delayed several times due to scripting issues. Filming finally began in October and wrapped up in early December. The pilot was not picked up by sponsors, who were nervous that the show would promote gambling and glamorize "Sin City."

Sheridan's only professional appearance during this time was a poorly received guest star spot opposite George Raft on *The Milton Berle Show* in May.

With no worthwhile movie or TV offers, Sheridan remained in Mexico City with Acosta during much of the year. In January 1955, it was reported, "Ann Sheridan, who hasn't made a movie in over a year, faces the cameras as the star of Republic's *Rebel Island*."[16] This feature was eventually released as *Flame of the Islands* in 1956 with Yvonne De Carlo, Howard Duff and Zachary Scott. Within months of that announcement, Sheilah Graham revealed that Sheridan was entertaining an offer from actor Steve Cochran to appear in his first independent production, *Come Next Spring*. This news brought considerable attention from the press, with Erskine Johnson stating the obvious: "Ann Sheridan, the one time 'Oomph' girl, will play her first mother role" (forgetting that Sheridan had already played a mother of two youngsters in *Good Sam*).[17] Johnson's comment indicated that the one-time glamour girl was now poised to move into the mother role territory that many actresses fought against.

A former Warner Brothers star, Cochran wanted to branch out into other areas of filmmaking. He formed the Robert Alexander Productions (using his real birth name). Cochran, along with co-producer Harrison "Red" Reader, entered into a deal with Herbert J. Yates, head of Republic, to release the feature.

The screenplay was written by Cochran's friend Montgomery Pittman; Pittman's stepdaughter Sherry Jackson was hired to play a significant role in the feature. The production began its shoot in June 1955, in various locations around Sacramento. Child actor Richard Eyer, who played Sheridan's son, recalled to this author, "It was very hot in Ione during the filming." Apparently, it wasn't just the temperature that heated things up as there were loud whispers of a sexual relationship between Sheridan and Cochran, well known for his highly publicized romantic escapades.

Making his acting debut was James Westmoreland (appearing under the name Rad Fulton). In an interview, he recalled that Sheridan was as lovely and classy as could be. Ann came up to me one day and said, "Rad, if you were only 20 years older, I could really go for you." She would often wink at me, and kiss me on the cheek. That woman was class personified. Working with her and all those wonderful people was one of the greatest experiences of my life.[18]

Jack Benny hoped to entice Sheridan to reunite with him on television for the *Shower of Stars* adaptation of "Time Out for Ginger." It was later reported that she turned down the role as the mother of a *teenage* daughter. Ruth Hussey, who did not let her vanity get in the way of an acting job, played the part instead.

Sheridan remained inactive on both the big and small screen for much of 1955, although it was frequently reported that she was going to produce a series of TV shows in Mexico City with Acosta. With the budget for this venture listed at $1.2 million, Sheridan and Acosta intended to reshoot the unsold *Assignment in Las Vegas* pilot under the title of *Assignment in Mexico* for Tara Films. That deal fell through; both Sheridan and Acosta were later sued by theatrical producer Edward Sartu for repayment of his loan of $16,000 toward the project. The matter was settled out of court in 1959. The *Assignment in Mexico* pilot was eventually filmed with Peggie Castle in the role intended for Sheridan.

In late 1955, Sheridan was offered a substantial supporting role in MGM's CinemaScope-Metrocolor remake of the brittle comedy *The Women* (1939). The 1939 original featured an all-female cast including Norma Shearer, Joan Crawford and Rosalind Russell. The updated version, conceived as a musical, was titled *The Opposite Sex* and featured June Allyson, Joan Collins, Dolores Gray, Ann Miller, Agnes Moorehead and Joan Blondell in important roles. With the high-powered lineup, the publicity department hoped for some on-the-set catfights, especially with the third wife of Dick Powell (Allyson) appearing alongside Powell's second wife (Blondell). No such luck. As Sheridan told interviewer Wanda Hale, "No fireworks. There wasn't one unpleasant moment. We were all angelic. Hedda [Hopper] paid me a visit, hoping to get a good story about a feud or an explosion of temper. She was so disappointed she left saying it was too dull for her."[19]

While working on *The Opposite Sex*, Sheridan was still on the lookout for a TV series to star in. "Finding a good series isn't easy," she told Bob Thomas. "I wish I could tell you how many times I have sat down and listened to ideas. 'Fine,' I say, 'but let me see a script.' When the script comes, it's awful."[20]

On February 1, 1956, *Come Next Spring* premiered in Little Rock, Arkansas, one month before its nationwide release. The movie takes place in Arkansas in 1927. A stranger coming into town turns out to be Matt Ballot (Cochran), an alcoholic who abandoned his family nine years earlier. Now sober, he wishes to reunite with his wife Bess (Sheridan) and mute daughter Annie (Jackson). Bess is reluctant to let Matt back into their lives and her heart, but she relents and allows him to stay there as hired hand. Matt is surprised that Bess bore him a son after his departure. It is not long before Bess and the children appreciate having Matt back in their lives, but the townsfolk are not so quick to forgive Matt for deserting his family. "Come next spring" (an oft-repeated phrase uttered throughout), Matt has proven himself a reformed man who wins back the respect of the community as well as his family.

Film Bulletin echoed the sentiments of many critics: "[It's] a warm and pleasant film. Heavy with sentiment, it also has a good deal of charm about it.... Under

R.G. Springsteen's competent, well-paced direction, and with fine performances by Ann Sheridan, Steve Cochran, and a topflight supporting cast, the story springs to life." Unfortunately, Republic chose to release the film on the bottom half of double bills. Despite the positive reviews and favorable word-of-mouth, Republic failed to market the feature properly. Republic's neglect prompted this response from *The Hollywood Reporter*: "Wake up, Republic. You have another *Marty* [1955] on your hands.... Or don't you care?"[21]

Sheridan later expressed her disappointment to John Kobal:

> That was a good little picture.... If it had been sold properly, it could have done well. But, unfortunately, it was part of Steve Cochran's package for Republic and Herbert Yates didn't care if it sold or not. It was supposed to

The fabled "Oomph Girl" surfaced briefly in this bathing scene from *Come Next Spring* (1956), a family drama she hoped would rejuvenate her motion picture career.

have A bookings all over the place. Well, it didn't. No point in crying over it, but it could have done well. But they had this personal feud going on between Steve and Yates, and the film paid for it. But I never got better word of mouth and reviews than for that.... It was a good part, a good picture. It was a sleeper that was never allowed to wake up.[22]

Sheridan always cited *Come Next Spring* as her favorite among her movies. It contains one of her most affecting and mature performances and is well worth the watch. Richard Eyer echoed her sentiments: "I agree that the movie is highly underrated. I think it was excellent." As far as his recollections of working with Sheridan, he admitted, "[M]y memories of Ann Sheridan, as well as Steve Cochran, are minimal. She was sweet and motherly, never a bad moment."

With the help of her agent, Sheridan appeared on several television programs, mostly in guest spots. On August 14, 1956, *Assignment in Las Vegas* was televised as *Calling Terry Conway*. The 30-minute pilot went unnoticed by the viewing public and critics. The producers' promise of another hit show had fallen flat.

While in production with *The Opposite Sex*, Sheridan was contacted about a new film project entitled *Woman and the Hunter*. She told Parsons, "I received the script a week ago and the same day I accepted Jack Gross and Phil Krasna's offer. You can imagine how I had to hurry since the picture starts June 11 and I was still busy on *The Opposite Sex*. In *Woman and the Hunter*, I play a woman who cares only for money and finally gets killed."[23] It certainly was a different type of role for Sheridan. What cinched the deal was the producers' plan to use color photography while filming on location in Nairobi. It was an offer she really could not refuse. Unfortunately, this project proved to be an unmitigated disaster from the start. At least she got an African trip out of the deal.

The shoot proved to be a low-budget affair after both Gross and Krasna bailed out. A new producer, Brian Robson, who had recently produced *Escape in the Sun* in Africa, was brought in to salvage the project. He instituted cost-cutting measures to minimize production cost. After some footage was shot, it was decided to ditch the costly color photography and resume filming in black-and-white. One wonders if Sheridan even knew of the switch as her garish makeup in some scenes would have been only suitable for color.

Filming lasted roughly a month and Sheridan took some time to explore Nairobi. By the time she arrived back in the States in September, she had fallen in love with Kenya.

Shortly after her return, she made a guest appearance on the show *I've Got a Secret*, in which she surprised panelist Henry Morgan with a trip to Africa so she could go back! She later told Hagen, "I adored Africa, would give my neck to go back tomorrow."[24]

While waiting for *Woman and the Hunter* to be released, Sheridan once again turned to television for acting jobs. A proposed pilot for a comedy series would have featured Sheridan as a widowed mother of two preteen boys, but the pilot was never shot. One of the most interesting projects was a television biography based on the life of Perle Mesta, a popular Washington, D.C., hostess and former U.S. ambassador to Luxembourg. Mesta was the inspiration for Ethel Merman's character in the Broadway production and movie version of *Call Me Madam*. The *Playhouse 90* episode was released in 1957 as "The Hostess with the Mostess'" with Shirley Booth as Sheridan's replacement.

Near the end of October, *The Opposite Sex* was released with great fanfare. Fourth-billed Sheridan (as Amanda) provides the voiceover narration as the storyline centers around Kay Hilliard (Allyson, in her last role as an MGM contract star), a former night club singer, who discovers that her husband Steve (Leslie Nielsen) is having an affair with crass showgirl Crystal Allen (Collins). Making the situation worse is that Kay learns she is the last in her circle of gossiping friends to learn of her husband's infidelity. After Kay obtains her Reno divorce, Steve marries the gold-digging Crystal, then realizes he has made a big mistake. When Kay finds out that Crystal is cheating on Stephen, she decides that it's time to win him back by any means necessary.

The Opposite Sex was immediately dismissed by many critics who compared it unfavorably to its predecessor. With a recorded loss of $1.5 million at the box office, the feature marked Sheridan's *eighth* motion picture that proved a box office loser.

With impeccable timing, as the subject of divorce played out on the big screen, Sheridan's own affair with Acosta became fodder for salacious gossip after his wife Jeanine filed for divorce. In the suit, she charged Sheridan with adultery. An arrest warrant in Mexico City was issued for Sheridan for failing to respond to several subpoenas regarding the charge. The matter was dropped after Acosta reunited with his wife. It was reported that Acosta, who had been estranged from Jeanine since 1950, had once threatened to kill her if she persisted with divorce proceedings. The couple continued their contentious marriage until he won his divorce decree in 1959 based on Jeanine's acts of cruelty. Meanwhile, it was reported that Sheridan found consolation in the arms of Jacques Mapes.

Sheridan turned once again to TV in hopes of a worthwhile series. She told Hagen, "Lots have been offered, and have been just plain bad. A lot had some halfway decent writing, but the minute an agent or producer tells me 'This is like *The Lucy Show*,' I don't want it. I don't want to compete with Lucy—I would be an idiot."[25] Until a series materialized, she had to settle for guest starring roles on anthology series like *Lux Video Theatre* and *The Ford Television Theatre.* One show that showed great promise was *Playhouse 90*'s "Without Incident," which reteamed her with her old friend Errol Flynn. It was earmarked as a special program as it was one of the few *Playhouse 90*s filmed on location in Arizona and shot on film instead of being filmed in front of a live audience. By this time, however, Flynn was in his late forties and in poor health. He had trouble remembering his lines, which caused frequent delays. It was also a sad waste of Sheridan's talents as her role was far less interesting than co-star Julie London's (London was cast as her promiscuous sister). Despite the sad state of affairs, however, the episode has bittersweet moments as we watch two former co-stars play together again. This effect has been referred as "doubling," a term originated by French film critic Andre Bazin. Author Marc Eliot defined doubling as a "cinematic phenomenon … wherein the characters in a film mirror the relationship between the characters in real life, with the resultant sparks supercharged— the reality of the actors' lives off-screen adding depth to the lives of the characters they portray."[26] "Without Incident" proved to be their last appearance together. Sheridan was greatly saddened when she learned of Flynn's death at the age of 50 in October 1959. She later reflected on her friend: "He was one of the wild characters of the world, but he had a strange, quiet side. He camouflaged himself completely. In all the years I knew him, I never really knew what lay underneath and I doubt if many people did."[27]

When film roles dwindled, Sheridan turned to television with increasing frequency. She is pictured here with Ernie Glucksman, who directed many of her television appearances.

"Without Incident" was presented on June 6 to indifferent criticism and lackluster viewership. Reportedly, Sheridan was so disheartened by her aging appearance, she underwent cosmetic surgery. She was not ready to settle into mother roles just yet.

Despite the recent disappointments, Sheridan's career appeared to be on the rebound with the constant stream of offers and publicity, leading one columnist to observe, "Annie's career is getting very bright again."[28]

The promise of a career revival, however, failed to materialize. With the release of *Woman and the Hunter* on hold indefinitely, Sheridan's movie future looked rather bleak. Television offers weren't all that hot either. Never one to give up, Sheridan left Mexico City behind and resettled in New York City. It was time to pursue acting opportunities in a new venue—the stage.

SEVENTEEN

Annie, Get Your Guy!

*I wish I had nerve enough to do a play, but going out there every single
night and giving what a stage performer has to give would terrify me.*[1]

Sheridan spoke these words in 1948, marveling at Ethel Merman's powerhouse
performance in the hit musical *Annie Get Your Gun*. While still at the peak of her
beauty and popularity, Sheridan did not need to leave the comforts of movie sound
stages to stretch her theatrical wings in front of a live audience. By 1957, however,
with film offers all but dried up and decent television roles hard to come by, Sheridan
decided that it was time to try her luck on the stage. The idea of retiring from acting
was unthinkable. Many of her peers from the Warner Brothers lot had long entered
into the theater world with varying degrees of success: Bette Davis, Joan Blondell,
Margaret Lindsay, Olivia de Havilland. Broadway was a far stretch for many, but there
was still an appreciative audience for the old favorites on stage around the country.

In May 1957, it was announced that Sheridan would assume the Rosalind Russell
role in *Auntie Mame* on a national tour, beginning in San Francisco. She must have
thought that a major touring production of the hit play was too daunting a risk, so
she backed out; no fewer than three actresses (Constance Bennett, Sylvia Sidney and
Eve Arden) toured the country with separate companies to great success. Sheridan
recalled also being offered Russell's role in a tour of *Wonderful Town*. "[H]oney, you
just don't walk in where Miss Russell has been," she told Kobal. "You cannot improve
on that."[2]

The play that finally brought Sheridan out of her year-long period of inactivity
was Norman Krasna's romantic comedy *Kind Sir*. The original production had a mod-
estly successful Broadway run during the 1953–54 season with Charles Boyer and
Mary Martin; it later came to the movies as the sparkling romantic comedy *Indis-
creet* (1958) with Cary Grant and Ingrid Bergman.

The director, Gus Schirmer, sent Sheridan the script and she loved it. She agreed
to the proposed run of 15 weeks of summer stock (often referred to as the "Straw-
hat Circuit"), with the opening scheduled for East Hampton, Long Island, on June
28. When asked why she took the engagement, Sheridan replied, "Because there is
a chance that *Kind Sir* will be made into a Broadway musical for me. Never having
appeared on Broadway, I thought I had better get my feet wet in summer stock, first!"[3]

The lightweight plot proved sufficient for summer stock fare. Sheridan was seen
to advantage as a glamorous actress who pursues a handsome diplomat (Scott McKay)
despite his proclamation that he is a married man. Sheridan recalled to Hagen that
the script veered away from the romantic feel of the original. Instead, the touring

production played it for sophisticated comedy. "I think we had a fairly good success with it," she noted with satisfaction.[4]

The early reviews were positive for the headliner. According to the *Syracuse Post-Standard*, "Movie star Ann Sheridan bewitched an audience." The play itself was mostly trifling and flimsy—which demonstrated that it was the Boyer-Martin combination that accounted for the length of its Broadway run. With less experienced actors, *Kind Sir* would have died a much earlier death on Broadway. Nonetheless, the early box office returns convinced the producers to depart from the normal engagement of smaller venues and take Detroit and Chicago by storm in late July.

The metropolitan critics proved much harder to please. The *Detroit Free Press* offered faint praise for both the play and its star: "Ann Sheridan ... decorates the role of Jane Kimball with her famed beauty and a dazzling array of costumes.... Miss Sheridan contributes to the salvage job, if for no other reason than being consistently on cue. Her staging is deliberate and her delivery of lines rather brittle." The *Chicago Sun-Times* praised Sheridan's physical charms, but sniped that her acting was "lamentably limited."[5]

Despite these harsh words, *Kind Sir* turned out to be a successful venture. The *Oneonta Star* duly noted, "Ann Sheridan got some of the worst reviews this side of the Cherry states when she opened in Chicago in *Kind Sir* but is proving more popular with the audiences than the critics."[6]

Kind Sir with Sheridan proved a major draw in a season that included film luminaries Mae West, Groucho Marx, Jeanette MacDonald, Don Ameche, Dorothy Lamour and Margaret Sullavan. The producers, still feeling the sting of the Detroit and Chicago critics, decided to cancel plans for a musical adaptation on Broadway.

The summer stock tour was a lark for those involved, especially for Sheridan's new leading man, Scott McKay. She recalled in 1966, "We had fun and laughed, and enjoyed the ten weeks we did together very much. I saw Scott off and on from then on."[7] The only fly in the ointment was the fact that McKay was married.

McKay accompanied Sheridan in her next theatrical appearance, William Saroyan's Pulitzer Prize–winning play *The Time of Your Life*, at the Brussels Universal Exposition; the week-long engagement began October 8. Almost on cue,

Sheridan's third husband was stage actor Scott McKay. Their relationship provided her with the happiness and security lacking in her prior marriages.

rumors of a Sheridan-McKay affair began circulating after the close of the production. Dorothy Kilgallen was one of the first to spread it: "Broadway's hottest rumor has it that Ann Sheridan will marry an actor en route to Brussels with her—as soon as he can get a divorce from his wife."[8]

McKay was born Carl Cose on May 28, 1915, in Pleasantville, Iowa. He attended the University of Colorado, majoring in English literature; at one time, he was a professor of English literature. His first experience in the theater was acting as the straight man for a magician. Bitten by the acting bug, he joined several stock companies to learn his craft.

After a stint with the Depression-inspired WPA (Federal) Theatre, Cose headed to New York City and made his Broadway debut as a member of the ensemble in the Fredric March starrer, *The American Way* (1939). The following year, he played a small speaking role in the national touring production of the hit comedy *The Man Who Came to Dinner*; next came small parts in several short-lived Broadway productions and bigger parts with summer stock work.

In the summer of 1940, Cose met Margaret Spickers while both were appearing at the Woodstock Playhouse in Woodstock, New York. Spickers and Cose tried their luck on Broadway, with Spickers (adopting the stage name Margaret Power) beating him in the publicity game when she was featured in a four-page pictorial in the October 20, 1941, issue of *Life* magazine. The article, titled "Broadway Hopeful Margaret Power Sets Out to Crash the Stage," touted her as an upcoming Broadway actress.[9] "Crash" she did, as the exposure failed to improve her Broadway prospects .

The couple married in October 1942 and had two sons, Anthony and Peter. Spickers retired from acting to care for their children, while Cose continued to act in Broadway productions. With his versatility in both dramas and comedies, he continued to be in great demand although most of the productions were short-lived. In 1943, he finally found success in a notable play, *The Eve of St. Mark*. That play caught the attention of Hollywood scouts, who scooped up Cose and the play's star, William Eythe.

Cose adopted the professional name Scott McKay and made his movie debut in *Thirty Seconds Over Tokyo* (1944). After three other less-than-inspiring film appearances (*Guest in the House*, 1944; *Kiss and Tell*, 1945; *Duel in the Sun*, 1946), McKay returned to Broadway to try his luck again.

His stint in motion pictures paid off: He now had no trouble securing acting jobs. After playing Oscar Hubbard in Broadway's *Another Part of the Forest* (1946), McKay finally hit his comic stride as the replacement for Gary Merrill in *Born Yesterday* as Paul Verrall, both on Broadway and the national touring company. During this time, McKay became acquainted with actress Joan Morgan (playing the role of Billie Dawn in *Born Yesterday*). After his divorce from Spickers in 1950, she became his second wife.

Morgan's success with *Born Yesterday* had her tagged as the latest Broadway "Cinderella" in the making. But like Spickers, she was stymied in her attempts at Broadway fame. She continued acting in small roles (at times, she found no better jobs than understudy), while McKay's career continued to surge with significant supporting roles in the successful Broadway production *Bell, Book and Candle* (1950) with Rex Harrison and Lilli Palmer; he replaced John Forsythe as Captain Fisby in *The Teahouse of the August Moon*; and appeared with Margaret Sullavan and Joseph

Cotten in *Sabrina Fair* (1953). He continued to act in touring productions and summer stock. McKay was also a regular face on television, appearing in several shows, including the short-lived Celeste Holm series *Honestly Celeste!* (1954). No one could accuse McKay of being lazy!

The McKay-Morgan union began to disintegrate due to professional jealousy and suspicions of marital infidelity. By the end of 1958, their marriage was in shambles and Morgan had strong reasons to believe that McKay was engaged in an affair with the glamorous Ann Sheridan.

Meanwhile, Sheridan had returned to Hollywood in December to film the episode "Dark Cloud" for the *Pursuit* anthology TV series. At that time, she spoke with Joe Finnigan about her career prospects. "I won't do a movie for another two years unless I find one I like," she stated. "Good stories are hard to come by. But that's nothing, there was a time when I didn't make a picture for five years." She also had some advice for the Silver Screen's new leading ladies: put some clothes on. "They would look a little better if they dressed up a little. The leading lady of today is aimed at the teenagers, but this too shall pass.... They emphasize the bustline more than they did when I started and they wear less clothes now.... I was as flat-chested as anything you could imagine." Looking back, Sheridan admitted, "I wasn't struggling to be a glamour girl. I wanted to be an actress."[10]

In July, Sheridan and McKay appeared together in *Kind Sir* at the Grist Mill Playhouse in Andover, New Jersey. The *Newark Star-Ledger* praised the "radiant, dynamic Ann Sheridan [who] proved last night that she is as talented an actress as she is a lovely woman."[11] The success of the week-long engagement showed that there was still money-making magic to be made with the Ann Sheridan name among theatergoers.

A play that attracted Sheridan's attention was the three-character *Odd Man In.* Playwright Robin Maugham had adapted the popular 1956 French farce, *Monsieur Masure*, and it played for a year in London starting in the summer of 1957. Its tried-and-true plot was simple (a bored wife becomes innocently involved with a traveler in need of a telephone in order to make her husband jealous). If handled with the right touch, it could be a solid moneymaker.

When initially approached, Sheridan doubted that the play would be good enough for Broadway. "When I read *Odd Man In*, I thought it delightful," she told interviewers. "I knew the part was for me."[12]

From the beginning, there was some disagreement between the producers and Sheridan about embarking on a long tour before hitting Broadway. Ross Hunter convinced Sheridan that touring would give her the stage experience she needed without the stress of combatting the hard-to-please Broadway critics. Hunter considered bringing his own play, *Vermillion O'Toole* to Broadway with Sheridan as his star.

Sheridan won out and a five-month tour was arranged prior to the Broadway engagement. "Why should we in the theater think only of one small island," she reasoned, "when the important theatre-goers by the millions are scattered all over the country? As far as I'm concerned, Broadway can wait. I've been grateful to my fans over the years and I'm happy that I shall be able to play for them in their towns."[13] The tour was sponsored by the Broadway Theatre League.

During the summer-long rehearsal, Sheridan spoke with interviewer Philip Scheuer about the differences between film and stage acting.

> Sure, the theater is harder in the sense that you have to sustain a mood over a longer period, but it's also easier for the same reason. On the stage, you have time to build an art and improve it from performance to performance until you can approach perfection. Not so in the films. There you jump from one scene to another, with each scene often requiring an entirely different mood from one preceding it. Yes, you can cut a poor scene and do it over, but once it's approved and on film, you have to live with it the rest of your life.

When asked if she was nervous about the opening night's performance of *Odd Man In*, Sheridan replied, "Of course I am nervous, but I'll be all right on stage. I've found if you just keep talking so you don't allow yourself to think too much, the potential problems melt away."[14]

But the problems were just beginning. When *Odd Man In* kicked off its tour in Wilmington, Delaware, on October 1, it was clear there was much work to be done. The *Variety* review of the Baltimore performance set the tone for the rest of the tour. The critic noted, "The plan to tour *Odd Man In* … throughout winter months before taking its Broadway presentation next spring, seems sensible for the show needs extensive revisions." The cast were lauded for their efforts: "There is little reason to carp with the players. Miss Sheridan displays a nice sense of comedy, which is no surprise. She handles her lines with ease and good timing." In the critic's final estimation, "*Odd Man In* is light-weight farce suitable for summer stock, but below par for Broadway." According to the *Baltimore News Post*, "Ann Sheridan is quite attractive, especially in her more serious moments. We trust that she will quickly acquire the deftly light, boisterous touch so essential to the performance of comedy."

The reviews in the early stands of the tour were mixed for both the play and its star. Sheridan shouldered some of the blame in her usual honest, self-deprecating fashion. "I don't have the characterization down yet," she admitted. "It will be a long time before I do."[15] She did know that the major fault lay with the script and pressured the producers to revise it, but to no avail. After its five-day Pittsburgh engagement, the producers decided to continue the tour in one- to two-night stands throughout the country. Sheridan quickly became disenchanted with the whole affair. "[The producers] only intended to make as much money as they could," she told Ray Hagen. "[It was the] hard way to learn about the theater…. I made the mistake in *Odd Man In* of accepting their word, which was strictly phony. I should have learned in Hollywood, about believing people."[16]

The ten-day engagements in various Texas cities during January, 1960, proved to be popular due to theatergoers wanting to see their own Texan girl in the flesh. The *Dallas Morning News* raved, "Miss Sheridan showed snappy timing, an assured and unabashed stage presence, and an ability to project the Sheridan qualities that have intrigued millions and still titillates. As for the 'Oomph,' it is still there in quantity."[17]

As the tour was winding down in late February, newspaper headlines suddenly exploded with the scandalous allegations of Sheridan's affair with McKay. McKay's wife's attorney claimed in New York Superior Court that McKay walked out on his wife due to an ongoing affair with Sheridan. McKay emphatically denied any wrongdoing: "There is nothing to comment on…. My lawyers have answered for me."[18] His lawyer Michael F. Mayer was quick to respond to the charges: "I object to this loose charge of adultery…. He is in a play with Ann Sheridan and there is nothing improper with their relationship."[19]

At first, Sheridan hid from the press and her manager declined to comment on the matter. After a few days, Sheridan spoke out, calling the rumors "a lot of nonsense, ridiculous." She also declared that she and McKay "are professional associates and that is all."[20]

Amidst the sensational news, the producers shut down *Odd Man In* in Burlington, Iowa, on March 5. With this trying experience behind her, Sheridan vented to the press: "The show stinks."[21] She laid much of the blame on the playwright who failed to rewrite the script as originally promised and the director, who had deserted the production shortly after the premiere. Sheridan told Kobal the play was an "atrocity" and called the experience "a period of tryouts and tribulations."[22]

Despite the play's failure, Maugham still harbored the hope of a Broadway run in the fall of 1960 and rewrote *Odd Man In*. The play eventually had a week-long summer stock engagement in Carlisle, Pennsylvania. After that fiasco, Maugham finally had enough sense to lay the whole wretched thing to rest.

Meanwhile, back on the Sheridan-McKay affair front, McKay gave newspapers his side of the story in late March: "In every instance, in every show that I was in, there was always somebody [my wife] was jealous of. She accused me on numerous occasions of having affairs. I never had an affair with Miss Sheridan then or now. I never told my wife that I did."[23]

After the failure of *Odd Man In*, the fallout from Joan Morgan's public shaming, and the ensuing bitter divorce battle, Sheridan was exhausted both mentally and physically. She limited her appearances to two guest spots (including singing "Guess Who I Saw Today" on *The Perry Como Show*) and a starring role in the *United States Steel Hour* episode "The Imposter." By midsummer, she decided she had had enough. It was time to quit the acting profession and devote her energy and time to her relationship with McKay.

EIGHTEEN

This Time It's Different

I'm terribly, terribly emotional about the old days at Warners and Paramount. The crews then and all the people were so wonderful to work with.[1]

From the early 1920s to the late 1950s, during the Golden Age of Hollywood, major studios dominated the motion pictures industry and amassed great fortunes by catering to the whims and wishes of moviegoers. Studio heads Louis B. Mayer, Darryl F. Zanuck and Jack L. Warner controlled every aspect of filmmaking from their roster of actors, screen material, production crew and the distribution of the final product.

That all changed with the historic 1948 *United States v. Paramount* case: The Supreme Court ruled that the major studios had violated anti-trust laws. This decision stipulated that the studios could no longer operate as they had for nearly three decades. The effect was not immediately felt but, with the combination of the growing popularity of television and rising costs of film production, the Golden Age was on a steady decline throughout the 1950s. The Studio Star System was fading away.

Sheridan recalled to John Kobal a time when she visited Warner Brothers in 1952. Cary Grant and his wife, actress Betsy Drake, were making *Room for One More* and invited a group of friends to the studio for lunch. "I was driving onto the lot, wondering if they'd let me on it even because I hadn't been there in so long I didn't know if the cop still knew me. Well—you could have shot a cannon down the street. There was nobody. No crew. None of the people I knew.... It was like an old friend dying."[2] By the early 1960s, that "friend" was no longer recognizable. Some of her dear friends like Bogart and Flynn passed away years prior and other former colleagues retired from the acting business. Only a handful like Bette Davis and Joan Crawford refused to go away. Hollywood just wasn't the same any more.

Her year-and-a-half sabbatical from acting was spent with McKay, who was still active on stage. On one occasion, she accompanied him on his summer stock engagements. Film historian–author James Robert Parish shared his recollections about his early theatrical experiences with this author:

The week of July 10–15, 1961, Scott McKay and Susan Oliver (along with William Redfield) came through with their tour of *Under the Yum Yum Tree*.... On the Sunday (July 9, 1961) before the July 10 opening, I was backstage at the theater up in the rafters area where there was a room in which permanent props were stored. As I was sorting through potential props to fill out the needed items for *Under the Yum Yum Tree*, I heard a very distinctive low voice on the stage below. It could only have been Ann Sheridan! I was able to peer down from the entrance to the prop room to the stage below and saw a woman dressed in black slacks with a black hooded jacket (and wearing sunglasses) walking about the stage with lead player Scott McKay. The two of them chatted a bit about the layout of the set for his play and then left. Scott McKay and Ann Sheridan were housed in a star cottage on a street within walking distance from the theater. During the week I never spotted Sheridan again, not even at the Cape Playhouse restaurant on the property where cast, theatergoers and Playhouse staff often went after the evening performance.

As Sheridan continued her self-imposed retirement, some genius decided it was time to unleash *Woman and the Hunter* on unsuspecting moviegoers. Throughout much of 1961 and 1962, it was shown as *Triangle on Safari* in England, Australia, Mexico and several Latin American countries on the bottom half of double bills. The feature was never released theatrically in the United States. Much to Sheridan's chagrin, however, it made its American television debut in 1966. "It made sense in the script," she admitted to Hagen, "but the way they cut it, it made no sense whatsoever."[3]

For once, Sheridan was not exaggerating. By far, *Woman and the Hunter* is Sheridan's worst film, and there were some strong contenders for that honor. The laughably absurd plot focuses on a predatory vixen (Sheridan) who bumps off the rich lover (he refused to marry her) so that she can marry his worthless son for his inheritance. Meanwhile, she tags along on a safari so she can seduce the tour guide on the side. This man she claims to really love—or does she? When she plots the husband's demise, the screenplay kills her off during an elephant stampede. It is all cheap, cheesy and not much fun to watch with Sheridan woefully miscast as the chain-smoking vixen.

Sheridan returned to acting when she appeared in *Kind Sir* at Chicago's Drury Lane Theatre on January 25, 1962. This performance marked the last time she appeared on the legitimate stage. She then returned to the small screen in June for a guest starring role in *Wagon Train.* She was assigned the title character in the episode "The Mavis Grant Story." "It's good to be back in the Old West again playing an old meanie," she joked in an interview. She was grateful for the job as "[t]hey're not making pictures for women my age." Coyly defining "age" as "mature," she lamented that the "only thing that comes along for a mature woman to play is a teenager's mother."[4]

On October 11, 1962, McKay's estranged wife Joan Morgan, 43 years old, was found dead in her Manhattan apartment. She was reportedly despondent over her stalled acting career and her failed marriage. The medical examiner ruled it an "apparent suicide from a possible overdose of an unknown drug, possibly sleeping pills."[5] There's reason to believe that Morgan suffered from mental illness, but that didn't stop the loud whispers that it was the Sheridan-McKay affair that drove her to self-destruction.

"The Mavis Grant Story" aired on October 24. Sheridan plays a hate-filled, greedy woman who offers access to her ample water supply to a band of thirsty travelers—but at an exorbitant price that the travelers can ill afford. The stand-off between Grant and the travelers become a life-and-death situation until the character's change of heart at the finale.

Ann Sheridan fans must have been shocked: Not only did she play an unsympathetic character, but the camera did little justice to her aging appearance. She looked nothing like the glamorous movie star they so fondly remembered. Seeing her image must have sparked a visit to the doctor for a facelift, because her appearance significantly improved afterwards. As McKay continued with his career in the wildly popular *Mary, Mary* on national tour before playing the role on Broadway, Sheridan was content to remain in the background. After he began rehearsals for *Once for the Asking* in the fall of 1963, Sheridan made TV appearances on the series *Missing Links, The Keefe Brasselle Show* and *Talent Scouts.* She accepted an offer from the producers of *To Tell the Truth* to join the panel. "Why am I going on? Because they asked me," she told an interviewer. "I haven't been on these shows in the past simply because they didn't ask me. Now, I feel that I'm working my way up to College Bowl." When asked if she was interested in resuming her acting career, she replied, "Oh, I'd like to do a musical, the right one. But movie musicals don't seem to come across, do they? I've seen a number of the old great ones on TV, and they've been terrifying. They don't hold up."[6] In her opinion, *Kings Row, City for Conquest* and *I Was a Male War Bride* have held up much better than most old films shown on television.

Sheridan continued making the rounds of daytime game shows from 1963 to 1965. These appearances didn't mean much, except to keep her face in front of television viewers. When asked if she would return to filmmaking, Sheridan replied with a wry, knowing smile. "Today it's all 'Singing in the Surf' pictures. If you can't ride a surfboard, you're out of work. There are a few good parts being written for women my age, but Roz Russell gets those. The rest of us stand in line."[7] Indeed, the pickings were pretty slim by this time. For every powerhouse role (such as in *Gypsy*), Russell had to contend with schlock like *Oh Dad, Poor Dad, Mamma's Hung You in the Closet and I'm Feelin' So Sad* (1967); Davis, Crawford and de Havilland had entered into the cheesy (but admittedly fun) horror film genre. Only Lana Turner clung tightly to her glamorous image, but unfortunately chose to grace such clunkers as *Bachelor in Paradise* (1961) and *Who's Got the Action?* (1962).

In 1964, there was talk that Sheridan would star in a musical play about Aimee Semple McPherson, the Pentecostal evangelist who became a celebrity in the 1920s and 1930s. When the project was pitched to Sheridan, she agreed to consider it as long as McPherson's life was accurately portrayed. She even met with McPherson's daughter, Mrs. David Salter, to gain insight into the woman. When the writers failed to develop the concept into a workable script, Sheridan, still feeling the sting of *Odd Man In*, decided against the play. She claimed that her agent had acted too hastily and "was out of his cotton-pickin' mind."[8] She elaborated to Hagen on the type of plays she would rather do: "I love comedy, I adore it. I'd like to find a good part in a straight play, I don't care whether it's a starring role or not."[9]

Pal Ross Hunter offered Sheridan the part of a French madam in a film, *The Art of Love* (1965). "I didn't feel right for that," she explained to Kobal. "I won't do just anything to have a job."[10] Ethel Merman took the part.

In 1966, Sheridan received an acting offer she couldn't refuse: the role of Katherine Corning in the daytime soap opera *Another World.* There was considerable news coverage as soap opera shows were considered something of a comedown for the actress. "Ann Sheridan Tumbles from Movie Queen to Soap Operas" was one headline.[11] She didn't care what the naysayers said. After all, former glamour girl Joan Bennett was also facing the daytime cameras with *Dark Shadows.* Sheridan was just glad to be acting again. "I'm going to love it!" she enthused. "There's no time to feel around in this medium of television."[12] There was talk of Sheridan starting on the show in mid–November, but her appearance was delayed when the producers realized there was a great deal of fan interest and decided to flesh out her role from its sporadic appearances to something more regular.

With the renewed attention from the press, there were the old references to the "Oomph Girl" title, such as this *New York Times* headline: "Actress Lends 'Oomph' to Soaps."[13] Sheridan asserted that she only wanted to be known as "[a] good actress. But I suppose I can't get away from that Ann Sheridan Oomph thing. I wish I could. But most people still come up and ask about that dumb—oh, it's horrible."[14]

Sheridan was asked if she would soon be working on the soaper. "Yes," she replied, "if I am not overexposed—if I don't have to be on every day, just once or twice a week."[15] After the initial episodes were filmed, Sheridan revealed that she was playing "a woman looking for a purpose. That's all I've done for several shows. I frankly don't know yet just what the character will be or which way it will go…. I thought I was going to be an actress playing an actress, but there's been no hint of that yet. The role can go any number of ways and that's another thing that makes daytime TV so interesting."[16]

Despite having to get up by 4 a.m., "I love the soaps," she told an interviewer. "It may be that the writing is not the greatest in the world, but the photography is good. I do my own makeup and my own hair."[17] Her initial trepidation in working with young TV actors proved to be unfounded as she appreciated their professional courtesy and helpfulness.

John Kobal recalled her appearance on the soap opera: "The face had edged where once it curved—for 'oomph' there was 'chic'— but an alertness about her acting made you sit up, and intelligence at work made her role believable, and though she had changed from the glamorous pinup, she looked very handsome."[18]

It wasn't until she began work on her own television series *Pistols 'n' Petticoats* that Sheridan told the truth about her experience with *Another World*:

> I'd never done a soap opera before, and, if I'd known what was in store for me, I'd have said "no" to the whole thing. I was

After years without any success, Sheridan finally landed a hit television series: a goofy take-off on Westerns, *Pistols 'n' Petticoats*.

supposed to work in the show just two days a week, but somehow I ended up doing it four days a week. That's several thousand lines a week to learn, and although I've always been able to learn easily, I found myself pushing harder than I've ever pushed before to stay ahead. It was hectic, but I've learned a lot from it.[19]

In December 1965, Sheridan received an offer from TV producer Joe Connelly about filming a pilot for a Western spoof called *Pistols 'n' Petticoats*. The show was created by George Tibbles, one of the writers of the popular Fred MacMurray sitcom *My Three Sons*. The script for the pilot appealed to her sense of humor: "I've had numerous pilot offers, but this felt like it would be great fun to do so I accepted producer Joe Connelly's offer."[20] Connelly was a prolific screenwriter-producer who, with Bob Mosher, was the team responsible for the hit TV series *Leave It to Beaver* and *The Munsters*. Excited by the creative talents involved, Sheridan agreed to fly out to Hollywood to film the pilot.

While doing so, she chatted with columnist Vernon Scott:

I hope the show sells. It could be a lot of fun. I play a mother in this one too.... My role is a combination of Annie Oakley and Calamity Jane. I guess I've worked in enough Westerns in my life to feel at home in the part. Like everyone else, I've read dozens of scripts for television series, but almost all of them are slush. But this pilot is a very funny show, the kind an actress can look forward to doing. I'm keeping my fingers crossed.[21]

While awaiting to hear if the pilot was picked up, Sheridan flew back to New York and continued on *Another World*. With the exposure to a younger audience, Sheridan experienced renewed interest from fans. She was inundated with requests for interviews. The Golden Age of Hollywood Nostalgia Craze was just beginning and Sheridan was pushed back into the limelight—and she loved every minute of it.

Ray Hagen interviewed her in 1966 for *Screen Facts* magazine. Interviewed by "John" of the "Remembering Ann Sheridan" website, Hagen fondly recalled his interviews with Sheridan:

What I was delighted to find was that the Ann Sheridan that I'd seen on the screen for all those years, that "good Joe" kinda girl, funny and bright, was exactly what she was like. The Ann Sheridan you saw in those movies was who I was talking to those many hours. That was her.... She looked great. She looked like I thought she'd look because I'd seen recent photographs of her—but better.[22]

In April 1966, Sheridan received the news that *Pistols 'n' Petticoats* had been picked up by a sponsor. At long last, she had her own TV series. She completed her commitment to *Another World*, packed up her bags and headed out to California.

With her acting career back on track and McKay's career still red-hot, it was time for the two of them to decide on the next step of their eight-year relationship. Both of them had been hesitant about marriage since both were twice married and endured bitter divorces. "I don't think I'm qualified to advise anybody on marriage," Sheridan admitted to interviewer James Gregory. "After all, I had two divorces in my life. I wanted to be moderately sure I'd found the right guy. I'm pretty sure I have...."[23] McKay felt the same way, and the couple finally tied the knot on June 5, 1966. The private wedding ceremony, held at the Bel-Air home of TV writer Robert Shaw, was attended by only a few personal friends. Sheridan gushed to an interviewer, "This is the one—I'm going to stay married to Scott forever."[24]

Nineteen

Saying Goodbye

Life is so great.[1]

After their secret wedding, the couple honeymooned in Hawaii. "We were supposed to stay two weeks," Sheridan told reporters, "but we stretched it to three."[2] During their honeymoon, Sheridan was thrown from her horse. X-rays of her rib cage revealed some ominous spots on the esophagus and liver. Further testing showed it was Stage 4 cancer. The doctor explained that the condition was terminal and that she most likely had only months to live. Treatment options were suggested only to manage the pain. The couple, devastated by the grim prognosis, struggled to make sense of it all, but were determined to make the best of the time she had left.

Sheridan decided to keep her condition a secret from everyone. Only her husband and attending physician knew. She vowed to keep working on the new TV series, because she felt she owed it to the cast and crew. If she left the show now, too many people would be out of work. To maintain a healthy appearance and positive mindset, Sheridan got a facelift before shooting began on July 1.

Carole Wells, who played Sheridan's daughter, recalled the cast, screenwriters and director sitting around a big table and reading the script every week. During these readings, Sheridan "was very charming but rather quiet … [and] down to earth."[3] Wells said that she and Sheridan often chatted on the set but that they never became close.

In the early days of filming, Sheridan maintained such a brave front, nobody suspected that anything was wrong. As a visitor to the set, Erskine Johnson noted, "When she walks toward you on the set of *Pistols 'n' Petticoats* … you'll notice that the Sheridan figure is as classy as ever, the large eyes just as luminous. The years have been kind in every way." According to Sheridan, filming the comedy series was a lark. "Now I come to the set laughing," she stated. "It's zany, crazy, ridiculous satire and I love it." Asked about McKay, Sheridan responded, "He's back East in summer stock [in *Mary, Mary*]. If this series makes it, we'll settle down in Hollywood. He should be in a series, too."[4]

When asked in another interview about the experience of starring in her first TV series, Sheridan was quick to quip, "I remember Ronnie [Reagan] telling all of us not to join TV because it was the enemy of the movies."[5] Reagan must have changed his mind as he was in the midst of a long-running gig hosting the Western anthology series *Death Valley Days*, which was his *second* stint after hosting *General Electric Theatre* for eight years from 1954 to 1962!

In an interview conducted by Bob Thomas, Sheridan explained what television viewers could expect from *Pistols 'n' Petticoats*:

The producer, Joe Connelly, describes it as the *Cat Ballou* of television, and that's a pretty good description. It's a satire on Westerns, but the people are real, not caricatures. It's sort of *Bonanza* and *Big Valley* [Barbara Stanwyck's series] gone crazy.... I feel at home in it. I did a few Westerns in my time, you know—things like *Silver River* and *Dodge City*.[6]

The interviews kept coming and Sheridan was gratified to be back in the spotlight. "I've had many television series offered to me but until I read the original script for *Pistols 'n' Petticoats* I didn't really feel I had something worthwhile. I've always loved westerns and this one happens to be the funniest one I've ever seen."[7]

The premise of the show was simple: the comic adventures of the Hawks family, who are better at keeping the peace in a Colorado town than the inept sheriff. Sheridan played Henrietta Hawks, a gun-totin', level-headed widow and the mother of teenage Lucy (Wells, who replaced Chris Noel). Also prominent in the cast were two veteran actors, Ruth McDevitt and Douglas Fowley, who played Grandma and Grandpa Hawks. Sheridan referred to them as "a couple of great old pros."[8]

Pistols 'n' Petticoats debuted on CBS on September 17, 1966. The initial reviews were terrible. "The name of Ann Sheridan (the one-time 'oomph' girl) also captured a sponsor swiftly," sniped one reviewer. "No one bothered to discover, apparently, that *Pistols 'n' Petticoats* was just one more imitation of *The Beverly Hillbillies.* Even with Miss Sheridan, the series is more 'ugh' than 'oomph.'"[9] "Ann Sheridan is in a hillbilly comedy," complained another, "and that's enough of a shock right there. It is called *Pistols 'n' Petticoats*, and is about a Western family in which the women are crack shots. If they were, they'd really know whom to plug. Miss Sheridan's fans must shudder."[10]

The highly anticipated *The Jean Arthur Show* reached the small screen five days before *Pistols 'n' Petticoats* made its bow. Arthur's show ranked near the bottom of the week's ratings and, after 12 episodes,

Sheridan fought a brave fight against cancer and, despite great pain, kept it a secret from friends and co-workers.

was cancelled. *Pistols 'n' Petticoats*, on the other hand, found an appreciative audience who enjoyed all the silliness. In early November, it was announced that the show was renewed for the rest of the 1966–67 season.

Therese Bushen, who was 12 or 13 years old at the time, recalled when Sheridan frequently visited her stepfather, Keith Vincents, an executive director, and her mother, Anna-Marie Hickey, at their home.

> I believe she came several times to watch the pilot and a few episodes of the show with our family. She was lovely and gracious, and she and my mom became friendly.... She suddenly stopped coming over, and I seem to remember something about her becoming very ill. My next memory is of Scott McKay coming over by himself for dinner, following the death of Ann.[11]

McKay and Hickey tied the knot in 1969. They remained together until his death in 1987.

After several *Pistols 'n' Petticoats* episodes were filmed, Sheridan became easily exhausted and was forced to reduce her workload. She worked as much as possible during the morning but, by noon, she was incapable of more. Connelly ordered chairs to be strategically placed around the set, so she could rest between takes. He also arranged for her scenes to be filmed while she sat down. Doubles took over for Sheridan in many scenes, and script adjustments were made to accommodate her absences.

On the set, Wells made it a point to greet Sheridan each day and ask how she was feeling. The answer was always the same: "I wish I felt as good as you do, sweetie."[12] Wells noticed that Sheridan smoked continuously on the set.

Despite her weakened state, Sheridan maintained a brave front and continued to give interviews on the set. "I didn't have to do a grinding TV series," she told one interviewer, "but I like to keep busy—when I can find something that isn't bogged down with messages."[13] In an interview conducted by James Gregory, she revealed, "When I finish work for the day, I go home, take off my makeup, eat a light dinner, and collapse.... These TV shows demand every bit of energy you have—but they're fun. That show is a lot of hard work, but I enjoy it."[14] During the weekend, she focused on resting to regain her energy for the Monday shoot. By this time, McKay, who had been touring the country in *Luv*, came home to be with his wife because it was apparent she was getting worse. They spent their time decorating their new San Fernando Valley house, giving her some pleasure in what would be the last months of her life.

In late November, it was announced that Sheridan would appear with Irene Dunne and Burt Lancaster in producer Ross Hunter's *Heaven Train*. By this time, Hunter and Sheridan had buried the hatchet and he was anxious to do another film with her.

Many people on the *Pistols 'n' Petticoats* set suspected something was seriously wrong with the actress. "We all knew then how very sick Ann was," Connelly told Chrys Haranis. "Ann was very weak, barely able to stand at times.... She had guts and courage. We thought somehow she'd pull through."[15] Of this time, Wells recalled, "She was very frail and thin and kept getting thinner as the series progressed. Basically, I watched her die in front of me. But with all she was going through, I never heard her complain and she was always very kind and respectful to me." Sheridan's clothes designer, Julie Heron, added padding to Sheridan's costumes when they began to hang on her frail frame.

By the start of the Christmas season, Sheridan, battling intense pain and chronic fatigue, was still determined to complete the full schedule of 26 episodes. By this time, however, she was stumbling on the set; some people thought she was drunk. Wells knew better: "I knew she wasn't going to be around much longer."[16]

When production resumed after Christmas, Sheridan found it more difficult to work and, one day, collapsed on the set. The stunned crew rushed to her aid. After much persuasion, she consented to being carried out to her limousine and going home. Within a few days, Sheridan notified Connelly she would not be able to return.

Sheridan sensed the end was imminent and made preparations with McKay by her side. Her doctor later revealed that the actress, although not religious, exhibited a strong sense of faith and bravery in her final days.

For several days, Connelly called the doctor and inquired about the nature of Sheridan's illness "and he would never tell me."[17] No one but the doctor, McKay and Sheridan knew she was dying.

In her last days, she made phone calls to many close friends, telling each person that she loved them. "I want to inform you that life is wonderful. And I have to say goodbye." She then hung up before the recipient had a chance to respond. Hunter told interviewer Ruth Waterbury that Sheridan's final words to him were "Ross, I'll be nostalgic over what you have meant to my life."[18]

On Saturday, January 21, Ann Sheridan died with her husband by her bedside. Her final words to her husband were reportedly, "I'm going to be all right."[19]

The tough-as-nails and sassy "Oomph Girl" was dead at the age of 51.

TWENTY

Remembering Ann Sheridan

Ann Sheridan left a rich legacy to Hollywood.
A very rich one for a gal who once had nothing but Oomph.[1]

When news of Sheridan's passing reached the newspapers, the entertainment world was stunned. She appeared so healthy on the show that it was assumed she had died from either undiagnosed cancer or emphysema. The official cause was later revealed as esophageal cancer with massive liver metastases.

It was disclosed that Sheridan had bravely kept those close to her in the dark about her condition. Her sister Kitty was one of the first to be notified of Ann's death. "I was just about to watch *Pistols 'n' Petticoats* (the 19th episode, entitled 'Beware the Hangman') when her manager called," she said. "That was the first any of us knew." It seemed that none of her surviving siblings, Kitty, Mabel and Georgia (brother George died in 1957), received a call from Sheridan prior to her death. Kitty revealed that their famous sister last visited Fort Worth three or four years prior. "We would meet her at Love Field in Dallas the times when she was flying through, but we haven't been able to see her too often."[2]

On January 22, a private funeral with only family members in attendance was held at the Pierce Brothers Mortuary in North Hollywood. Sheridan wished for her body to be cremated. Her ashes were then stored at the Chapel of the Pines Cemetery.

Almost immediately, tributes poured in from many who knew her well. Former co-star Ronald Reagan, then the governor of California, said, "I am deeply shocked and saddened. Although I have not seen her in recent years, I remember her with affection and warmth. This is a personal loss."[3] Syndicated columnist Jack O'Brian noted, "Ann Sheridan's death was a real shocker ... she was a rare film star; not an inch of phoniness in her beautiful makeup; our old Stork Club gang will miss this fine girl."[4]

In a *Los Angeles Times* tribute, the writer called Ann

> the saving grace of dozens of formula films which would have seemed all the worse without her radiance and style. She was no Bette Davis or Eleanor Parker as an actress; no Virginia Mayo or Alexis Smith as a beauty.... But, the quality that set her apart from the dozens of older movie heroines was how well she could hold her own with the tough guys who dominated the screen in the late 1930s."[5]

Most of the cast members and crew of *Pistols 'n' Petticoats* were shocked by the news. Connelly reflected on Sheridan's passing: "I don't think Miss Sheridan knew how sick she was until about ten days ago. She never admitted it."[6] In a separate interview, Connelly admitted that, as a rule, he was not fond of actresses, finding them difficult to work with. Not so with Sheridan. "Of this one I was [fond]. She was a great, wonderful human being."[7] Co-star Wells believed that, for Sheridan, "being part of the show might have helped her live a little longer."[8] After hearing of Sheridan's death, the cast members held a lunch to memorialize her life.

With Sheridan's passing, there was the issue of how to proceed with *Pistols 'n' Petticoats* as there were a few episodes still to be made (the actual number ranges from one to five). The remaining episode (or episodes) were altered in order to explain Sheridan's limited footage. Another aspect of the production was reported by Bob Thomas in November 1967. In an article on voiceover actress June Foray, Thomas noted, "Ann Sheridan died before she could re-record dialogue for her last television show that extraneous noises had ruined in the sound track. Miss Foray, after listening carefully to Miss Sheridan's voice, did the re-recording, matching the words to Ann's lip movements."[9]

The final episode of *Pistols 'n' Petticoats* was aired on March 11, 1967. Later, the producers edited some of the episodes into a 100-minute feature film called *The Far Out West*. This feature was sold to television and is often shown. Currently, both Universal Home Video and Echo Bridge Home Video hold home video rights to the full series.

Sheridan made a will months before her death. In the document, she stated her desire to have her cremated remains interred in a niche in a columbarium in Los Angeles. For 38 years, however, her ashes were stored in an unpretentious metal container inside a storage drawer along with some diamond earrings and her wedding ring from McKay. Researcher-biographer Karen McHale was instrumental in fulfilling Sheridan's final wish; it is not known why McKay failed to make this happen. In 2005, Sheridan's ashes were interned in a niche in the Chapel Columbarium at the Hollywood Forever Cemetery. "We're deeply honored Ann Sheridan's family has chosen our cemetery as her final resting place," said Hollywood Forever owner Tyler Cassity. "She truly embodied the beauty, intelligence, patriotism and glamour of Hollywood's Golden Age."[10]

A service was held at Hollywood Forever on February 21, 2005 (which would have been her 90th birthday). A celebration of Sheridan's life and career, it was officiated by her cousin, Presbyterian Pastor Sallie Watson of Denton. Among the invited guests were Carole Wells and director Vincent Sherman. Today, her grave is part of the walking tour at Hollywood Forever.

* * *

At the time of Sheridan's death, the *London Times* obituary said it best, astutely noting, "Without ever quite achieving the mythic status of a super-star, she was always a pleasure to watch and, as with all true stars, was never quite like anyone else."[11]

Nearly half a century after her untimely death, Sheridan remains a little-known actress except for fervent fans of Hollywood's Golden Age. Like most of her contemporaries, she is often eclipsed by the bright glare of Legendary Stars (Swanson, Davis, Crawford, Hepburn) or Cult Favorites (Kay Francis, Rita Hayworth, Vivien Leigh). While there are dozens of biographies written on many of these ladies, Ann Sheridan has only rated a few well-written chapter-long entries in books. Every now and then, Turner Classic Movies makes her their "Star of the Month."

She is honored with a star on the Hollywood Walk of Fame at 7024 Hollywood Boulevard. The University of North Texas has opened a museum showcasing the actress's photograph collection.

The fact this is the first full-length biography (not counting Margie Schultz's excellent reference book) speaks loudly to the fact that the time has come for Ann Sheridan's re-emergence. For me, what started out as a teenage crush back in the mid–1970s has developed into quite the labor of love—and the quest to give an unjustly neglected star her due.

In the course of writing this book, some "truths" have emerged. First, Ann Sheridan was an accomplished actress in her own right. She was at home in *all* genres— thus making her far more versatile than the likes of Davis, Crawford and many other, better-known stars. Sec-

The "Oomph Girl" as movie fans remember her.

ond, Sheridan lived life on her own terms. Her motto was to always live life to the fullest. Perhaps she was guilty of making poor decisions regarding her career and in her choice of men, but she lived her life without regrets and made no apologies.

As a history buff, I have always lamented being unable to travel back in time. Motion pictures, on the other hand, offer the perfect opportunity to experience a piece of history with all the magic and fanfare of being there. With easy accessibility to nearly all of her films, anyone can become acquainted with this delightful actress. The best way to experience her beguiling allure is to start with this list of representative films and performances—and it's ranked in order of importance and relevance:

It All Came True
Torrid Zone
Kings Row
The Man Who Came to Dinner
I Was a Male War Bride
Woman on the Run

They Drive by Night
Angels with Dirty Faces
The Unfaithful
Take Me to Town
Come Next Spring
Good Sam
City for Conquest
Edge of Darkness
The Footloose Heiress
Black Legion

Given the sheer number of motion pictures and television programs on Ann Sheridan's résumé, a more detailed look at her career is warranted. For now, this biography is a good start. To paraphrase Cagney's great line: "Here's to you and your 14-carat Oomph."

Chapter Notes

Introduction

1. Ann Sheridan, "This Is Myself," *Movieland*, April 1944, 34.
2. Ray Hagen and Laura Wagner, *Killer Tomatoes: Fifteen Tough Film Dames* (Jefferson, NC: McFarland, 2004), 199.
3. Humphrey Bogart, "Sister Annie," *Silver Screen*, March 1943, 26.
4. Hedda Hopper, "Looking at Hollywood," *Alfred Sun*, July 22, 1944.
5. William Donati. *Ida Lupino: A Biography* (Lexington: University Press of Kentucky, 1996), 75.
6. Fredda Dudley. "Ann Sheridan Marries George Brent!" *Modern Screen*, March 1942, 73.
7. Joseph McBride. *Hawks on Hawks* (Oakland: University of California Press, 1982), 71.
8. Michael D. Rinella, *Margaret Sullavan: The Life and Career of a Reluctant Star* (Jefferson, NC: McFarland, 2019), 2.
9. David Shipman. *The Great Movie Stars: The Golden Years* (New York: Crown Publishers, 1970), 492.

Chapter One

1. Hagen and Wagner, 170.
2. Edward MacLysaght. "Irish Families," posted May 13, 2014, https://www.facebook.com/SheridanFamilyHistory.
3. Louella Parsons, "Ann Sheridan's Sense of Humor and Friendliness Keeps Her on Top," *Indianapolis Star*, March 30, 1952.
4. Sheridan, 32.
5. Robert Higgins, "The Oomph Girl Is 51," *TV Guide*, May 21, 1966, 26.
6. Ann Sheridan, "Take My Word For It!," *Modern Screen*, July 1953, 60.
7. Francis Hyland, "From Main Street to Hollywood in Few Months Is Remarkable Record Made by Local Personality Girl," *Denton Record-Chronicle*, December 13, 1933.
8. Sheridan, "This Is Myself," 32.
9. Sheridan, 34.
10. Chrys Haranis, "Ann Sheridan: She Had Oomph and Courage," *Photoplay*, April 1967, 18.
11. Marian Rhea, "Texas Bombshell," *Movie Mirror*, May 1939, 72.

12. "Red-Haired 'Ludie' Sheridan Grew Up to Become a Star," *Denton Record-Chronicle*, February 3, 1957.
13. Francis Hyland, "From Main Street to Hollywood...," *Denton Record-Chronicle*, December 13, 1933.
14. Higgins, 25.
15. Annette Bochenek, "Hometowns to Hollywood: Ann Sheridan," retrieved April 14, 2023; https://hometownstohollywood.com/2020/06/29/ann-sheridan/.
16. Ruth Rankin, "From Ranch to Riches," *Photoplay*, June 1939, 16.
17. Hagen and Wagner, 170.
18. Betty Colfax, "They Made Her What She is Today," *Modern Screen*, January 1940, 70.
19. Margie Schultz, *The Ann Sheridan Bio-Bibliography* (Westport, CT: Greenwood Press, 1997), 57.
20. John C. Merriman, "School Marm From Texas Who is Learning All About Hollywood," *Rochester Democrat and Chronicle*, August 6, 1937.

Chapter Two

1. Untitled article, *Hartford Courant*, May 29, 1948.
2. Cliff Allperti, "Ann Sheridan—Search for Beauty Contest Winner Before the Oomph," retrieved February 2, 2021, https://immortalephemera.com/31105/ann-sheridan-search-for-beauty/.
3. Higgins, 25.
4. Perry Stewart, "Voice Made Ann Sheridan," *Fort Worth Star-Telegram*, January 23, 1967.
5. "Sheridan's Pride," *Chicago Sunday Tribune*, July 9, 1944.
6. "Miss Sheridan is Winner in Screen Contest," *Denton Record-Chronicle*, July 19, 1933.
7. *Dallas Semi Weekly Campus*, October 11, 1933.
8. Francis Hyland, "From Main Street to Hollywood...," *Denton Record-Chronicle*, December 13, 1933.
9. Edith Linderman, "Ann Sheridan Had Oomph Before She Ever Saw Films," *Richmond Times-Dispatch*, June 29, 1939.

10. Sheridan, 76.

11. Marian Rhea, "Texas Bombshell–Part 2," *Movie Mirror*, June 1939, 72.

12. John C. Merriman, "School Marm From Texas," *Rochester Democrat and Chronicle*, August 6, 1937.

13. Hagen and Wagner, 170.

14. James Robert Parish and Don E. Stanke, *The Forties Gals* (New Rochelle: Arlington House Publishers, 1980), 135.

15. Hagen and Wagner, 180.

16. Dan Thomas, "Hollywood Gossips," *Burlington Daily Times News*, January 8, 1934.

17. Film Review, *Denton Record-Chronicle*, February 23, 1934.

Chapter Three

1. Gladys Hall, "Confessions of a Contest Winner," *Motion Picture*, December 1938, 66.

2. Rhea, 73.

3. Jacques Mapes, "What's It Like Dating Ann," *Screenland*, December 1949, 66.

4. Hagen and Wagner, 169.

5. Phillip T. Crosland, "Ann Sheridan Scorns Scorners of Filmland Talent," *Wilmington News Journal*, September 28, 1959.

6. Jerry Vermilye, *Buster Crabbe: A Biofilmography* (Jefferson, NC: McFarland, 2014), 19.

7. John Kobal, *People Will Talk* (New York: Knopf Publishers, 1986), 419.

8. Kobal, 417.

9. Hagan and Wagner, 170.

10. Hagen and Wagner, 180.

11. Kobal, 417.

12. *The Hollywood Reporter*, June 20, 1934, 7–10.

13. Picture caption, *Muncie Post Democrat*, July 20, 1934.

14. "Clara Lou Sheridan Possess Perfect Camera Face, Says Movie Camera-man," *Denton Record-Chronicle*, July 13, 1934.

15. "*College Rhythm* at Palace Next Week, Clara Lou Sheridan Has Part," *Denton Record-Chronicle*, November 24, 1934.

16. "Denton Girl is Given Contract With Paramount." *Pampa Daily News*, September 27, 1934.

17. Roy Catesby Flannagan, "TheWhipping," retrieved January 31, 1921, https://www.goodreads.com/book/show/17623507-the-whipping.

Chapter Four

1. Sheilah Graham, "Ann Sheridan is Back," *Baltimore Sun*, April 28, 1946.

2. "Clara Lou Sheridan Shortens Name, Lengthens Contract with Movies Simultaneously," *Denton Record-Chronicle*, September 27, 1934.

3. Hagen and Wagner, 272.

4. Kobal, 419.

5. Scott O'Brien, *Sylvia Sidney: Paid By the Tear* (Albany, GA: Bear Manor Media, 2016), 121.

6. Kobal, 419.

7. Frank Neil, "In Hollywood," *Long Beach Independent*, June 5, 1949.

8. "Mrs. Leslie Carter," retrieved March 5, 2021, https://www.Britannica.com/biography/Mrs-Leslie-Carter.

9. Hagen and Wagner, 172.

10. Robert Nott, *The Films of Randolph Scott* (Jefferson, NC: McFarland, 2004), 40.

11. James Robert Parish and Don E. Stanke, *The All-Americans* (New Rochelle: Arlington House Publishers, 1977), 257.

12. Hall, 66.

13. Rhea, 74.

14. Untitled article, *Oakland Tribune*, May 12, 1935.

15. Hall, 63

16. Untitled article, *Denton Record-Chronicle*, March 27, 1935.

17. *Oakland Tribune*, May 12, 1935.

18. Daniel Bubbeo, *The Women of Warner Brothers: The Lives and Careers of 15 Leading Ladies* (Jefferson, NC: McFarland, 2002), 193.

19. Kobal, 417.

20. Alan Gill, "Ann Sheridan Accepts Daytime Panel Bid," *Bradenton Manatee County Call*, August 29, 1963.

21. Colfax, 70.

Chapter Five

1. Kobal, 416.

2. Colfax, 70.

3. McBride, 71.

4. Jerry Jerome, "Ann Sheridan's in Love with Living," *Movieland*, March 1947, 98.

5. Wood Soames, "Hollywood's Looking at Her!" *Oakland Tribune*, April 11, 1937.

6. Rhea, 74.

7. Dan Van Neste (2019). *They Coulda Been Contenders* (Albany, GA: Bear Manor Media, 2019), 267.

8. Van Neste, 264.

9. Elizabeth Yeaman, "Warner Newcomer Scores," *Hollywood Citizen-News*, July 16, 1936.

10. Hall, 66.

11. Van Neste, 268.

12. Bubbeo, 193.

13. Wood Soames, "Hollywood's Looking at Her!" *Oakland Tribune*, April 11, 1937.

Chapter Six

1. Kobal, 421.

2. Sybil Jason, *My Fifteen Minutes: An Autobiography of a Child Star in the Golden Era of Hollywood* (Albany, GA: BearManor Media, 2005), 67.

3. "Warner Dies; Movie Tycoon." *The Youngstown Vindicator*, September 11, 1978.

4. Hal Wallis and Charles Higham, *Starmaker: The Autobiography of Hal Wallis* (New York: Macmillan Publishing, 1980), 14.

5. Hagen and Wagner, 190.

6. "Jane Wyman—The Joan Blondell of the Bs" (TCM interview, 7:04–7:08; 7:41–7:52), retrieved March 20, 2021; htps://www.youtube.com/watch?v=MSzI99xMN8w

7. Higgins, 26.

8. Kobal, 422.

9. *Sing Me a Love Song* advertisement, *Dayton Daily Times*, December 31, 1936.

10. Ann Sheridan, "Brother Bogie," *Silver Screen*, January 1943, 22.

11. Frederick James Smith, "The Real Oomph Girl," *Liberty*, July 20, 1940, 41.

12. Hagen and Wagner, 198–199.

13. Sheridan, "Brother Bogie," 61.

14. Sheridan, "Brother Bogie," 22.

15. Bogart, 64.

16. Bogart, 26.

17. Jerry Asher, "This is Bogart," *Photoplay*, January 1944, 96.

18. Jason, 61.

19. Van Neste, 268.

20. Louella O. Parsons, "Leslie Howard Accepts Role for Daughter," *Pittsburgh Post-Gazette*, October 5, 1936.

21. Hagen and Wagner, 174.

22. Bryan Senn, *Golden Horrors* (Jefferson, NC: McFarland, 1996), 430.

23. Review of *The Footloose Heiress*. *Motion Picture Herald*, April 10, 1937, 49.

24. Picture of Craig Reynolds. *Picture Play*, April 1937, 64.

25. "Gropper v. Warner Bros. Pictures, 38 F. Supp. 329 (S.D.N.Y. 1941)," retrieved February 16, 2021; https: //law. justia.com/cases/federal/dis-trictcourts/FSupp/38/329/2096542/.

Chapter Seven

1. Elizabeth Wilson, "Get Sheridan," *Screenland*, August 1939, 25.

2. John C. Merriman, "School Marm From Texas Who Is Learning All About Hollywood," *Rochester Democrat and Chronicle*, August 6, 1937.

3. *Hollywood Citizen-News*, February 4, 1937.

4. Robbin Coons, "Bad Fortune Strikes at Edward Norris," *The Manhattan Mercury*, April 16, 1937.

5. Schultz (B-304), 302.

6. H. H. Niemeyer, "Hollywood Puzzle," *St. Louis Post-Dispatch Women's Sunday Magazine*, May 1, 1938.

7. Smith, 41.

8. "They're Talking About …," *Photoplay*, March 1939, 69.

9. Hall, 66.

10. Hagen and Wagner, 174.

11. "Ann Sheridan Assigned to Feminine Lead in Warners' *Heart of North*," *Hollywood Citizen-News*, June 22, 1938.

12. *Brainerd Daily Dispatch*, August 31, 1938.

13. "Jimmie Fidler in Hollywood," *Joplin Sunday Globe*, September 11, 1938.

14. Untitled article, *Defiance Crescent News*, October 8, 1938.

15. "What Keeps Ann's Figure That Way?" *Oakland Tribune*, November 6, 1938.

16. Ruth Rankin, "From Ranch to Riches," *Photoplay*, June 1939, 16.

17. Van Neste, 269.

18. Sheilah Graham, "Ann Sheridan Is Back," *Baltimore Sun*, April 28, 1946.

19. Hagen and Wagner, 178.

20. Colfax, 70.

21. Smith, 41.

22. Colfax, 70.

23. James Cagney, *Cagney by Cagney* (New York: Doubleday, 1976), 89.

24. Louella O. Parsons, "Ann Sheridan, Texas Girl, May Get Role in G.W.T.W," *San Antonio Light*, January 26, 1939.

25. Jimmie Fidler, "Garfield, Lynn, Sheridan, and Payne—Watch Out for Them in 1939, Writes Fidler," *Salt Lake Tribune*, January 19, 1939.

26. Lucie Neville, "Who's a Lady—Me?" *Asbury Park Press*, January 1, 1939.

27. "Sidney Skolsky Presents…," *Hollywood Citizen-News*, September 27, 1938.

28. Hagen and Wagner, 176.

29. Errol Flynn, *My Wicked, Wicked Ways* (New York: G.P. Putnam's Sons, 1959), 290.

30. Flynn, 296.

31. Hagen and Wagner, 175.

32. Lucie Neville, "Who's a Lady—Me?" *Asbury Park Press*, January 1, 1939.

33. Rankins, "Ranch to Riches," 18.

34. Sheilah Graham, "Jack Warner Speaks Frankly on Movies," *St. Louis Globe-Democrat*, January 28, 1939.

35. Neville, "Who's a Lady—Me?"

36. Paul Harrison, "Ann Sheridan, Treated as 'Cute-Savage' for 5 Years, Finally Rewarded for 'Umph,'" *Pittsburgh Press*, July, 23, 1938.

37. Richard G. Hubler and Ronald Reagan, *Where's the Rest of Me? The Autobiography of Ronald Reagan* (New York: Hawthorn, 1973), 101.

Chapter Eight

1. "Ann Sheridan Now Indian Placater," *Biddeford Journal*, September 10, 1966.

2. "It? No! Umph Now" (picture caption), *Bangor Daily News*, October 13, 1936.

3. Paul Harrison, "Hollywood's New Queen of 'Umph,'" *The Montana Standard*, November 28, 1937.

4. Walter Winchell, "Walter Winchell on Broadway," *The Morning Post*, March 25, 1938.

5. Paul Harrison, "Ann Sheridan, Treated as 'Cute Savage.'..," *Pittsburgh Press*, July, 23, 1938.

6. Paul Harrison, "With Ballyhoo Ruled Out, Lovely Newcomers Went It Alone," *Muncie Evening Press*, December 21, 1938.

7. Hagen and Wagner, 175.

8. Whitney Stine and George Hurrell, *The Hurrell Style: 50 Years of Photographing Hollywood* (New York: John Day, Co., 1976), 159.

9. Hagen and Wagner, 175.

10. Joe Finnigan, "Ann Sheridan in Hollywood for TV Show," *Corsicana Daily Sun*, December 23, 1958.

11. Ad in *Hollywood* magazine, July 1939, 55.

12. Kay Proctor, "Oomph (pronounced 'ouch!')," *Hollywood*, September 1939, 50.

13. Proctor, 19.

14. "Ann Sheridan Is New Oomph Girl," *San Antonio Light*, March 17, 1939.

15. "Jimmie Fidler in Hollywood," *Richmond Times-Dispatch*, April 1, 1939.

16. James Carson, "Annie Meets the Boys," *Modern Screen*, July 1940, 30.

17. https://www.ann-sheridan.com/Ann_Sheridan_Quotations/Ann_Sheridan_Quotations.html., retrieved April 12, 2020.

18. Hagen and Wagner, 177.

19. Stuart Jerome, *Those Crazy Wonderful Years When We Ran Warner Bros* (New York: Lyle Stuart, Inc., 1983), 223.

20. Van Neste, 315.

21. Erskine Johnson, "Ann Sheridan Is Still Around for Fall Debut," *North Adams Transcript*, August 27, 1966.

22. *Film Daily*, April 5, 1939, 6.

23. http://annsheridan.com/Ann_Sheridan_Articles/Ann_Sheridan_Life_Story.html, retrieved April 16, 2020.

24. "Ann Sheridan Restricts Goal," *South Bend Tribune*, May 1, 1939.

25. Erskine Johnson, "Ann Sheridan Is Chuckling," *Bakersfield Californian*, November 3, 1951.

26. "Ann Sheridan Becomes a Different Personality," *Washington Star*, June 25, 1939.

27. Frederick C. Othman, "Actress Sorry She Received 'Oomph' Title," *Jefferson City Daily Capital News*, January 12, 1940.

28. Bogart, 27.

29. "Ann Sheridan Named in Suit," *Oakland Tribune*, July 25, 1939.

30. "Oomph-Girl Ann Sheridan, Veteran Movie-Goer, Dodges All Romantic Films," *Lexington Herald-Leader*, September 29, 1940.

31. Jimmie Fidler's column, *Los Angeles Times*, August 2, 1939.

Chapter Nine

1. "Ann Sheridan Faces Crisis: Actress Knows She Will Have to Deliver More Than 'Oomph,'" *Charlotte Observer*, April 7, 1940.

2. Colfax, 29.

3. Mel Heimer, "My New York," *Wilmington Daily Press Journal*, November 8, 1950.

4. "Oomph-Girl Ann Sheridan, Veteran Movie-Goer, Dodges All Romantic Films," *Lexington Herald-Leader*, September 29, 1940.

5. Louella Parsons, "Hollywood," *Syracuse Herald-Journal*, November 27, 1939.

6. Hagen and Wagner, 184.

7. Mark Hellinger, "The lady's name is Ann Sheridan...," http://www.ann-sheridan.com/Ann_Sheridan_Arti-cles/Mark_Hellinger_on_Ann_Sheridan.htm, retrieved January 10, 2023.

8. Jim Bishop, *The Mark Hellinger Story: A Biography of Broadway and Hollywood* (Whitefish, MT: Literary Licensing, LLC, 2012), 14.

9. *Syracuse Herald-American*, October 15, 1939.

10. Louella Parsons' column, *San Antonio Light*, October 9, 1939.

11. *Tucson Daily Citizen*, February 29, 1940.

12. Frederick C. Ottmann, "Harvard Sneers at Ann; She Hints College Could Use Some Oomph," *Oakland Tribune*, March 5, 1940.

13. "Ann Sheridan Sharpshoots at Lampy; Calls Harvard Humor Sheet Sad Rag," *The Harvard Crimson*, March 6, 1940. https://www.thecrimson.com/article/1940/3/6/ann-sheridan-sharpshoots-at-lamp-calls/, retrieved June 12, 2021.

14. "Movie Oomph-Girl Invited to Dance By 'Record' Boss," *The Yale Daily News*, March 7, 1940. https://ydnhistorical.library.yale.edu/?a=d&d=YDN19400307-01.2.5&e=-en-20-1-txt, retrieved June 12, 2021.

15. "University Authorities Balk at Oomph Girl Premiere at U.T.," *The Harvard Crimson*, March 18, 1940. https://www.thecrimson.com/article/1940/3/18/university-authorities-balk-at-oomph-girl/, retrieved June 11, 2021.

16. Louella Parsons, "Screen and Drama: Pretty Samaritan—It's Ann Sheridan," *San Francisco Examiner*, May 12, 1940.

17. The Bogie Film Blog, https://bogiefilmblog.wordpress.com/2013/06/14/it-all-came-true-1940/, retrieved January 14, 2023.

18. Louella Parsons, "Screen and Drama: Pretty Samaritan ...," *San Francisco Examiner*, May 12, 1940.

19. Katharine Hartley Frings, "Will the 'Oomph' Title Hurt Her?" *Motion Picture*, August 1939, 29.

20. Wilson, "Get Sheridan!" 92.

21. James Robert Parish, *Hollywood's Great Love Teams* (New Rochelle, NY: Arlington House Publishers, 1974), 466.

22. Louella Parsons, "Screen and Drama: Pretty Samaritan ...," *San Francisco Examiner*, May 12, 1940.

23. Lewis Yablonsky, *George Raft* (New York: New American Library, 1974), 136.

24. Parish and Stanke, *The Forties Gals*, 276.

25. The Bogart Film Blog, retrieved January 14, 2023.

26. Wood Soames, "Interview with Author and Adapter Reveals Strange Revisions," *Oakland Tribune*, October 17, 1940.

27. "Sheridan to the Orpheum," *Wichita Eagle*, October 20, 1940.

28. Hagen and Wagner, 178.

29. Dickens, 155.

30. http://www.ann-sheridan.com/Ann_ Sheridan_Quotations/Ann_Sheridan_Quotations. html, retrieved November 23, 2022.

Chapter Ten

1. Smith, 41.

2. James Carsons, "Annie Meets the Boys," *Modern Screen*, July 1940, 86.

3. Frings, 75.

4. Helen Hover, "Forecasts for 1940," *Hollywood*, January 1940, 21.

5. "George Brent Mystery Man of Hollywood," *Syracuse Herald-Journal*, 1940 (date illegible).

6. Jimmie Fidler, "In Hollywood," *State Times Advocate*, January 26, 1940.

7. Whitney Stine and Bette Davis, *Mother Goddam: The Story of the Career of Bette Davis* (London: W.H. Allen and Co., 1974), 31.

8. Elizabeth Wilson, "Hollywood's Gayest Romance!" *Screenland*, September 1940, 86.

9. George Brent, "Categorically Speaking: Ann—As Seen by George Brent," *Photoplay*, September 1940, 85.

10. Ann Sheridan, "Categorically Speaking: George—As Seen by Ann Sheridan," *Photoplay*, September 1940, 85.

11. "Oomph Girl, Brent Break Record with 56-Seconds Kiss," *Omaha World-Herald*, August 8, 1940.

12. Scott O'Brien, *George Brent: Ireland's Gift to Hollywood and Its Leading Ladies* (Albany, GA: BearManor Media, 2014), 195.

13. Sheilah Graham, "Ann Sheridan Hangs Up Mistletoe, Complains," *Cleveland Plain Dealer*, December 21, 1940.

14. Anita Blake, "Learned in Exile," *Photoplay*, June 1941, 43.

15. O'Brien, *George Brent...*, 198.

16. Blake, 43.

17. Maude Cheatham, "George Tells Why, Ann Sheridan and I Won't Marry," *Photoplay*, September 1941, 31.

Chapter Eleven

1. Blake, 43.

2. Blake, 43, 99.

3. Jerome, 221.

4. Kobal, 421.

5. Hagen and Wagner, 178.

6. http://www.ann-sheridan.com/Ann_ Sheridan_Articles/Ann_Sheridan_ The_Role _I_ Liked_Best.html, retrieved February 23, 2021.

7. Kobal, 422.

8. "Jimmie Fidler in Hollywood," *St. Louis Star and Times*, March 24, 1941.

9. Jack E. Anderson, "The Oomph Girl Is Back," *Miami Herald Sunday Magazine*, August 7, 1966.

10. Jerome, 52, 55.

11. Kobal, 422.

12. Cheatham, 31.

13. Cheatham, 90.

14. https://catalog.afi.com/Film/27013-KINGS-ROW?cxt=filmography.

15. Hagen and Wagner, 181.

16. http://www.ann-sheridan.com/Ann_ Sheridan_Articles/Ann_Sheridan_ The_Role _I_ Liked_Best.html.

17. Kobal, 422.

18. Smith, 41.

19. Ann Sheridan, "My Favorite Screen Stars," *St. Louis Globe-Democrat*, December 24, 1944.

20. Stine and Davis, 153.

21. Stine and Davis, 154.

22. Lawrence J. Quirk, *Fasten Your Seat Belts: The Passionate Life of Bette Davis* (New York: William Morrow and Company, Inc., 1990), 236.

23. Hagen and Wagner, 180.

24. Reagan, 103.

25. http://ann-sheridan.com/About_Ann _ Sheridan/Comments_about_Ann_Sheridan. html, retrieved February 27, 2021.

Chapter Twelve

1. Richard Bard, "We Didn't Part Friends!" *Hollywood*, February 1943, 25.

2. Fredda Dudley, "Ann Sheridan Marries George Brent!" *Modern Screen*, March 1942, 36.

3. Ida Zeitlin, "I, Clara Lou Take Thee, George," *Screenland*, May 1942, 59.

4. Hagen and Wagner, 182.

5. Quirk, 55.

6. "Fox Will Show *The Juke Girl*," *Spokesman-Review*, June 12, 1942.

7. Liza, "Why the Sheridan-Brent Marriage Failed?" *Screenland*, January 1943, 80.

8. Mary Livingston Benny, Hilliard Marks and Marcia Borie, *Jack Benny* (New York: Doubleday and Company, Inc. 1978), 47–48.

9. Benny, Marks and Borie, 220–221.

10. Benny, Marks and Borie, 48.

11. Benny, Marks and Borie, 49.

12. Liza, 80.

13. Louella Parsons, "Sheridan, Brent Split Up," *San Diego Union*, September 29, 1942.

14. Liza, 81.

15. Bard, 25.

16. Liza, 81.

17. Haranis, 78.

18. James Robert Parish and Don E. Stanke, *The Debonairs* (New Rochelle, NY: Arlington House Publishers, 1975), 48.

Chapter Thirteen

1. Hagen and Wagner, 190.

2. Liza, 81.

3. Ezra Goodman, "Hollywood: Norway to Monterey," *New York Times*, September 27, 1942.

4. Charles Higham and Joel Greenberg, *The*

Celluloid Muse: Hollywood Directors Speak (Washington D.C.: Regnery, 1971), 184.

5. Hagen and Wagner, 183.

6. "My Secret Dream," *Photoplay* October 1943, 54.

7. "Flynn Denies Plans to Wed Ann Sheridan," *Augusta Chronicle*, January 1, 1943.

8. Frederick C. Othman, "Ann Sheridan Discovers That She Is Allergic to Snow of the Gypsum-Cornflakes Variety," *Miami Herald*, May 7, 1943.

9. Louella Parsons, "Ann Sheridan May—or May Not—Wed Flynn," *San Francisco Examiner*, April 12, 1943.

10. Harrison Carroll, "Your Hollywood," *The Bernice Times*, April 13, 1943.

11. Louella Parsons, "Sheridan Scorns Flynn Romance Rumors," *Rochester Democrat and Chronicle, April,* 21, 1943.

12. Louella Parsons, "Van Johnson Gets Lead in New Film," *Philadelphia Inquirer*, April 24, 1943.

13. Erskine Johnson, "In Hollywood: Ann Sheridan Still Capable of Dishing Out the 'Oomph,'" *Kalispell Daily Inter Lake*, November 9, 1952.

14. Alyce Canfield, "The Next Time I Love," *Movieland*, March 1943, 52.

15. "Steve Hannagan—An American Success Story" *Syracuse Herald Journal*, February 7, 1953.

16. "Steve Hannagan: The Prince of Press Agents," https://go.gale.com/ps/i.do?id=GA LE%7CA673020844&sid=googleScholar&v =2.1&it=r&linkaccess=abs&issn=1040788X &p=AONE&sw=w&userGroupName=nysl_ oweb&isGeoAuthType=true, retrieved November 21, 2022.

17. Louella Parsons, "Hannagan's Romance with Ann Recalled," *Miami Herald*, February 22, 1953.

18. http://www.ann-sheridan.com/ About_ Ann_Sheridan/Comments_about_Ann_Sheri-dan.Html, retrieved July 15, 2022.

19. Hagen and Wagner, 184.

20. Bogart, 26.

21. http://www.ann-sheridan.com/About_ Ann_Sheridan/Comments_about_Ann_ Sheri-dan.html, retrieved July 15, 2021.

22. Alyce Canfield, "Ann Sheridan X-Rayed!" *Screenland*, August 1944, 85.

23. Helen Louise Walker, "I Wish I Were...," *Photoplay*, March 1943, 55.

24. Lawrence J. Quirk, *Jane Wyman: The Actress and the Woman* (New York: W.W. Norton & Co., 1987), 85.

25. Joe Morelle and Edward Z. Epstein, *Jane Wyman: A Biography* (New York: Delacorte Press, 1985), 71.

26. "Ann Sheridan USO Tour CBI," retrieved January 16, 2023, https://www.thefedoralounge. com/threads/ann-sheridan-uso-tour-cbi.46973/.

27. Jane Corby, "Boys in Burma, Ann Sheridan Reports, Are as Quick to Wolf-Howl as Ever," *Brooklyn Daily Eagle*, September 10, 1944.

28. https://www.uso.org/stories/1755-america-s-oomph-girl-was-a-uso-tour-star-too, retrieved August 12, 2022.

29. Schultz (B-528), 322.

30. "GI's in China Want Beer, Says Ann Sheridan," *Santa Cruz Sentinel*, September 9, 1944.

31. Schultz (B-25), 272.

32. Darrell Berrigan, "CBI Roundup Fires Parting Broadside at Stars, Quits," *Tucson Citizen*, October 20, 1944.

33. Ann Sheridan, "My Life on the Burma Front," *St. Louis Post-Dispatch*, October 22, 1944.

34. Harold V. Cohen, "The Drama Desk," *Pittsburgh Post-Gazette*, November 16, 1944.

Chapter Fourteen

1. Louella Parsons, "Ann Sheridan Says She's Too Old for 'Oomph' Roles," *Waterloo Daily Courier*, January 12, 1947.

2. Louella Parsons, "Ann Sheridan Makes Up with Warners," *San Antonio Light*, January 23, 1945.

3. *Bluefield Daily Telegraph*, April 8, 1945.

4. Sherman, 155.

5. Bob Thomas, "Ann Sheridan Back at Warners with Still Plenty of Oomph," *Paris News*, January 28, 1946.

6. Sheilah Graham, "Explosive Ann Sheridan at Peace with Movies," *Boston Globe*, February 24, 1946.

7. Sherman, 156.

8. Parsons, "Ann Sheridan Says ..."

9. *Nora Prentiss* ad, *Photoplay*, February 1947, 7.

10. Sherman, 162.

11. Parsons, "Ann Sheridan Says ..."

12. Hagen and Wagner, 187.

13. Hubler and Reagan, 96.

14. Danny Peary, editor, *Close-Ups: The Movie Star Book* (New York City: Workman Publishing Company, 1978), 158.

15. Peary, 159.

16. Herb Howe, "Sheridan Preferred," *Photoplay*, October 1947, 117.

17. Hattie Bilson, "Good Time Annie," *Screenland*, March 1947, 59.

18. Howe, 117.

19. Leo McCarey, "My Love Affair with Ann Sheridan," *Modern Screen*, November 1948, 107.

20. Ann Sheridan, "Happy Annie," *Modern Screen*, July 1948, 92.

21. McCarey, 104.

22. Hagen and Wagner, 188.

23. Hedda Hopper, "Why Don't You Two Get Married?" *Modern Screen*, December 1947, 99.

24. Hagen and Wagner, 187–188.

25. McCarey, 106.

26. Hal Humphrey, "Horseless Series for Ann Sheridan," *Los Angeles Times*, August 2, 1966.

27. "Oonph Girl Ann Sheridan Visits in S.L.," *Salt Lake Tribune*, May 7, 1948.

Chapter Fifteen

1. Bob Thomas, "Ann Sheridan Starts Another Film While Cary Grant Rests," *Del Rio News Herald*, June 3, 1949.
2. McCarey, 106.
3. Hopper, 100.
4. McCarey, 119.
5. Annette Ramsey, "Ann Sheridan, Denton Girl at Heart, Tackled Hollywood Her Way," https:per://dentonrc.com/news/ann-sheridan-denton-girl-at-heart-tackled-hollywood-her-way/article_0690af8f-a80d-5dc4-a964-bf8482a323f0.html, retrieved July 12, 2021.
6. http://ann-sheridan.com/About_Ann_Sheridan/Comments_about_Ann_Sheridan.html, retrieved August 14, 2021.
7. Sheilah Graham, "Annie, Get Your Guy," *Modern Screen*, December 1949, 46.
8. Sheilah Graham, "Ann Sheridan Is Fond of Travel," *Kansas City Star*, November 12, 1950.
9. Mapes, 66.
10. McBride, 72.
11. Hagen and Wagner, 188.
12. Frank Neill, "In Hollywood," *Long Beach Independent*, June 5, 1949.
13. "Movie Actress Ann Sheridan Seriously Ill," *Lowell Sun*, December 30, 1948.
14. Kobal, 423–424.
15. Frank Neill, "In Hollywood," *Long Beach Independent*, June 5, 1949.
16. Mapes, 67.
17. "Star Asks $350,000 for Job Loss," *Bakersfield Californian*, January 31, 1951.
18. *New York Times*, 8/20/49.
19. https://catalog.afi.com/Film/50216-MY-FORBIDDEN-PAST?cxt= filmography, retrieved November 15, 2022.
20. "Ann Sheridan Awarded Damages from Studio," *Corpus Christi Times*, February 7, 1951.
21. Hagen and Wagner, 191.
22. "Ann Sheridan Is Skid Row Club Angel," *Oakland Tribune*, June 15, 1950.
23. Bob Thomas, "Ann Sheridan Enjoys Home Without Husband," *Abilene Reporter News*, March 31, 1950.
24. Sheilah Graham, "Ann Sheridan Is Fond of Travel," *Kansas City Star*, November 12, 1950.
25. Louella Parsons, "Ann Sheridan's Sense of Humor and Friendliness Keeps Her on Top," *Indianapolis Star*, March 30, 1952.
26. Charles Denton, "Ann Sheridan Sees Big Test Due for Marilyn Monroe," *Rochester Democrat and Chronicle*, September 16, 1952.
27. Sheilah Graham's column, *Bluefield Daily Telegraph*, May 8, 1951.
28. Louella Parsons' column, *San Antonio Light*, April 5, 1951.
29. Erskine Johnson, "In Hollywood," *Bakersfield Californian*, November 8, 1951.
30. Erskine Johnson, "In Hollywood," *Portsmouth Herald*, May 12, 1951.
31. Dorothy Kilgallen, "The Voice of Broadway," *Middletown Journal*, June 8, 1951.
32. Herb Stein, "What Hollywood's Whispering About," *Photoplay*, September 1951, 14.
33. Marsha Saunders, "Storm Clouds for Jeff," *Modern Screen*, June 1951, 58.
34. Parsons, "Ann Sheridan's Sense of Humor and..."
35. Parsons, "Ann Sheridan's Sense of Humor and..."
36. Erskine Johnson, "In Hollywood," *Redlands Daily Facts*, March 11, 1952.
37. Norma Lee Browning, "Three Cheers For Ross Hunter," *Chicago Tribune*, April 28, 1968.
38. Erskine Johnson, "In Hollywood: Ann Sheridan Still Capable of Dishing Out the 'Oomph,'" *Kalispell Daily Inter Lake*, November 9, 1952.
39. *Lubbock Avalanche Journal*, January 4, 1953.

Chapter Sixteen

1. Erskine Johnson, "Ann Sheridan Likes Character Role," *Rhinelander Daily News*, September 28, 1955.
2. "Ann Sheridan Mourns for Steve Hannagan," *Lowell Sun*, February 6, 1953.
3. Louella Parsons, "Louella's Merry-Go-Round," *Albuquerque Journal*, February 8, 1953.
4. Louella Parsons, "Hannagan's Romance with Ann Recalled," *Miami Herald*, February 22, 1953.
5. Harrison Carroll, "Behind the Scenes in Hollywood," *Bradford Era*, April 20, 1953.
6. Bob Thomas, "Ann Sheridan Falls in Love with Mexico and Lives There," *Massillion Evening Independent*, December 28, 1955.
7. Bob Thomas, "Ann Sheridan to Leave Tense Hollywood for Mexico," http://www.ann-sheridan.com/Ann_Sheridan_Articles/Ann_Sheridan_to_Leave_Tense_Hollywood_for_Mexico.html, retrieved November 27, 2021.
8. Aline Mosby, "So Ann Sheridan Heads for Mexico," *Moline Daily Dispatch*, July 1, 1953.
9. Hagen and Wagner, 192.
10. Erskine Johnson, "If Role Calls for It, Ann Sheridan Looks Disheveled," *Sacramento Bee*, June 30, 1953.
11. Erskine Johnson, "Glenn Ford and Ann Sheridan May Take Their Bitter Feud to the Screen Actor's Guild," *Lubbock Avalanche Journal*, July 5, 1953.
12. Cal York, "Inside Stuff," *Photoplay*, October 1953, 99–100.
13. Hedda Hopper, "The Talk of Hollywood," *Baltimore Sun*, June 18, 1953.
14. "TV Is Idea-Free for Ann Sheridan," *Annapolis Capital*, May 30, 1953.
15. Louella Parsons' column, *Corsicana Daily Sun*, May 20, 1954.
16. *Miami Daily News Record*, January 12, 1955.

17. Erskine Johnson, "Ann Sheridan Gets First Mother Role in New Film," *Fresno Bee Republican*, May 16, 1955.

18. Jack O'Dowd, "Rad Fulton (aka James Westmoreland)," *Classic Images*, January 2023, 14.

19. Wanda Hale, "Ann Sheridan Has New Love—It's Africa!" *New York Daily News,* January 2, 1956.

20. Bob Thomas, "Ann Sheridan Loves Mexico," *Miami Herald*, January 7, 1956.

21. https://catalog.afi.com/Film/51786-COME-NEXTSPRING?cxt=filmography, retrieved November 12, 2022.

22. Kobal, 424.

23. Louella Parsons, "Ann Sheridan Leaves for Nairobi," *Waterloo Daily Courier*, May 31, 1956.

24. Hagen and Wagner, 193.

25. Hagen and Wagner, 168.

26. Marc Eliot, *Jimmy Stewart: A Biography* (New York: Rebel Road, 2006), 143.

27. http://www.ann-sheridan.com/Ann_Sheridan_Quotations/Ann_Sheridan_Quotations.Html, retrieved January 20, 2023.

28. Dorothy Masters, "Ann Sheridan Turns Singer in Film Now Being Shot in Darkest Africa," *Lubbock Morning Avalanche*, August 6, 1956.

Chapter Seventeen

1. Ann Sheridan, "Happy Annie," *Modern Screen*, July 1948, 91.

2. Kobal, 414.

3. Lucy Key Miller, "Front Views and Profiles," *Chicago Tribune*, August 12, 1958.

4. Hagen and Wagner, 193.

5. Schultz, 66.

6. *Oneonta Sun*, September 15, 1958.

7. James Gregory, "Ann Sheridan: Goodbye to a Great Redhead," retrieved January 15, 2021, http://ann-sheridan.com/Death_of_Ann_Sheridan/Ann_Sheridan_Goodbye_to_a_Great_Redhead.html, retrieved January 15, 2021.

8. Dorothy Kilgallen, "Broadway: Ann Sheridan May Wed," *Lancaster New Era*, October 8, 1958.

9. https://www.originallifemagazines.com/product/life-magazine-october-20-1941/, retrieved January 12, 2023.

10. Joe Finnigan, "Ann Sheridan in Hollywood for TV Show," *Corsicana Daily Sun*, November 23, 1958.

11. Schultz, 68.

12. "Parisian Comedy Coming on Jan. 26," *Amarillo Sunday News Globe*, January 17, 1960.

13. "Ann Sheridan Says She's Happy to Tour Country," *Corpus Christi Times*, January 18, 1960.

14. Philip K. Scheuer, "Hunter Promoting Play From Movie," *Los Angeles Times*, August 5, 1959.

15. "La Sheridan Debut Is Fair Say Critics," *Rochester Democrat and Chronicle*, October 7, 1959.

16. Hagen and Wagner, 194.

17. Schultz, 70.

18. "McKay Denies Charges Involving Ann Sheridan," *Waterloo Daily Courier*, February 24, 1960.

19. "Estranged Wife Names Ann as 'Other Woman,'" *Racine Journal Times*, February 24, 1960.

20. "Actress Brands Report Nonsense," *Miami Herald*, February 29, 1960.

21. Schultz, 71.

22. Kobal, 414.

23. "Actor Denies Affair with Ann Sheridan," *Los Angeles Times*, March 30, 1960.

Chapter Eighteen

1. Kobal, 422.

2. Kobal, 422.

3. Hagen and Wagner, 193.

4. Joseph Finnegan, "No More Glamour for Ann Sheridan," *Hayward Daily Review*, June 26, 1962.

5. *San Francisco Chronicle*, October 12, 1962.

6. Alan Gill, "Ann Sheridan Accepts Daytime Panel Bid," *Bradenton Manatee County Call*, August 29, 1963.

7. Parish and Stanke. *The Forties Gals*, 299.

8. Hagen and Wagner, 194.

9. Hagen and Wagner, 195.

10. Kobal, 416.

11. *Lincoln Daily Citizen*, December 15, 1965.

12. Richard Doan, "Out of the Air: Ann Sheridan in 'Another World,'" *East Liverpool Review*, November 16, 1965.

13. *New York Times*, November 21, 1965.

14. Kobal, 420.

15. "Detergent Dramas Draw the Stars," *Mount Pleasant News*, December 23, 1965.

16. Aileen McMinn, "Film Stars Clean Up in Soap Operas," *Los Angeles Times*, December 30, 1965.

17. "What Ever Happened to Ann Sheridan?" *Ogden Standard Examiner*, January 30, 1966.

18. Kobal, 413.

19. "Ann Sheridan Finds New Show a 'Snap,'" *Stroudsburg Pocono Record*, September 30, 1966.

20. "Sheridan (Ann) Rides Again," *Salt Lake Tribune*, September 11, 1966.

21. Vernon Scott, "Ann Sheridan Takes Decline in Stride," *Kittanning Leader Times*, December 15, 1965.

22. "My interview with Ray Hagen," retrieved January 22, 2023, http://www.ann-sheridan.com/Ann_Sheridan_Interviews/Ray_Hagen_Interview.html, retrieved January 22, 2023.

23. James Gregory, "Ann Sheridan: Goodbye to a Great Redhead."

24. Haranis, 78.

Chapter Nineteen

1. Ruth Waterbury, "We Say Goodbye to a Valiant Lady," *Modern Screen*, April 1967, 80.

2. Bob Thomas, "Ann Sheridan Shows She Still

Has Plenty Oomph Left," *Appleton Post Crescent*, July 29, 1966.

3. Nick Thomas, "Carole Wells Remembers 'Oomph Girl' Ann Sheridan," https://www.mansfieldnewsjournal.com/story/entertainment/2020/02/18/entertainment-carole-wells-remembers-oomph-girl-ann-sheridan/4793599002/, retrieved December 20, 2022.

4. Erskine Johnson, "Ann Sheridan Is Still Around for Fall Debut," *North Adams Transcript*, August 27, 1966.

5. "Ann Sheridan, Scott McKay Secretly Wed," *Eureka Humboldt Times*, June 14, 1966.

6. Nick Thomas, "Carole Wells Remembers 'Oomph Girl" Ann Sheridan."

7. "Portrait of a Star: Ann Sheridan Finds Series," *Lima News*, October 28, 1966.

8. "Sheridan (Ann) Rides Again," *Salt Lake Tribune*, September 11, 1966.

9. *Des Moines Register*, September 24, 1966.

10. "Big Stars Running Aground," *Scottsdale Progress*, September 24, 1966.

11. Therese Bushen, "Scott McKay Post Ann Sheridan," http://www.ann-sheridan.com/Scott_McKay/Scott_McKay.html, retrieved January 15, 2023.

12. Hagen and Wagner, 199.

13. Schultz (B-303), 302.

14. James Gregory, "Ann Sheridan: Goodbye to a Great Redhead."

15. Haranis, 78.

16. Nick Thomas, "Carole Wells Remembers "Oomph Girl" Ann Sheridan."

17. http://www.ann-sheridan.com/Death_of_Ann_Sheridan/Ann_Sheridan_Kept_Fatal_Illness_Secret.html, retrieved February 1, 2023.

18. Waterbury, 8.

19. "Ann Sheridan: The 'Oomph Girl,'" https://www.dametown.com/ann-sheridan/, retrieved December 28, 2022.

Chapter Twenty

1. Haranis, 78.

2. "Call Tells Ann's Kin of Death," *Fort Worth Star-Telegram*, January 23, 1967.

3. "Texas' Own Ann Maintained to Last Her Independence," *Corpus Christi Caller-Times*, January 23, 1967.

4. Jack O'Brian, "Ann Sheridan's Death Was Unexpected by Her Friends," *Fort Worth Star-Telegram*, January 27, 1967.

5. John C. West, "Ann Sheridan Was a Lady," *Los Angeles Times*, February 12, 1967.

6. Schultz (B-711), 340.

7. Waterbury, 8.

8. Nick Thomas, "Carole Wells Remembers 'Oomph Girl' Ann Sheridan."

9. Bob Thomas, "Hollywood Highlights," *Bryan Eagles*, November 3, 1967.

10. Diana Saenger, "Film Star Ann Sheridan's Cremains Interred 38 Years After Her Death," https://web.archive.org/web/20060209155808/http://classicfilm.about.com/od/classicfilmactresses/a/ann shrdan20705.htm, retrieved February 2, 2023.

11. "Ann Sheridan," *London Times*, January 23, 1967.

Bibliography

Books

Aaker, Everett. *The Films of George Raft*. Jefferson, NC: McFarland, 2013.

Benny, Jack, and Joan Benny. *Sunday Nights at Seven: The Jack Benny Story*. New York: Warner Books, Inc., 1990.

Benny, Mary Livingston, Hilliard Marks, and Marcia Borie. *Jack Benny*. New York: Doubleday and Company, Inc., 1978.

Bergman, Andrew. *James Cagney*. New York: Galahad Books, 1973.

Bishop, Jim. *The Mark Hellinger Story: A Biography of Broadway and Hollywood*. Whitefish, MT: Literary Licensing, LLC, 2012.

Bubbeo, Daniel. *The Women of Warner Brothers: The Lives and Careers of 15 Leading Ladies*. Jefferson, NC: McFarland, 2002.

Chierichetti, David, and Dorothy Lamour. *Mitchell Leisen: Hollywood Director*. Los Angeles: Photoventures Co., 1995.

Dickens, Homer. *The Films of James Cagney*, New York: Citadel Press, 1972.

Donati, William. *Ida Lupino: A Biography*. Lexington: University Press of Kentucky, 1996.

Eames, Douglas Michael. *The Paramount Story*. London: Octopus Publishers Limited, 1995.

Flynn, Errol. *My Wicked, Wicked Ways*. New York: G. P. Putnam's Sons, 1959.

Hagen, Ray, and Laura Wagner. *Killer Tomatoes: Fifteen Tough Film Dames*. Jefferson, NC: McFarland, 2004.

Hardy, Phil, ed. *The Overlook Film Encyclopedia: The Westerns*. New York: Overlook Books, 1994.

Higham, Charles, and Joel Greenberg. *The Celluloid Muse; Hollywood Directors Speak*. New York: Regnery, 1971.

Hirschborn, Clive. *The Warner Bros. Story*. New York: Crown Publishing, Inc., 1979.

Hirschhorn, Clive. *The Universal Story*. New York: Crown Publishing, Inc., 1983.

Hubler, Richard G., and Ronald Reagan. *Where's the Rest of Me? The Autobiography of Ronald Reagan*. New York: Karz Publishers, 1981.

Jason, Sybil. *My Fifteen Minutes: An Autobiography of a Child Star of the Golden Era of Hollywood*. Albany, GA: BearManor Media, 2005.

Jerome, Stuart. *Those Crazy Wonderful Years When We Ran Warner Bros.*, New York: Lyle Stuart, Inc., 1983.

Jewell, Richard B., and Vernon Hardin. *The RKO Story*. New Rochelle, NY: Arlington House, 1985.

Kear, Lynn, and James King. *Evelyn Brent: The Life* and *Films of Hollywood's Lady Crook*. Jefferson, NC: McFarland, 2009.

Kobal, John. *People Will Talk*. New York: Knopf Publishers, 1986.

McBride, Joseph. *Hawks on Hawks*. Oakland: University of California Press, 1982.

McNulty, Thomas. *Errol Flynn: The Life and Career*. Jefferson, NC: McFarland, 2011.

Morelle, Joe, and Edward Z. Epstein. *Jane Wyman: A Biography*. New York: Delacorte Press, 1985.

Nott, Robert. *The Films of Randolph Scott*. Jefferson, NC: McFarland, 2004.

O'Brien, Scott. *George Brent: Ireland's Gift to Hollywood and Its Leading Ladies*. Albany, GA: BearManor Media, 2014.

O'Brien, Scott. *Sylvia Sidney: Paid By the Tear*. Albany, GA: BearManor Media, 2016.

Parish, James Robert. *The George Raft File: The Unauthorized Biography*. Minot, ND: Drake Publishers, 1973.

Parish, James Robert. *Hollywood's Great Love Teams*. New Rochelle, NY: Arlington House Publishers, 1974.

Parish, James Robert, and Don E. Stanke. *The All-Americans*. New Rochelle, NY: Arlington House Publishers, 1977.

Parish, James Robert, and Don E. Stanke. *The Forties Gals*. New Rochelle, NY: Arlington House Publishers, 1980.

Parish, James Robert, and Don E. Stanke. *The Debonairs*. New Rochelle, NY: Arlington House Publishers, 1975.

Peary, Danny, ed. *Close-Ups: The Movie Star Book*. New York: Workman Publishing Company, Inc., 1978.

Quirk, Lawrence J. *Fasten Your Seat Belts: The Passionate Life of Bette Davis*. New York: William Morrow and Company, Inc., 1990.

Quirk, Lawrence J. *Jane Wyman: The Actress and the Woman*. New York: W.W. Norton & Co., 1987.

Rinella, Michael D. *Margaret Sullavan: The Life*

and Career of a Reluctant Star. Jefferson, NC: McFarland, 2019.

Schultz, Margie. *Ann Sheridan: A Bio-Bibliography.* Westport, CT: Greenwood Press, 1997.

Sherman, Vincent. *Studio Affairs: My Life as a Film Director.* Lexington: University Press of Kentucky, 1996.

Shipman, David. *The Great Movie Stars: The Golden Years.* New York: Crown Publishers, 1970.

Sperber, A. M., and Eric Lax. *Bogart.* New York: HarperCollins, 2011.

Stine, Whitney, and Bette Davis. *Mother Goddam: The Story of the Career of Bette Davis.* New York: W.H. Allen and Co., 1974.

Stine, Whitney, and George Hurrell. *The Hurrell Style: 50 Years of Photographing Hollywood.* New York: John Day, Co., 1976.

Van Neste, Dan. *They Coulda Been Contenders: Twelve Actors Who Should Have Become Cinematic Superstars.* Albany, GA: BearManor Media, 2020.

Vermilye, Jerry. *Bette Davis.* New York: Galahad Books, 1973.

Vermilye, Jerry. *Buster Crabbe: A Biofilmography.* Jefferson, NC: McFarland, 2014.

Wallis, Hal, and Charles Higham. *Starmaker: The Autobiography of Hal Wallis.* New York: Macmillan Publishing, 1980.

Wansell, Geoffrey. *Haunted Idol: The Story of the Real Cary Grant.* New York: William Morrow & Co., 1987.

Periodicals

Asher, Jerry. "This is Bogart," *Photoplay* January 1944.

Bard, Richard. "We Didn't Part Friends!," *Hollywood* February 1943.

Bilson, Hattie. "Good Time Annie," *Screenland* March 1947.

Blake, Anita. "Learned in Exile," *Photoplay* June 1941.

Bogart, Humphrey. "Sister Annie," *Silver Screen* March 1943.

Brent, George. "Categorically Speaking: Ann—as seen by George Brent," *Photoplay* September 1940.

"Broadway Hopeful Margaret Power Sets Out to Crash the Stage," *Life* October 20, 1941.

Busch, Noel F. "Ann Sheridan's Life Story," *Life* July 24, 1939.

Canfield, Alyce. "The Next Time I Love," *Movieland* March 1943.

Canfield, Alyse. "Ann Sheridan X-Rayed!," *Screenland* August 1944.

Carroll, Avery. "Down to Earth Annie," *Movieland* July 1948.

Carsons, James. "Annie Meets the Boys," *Modern Screen* July 1940.

Cheatham, Maude. "George Tells Why, Ann Sheridan and I Won't Marry," *Photoplay* September 1941.

Colfax, Betty. "They Made Her What She Is Today," *Modern Screen* January 1940.

Dudley, Fredda. "Ann Sheridan Marries George Brent!," *Modern Screen* March 1942.

Dudley, Fredda. "The Marriage That Couldn't Happen," *Modern Screen* May 1942.

Fletcher, Adele Whitely. "Gay Companions," *Photoplay* March 1944.

Frings, Katharine Hartley. "Will the 'Oomph' Title Hurt Her?," *Motion Picture* August 1939.

Graham, Sheilah. "Annie, Get Your Guy," *Modern Screen* December 1949.

Hall, Gladys, "Confessions of a Contest Winner," *Motion Picture* December 1938.

Haranis, Chrys. "Ann Sheridan: She Had Oomph and Courage," *Photoplay* April 1967.

Higgins, Robert. "The Oomph Girl Turns 51," *TV Guide* May 21, 1966.

Hopper, Hedda. "Why Don't You Two Get Married?," *Modern Screen* December 1947.

"Hot From Hollywood," *Screenland* April 1946.

Hover, Helen. "Forecasts for 1940," *Hollywood* January 1940.

Howe, Herb. "Sheridan Preferred," *Photoplay* October 1947.

Jerome, Jerry. "Ann Sheridan's in Love with Living," *Movieland* March 1947.

Liza. "Why the Sheridan-Brent Marriage Failed," *Screenland* January 1943.

"Look Out Mr. Gable!," *Silver Screen* March 1936.

Mapes, Jacques. "What's It Like Dating Ann," *Screenland* December 1949.

McCarey, Leo. "My Love Affair with Ann Sheridan." *Modern Screen* November 1948.

"My Secret Dream," *Photoplay* October 1943.

O'Dowd, Jack. "Rad Fulton: aka James Westmoreland," *Classic Images* January 2023.

Pieck, Karen. "When Love Died," *Modern Screen* January 1943.

Proctor, Kay. "Girl Crazy," *Hollywood* November 1938.

Proctor, Kay. "Oomph (pronounced 'Ouch'!)," *Hollywood* September 1939.

Rankin, Ruth. "From Ranch to Riches," *Photoplay* June 1939.

Rhea, Marian. "Texas Bombshell—Part 2," *Movie Mirror* June 1939.

Rhea, Marian. "Texas Bombshell," *Movie Mirror* May 1939.

Schaffer, Rosalind. "Marriage and Ann Sheridan," *Movieland* September 1946.

"Screenland Salutes New Screen Siren," *Screenland* December 1938.

Sheridan, Ann. "Brother Bogie," *Silver Screen* January 1943.

Sheridan, Ann. "Categorically Speaking: George—as seen by Ann Sheridan," *Photoplay* September 1940.

Sheridan, Ann. "Happy Annie," *Modern Screen* July 1948.

Sheridan, Ann. "It's a Man's World, Says Ann Sheridan," *Hollywood* August 1941.

Sheridan, Ann. "Most Men Don't Like Love," *Hollywood* June 1939.

Sheridan, Ann. "Take My Word For It!," *Modern Screen* July 1953.

Sheridan, Ann. "This is Myself," *Movieland* April 1944.

Shupper, Alyce. "Ann How!," *Silver Screen* November 1938.

Smith, Frederick James. "The Real Oomph Girl," *Liberty* July 20, 1940.

Stein, Herb. "What Hollywood's Whispering About," *Photoplay* September 1951.

"They're Talking About…," *Photoplay* March 1939.

Walker, Helen Louise. "I Wish I Were…," *Photoplay* March 1943.

Waterbury, Ruth. "We Say Goodbye to a Valiant Lady," *Modern Screen* April 1967.

Weller, Helen. "The Jinx Behind the Filming of 'Kings Row,'" *Hollywood* January 1942.

Wilson, Elizabeth. "Get Sheridan," *Screenland* August 1939.

Wilson, Elizabeth. "Hollywood's Gayest Romance!," *Screenland* September 1940.

York, Cal. "Inside Stuff," *Photoplay* October 1953.

Zeitlin, Ida. "I, Clara Lou Take Thee, George," *Screenland* May 1942.

Online Sources

Allperti, Cliff. "Ann Sheridan—Search for Beauty Contest Winner Before the Oomph." https://immortalephemera.com/31105/ann-sheridan-search-for-beauty/

"Ann Sheridan Sharpshoots at Lampy; Calls Harvard Humor Sheet Sad Rag," The Harvard Crimson, 3/6/40. https://www.thecrimson.com/article/1940/3/6/ann-sheridan-sharpshoots-at-lampy-calls/"Ann Sheridan USO Tour CBI," https://www.thefedoralounge.com/threads/ann-sheridan-uso-tour-cbi.46973/

Bochenek, Annette. "Hometown to Hollywood: Ann Sheridan," https://hometownstoholly-wood.com/2020/06/29/ann-sheridan/

"The Bogie Film Blog," https://bogiefilmblog.wordpress.com/2013/06/14/it-all-came-ue-1940.

Gregory, James. "Ann Sheridan: Goodbye to a Great Redhead," http://ann-sheridan. com/Death_of_Ann_ Sheridan/Ann_Sheridan_Goodbye_to_a_Great_Redhead.html.

Metz, Nina. "'Woman on the Run' a noir treasure that was nearly lost," https://www.chicagotribune. com/entertainment/movies/ct-noir-city-film-fest-chicago-woman-on-"

Movie Oomph-Girl Invited to Dance By 'Record' Boss," The Yale Daily News, 3/7/40. https://ydnhistorical.library.yale.edu/?a=d&d=-YDN19400307-01.2.5&e=-en-20-1-txt.

"My interview with Ray Hagen," http://www.ann-sheridan.com/Ann_Sheridan_Interviews / Ray_Hagen_Interview.html.

"Remembering Ann Sheridan," http://www.ann-sheridan.com/index.html.

"Steve Hannagan: The Prince of Press Agents," https://go.gale.com/ps/i.do?id=GALE%7CA673020844&sid=googleScholar&v=2.1&it=r&linkaccess=abs&issn=1040788X-&p=AONE&sw=w&userGroupName=nysl_oweb&isGeoAuthType=true.

Thomas, Nick. "Carole Wells remembers 'Oomph Girl' Ann Sheridan," https://www.msn.com/en-us/movies/news/carole-wells-remembers-oomph-girl-ann-sheridan/ar.

"The time Ann Sheridan sued Howard Hughes and won," TopBilledhttps://forums.tcm.com/topic/35963-the-time-ann-sheridan-sued-howard-hughes-and-won/

Index

9 781476 694184